IT HAPPENED TO ME

Series Editor: Arlene Hirschfelder

Books in the It Happened to Me series are designed for inquisitive teens digging for answers about certain illnesses, social issues, or lifestyle interests. Whether you are deep into your teen years or just entering them, these books are gold mines of up-to-date information, riveting teen views, and great visuals to help you figure out stuff. Besides special boxes highlighting singular facts, each book is enhanced with the latest reading lists, websites, and an index. Perfect for browsing, there are loads of expert information by acclaimed writers to help parents, guardians, and librarians understand teen illness, tough situations, and lifestyle choices.

16. *Gender Identity: The Ultimate Teen Guide*, by Cynthia L. Winfield, 2007.
17. *Physical Disabilities: The Ultimate Teen Guide*, by Denise Thornton, 2007.
18. *Money—Getting It, Using It, and Avoiding the Traps: The Ultimate Teen Guide*, by Robin F. Brancato, 2007.
19. *Self-Advocacy: The Ultimate Teen Guide*, by Cheryl Gerson Tuttle and JoAnn Augeri Silva, 2007.
20. *Adopted: The Ultimate Teen Guide*, by Suzanne Buckingham Slade, 2007.
21. *The Military and Teens: The Ultimate Teen Guide*, by Kathlyn Gay, 2008.
22. *Animals and Teens: The Ultimate Teen Guide*, by Gail Green, 2009.
23. *Reaching Your Goals: The Ultimate Teen Guide*, by Anne Courtright, 2009.
24. *Juvenile Arthritis: The Ultimate Teen Guide*, by Kelly Rouba, 2009.
25. *Obsessive-Compulsive Disorder: The Ultimate Teen Guide*, by Natalie Rompella, 2009.
26. *Body Image and Appearance: The Ultimate Teen Guide*, by Kathlyn Gay, 2009.
27. *Writing and Publishing: The Ultimate Teen Guide*, by Tina P. Schwartz, 2010.
28. *Food Choices: The Ultimate Teen Guide*, by Robin F. Brancato, 2010.
29. *Immigration: The Ultimate Teen Guide*, by Tatyana Kleyn, 2011.
30. *Living with Cancer: The Ultimate Teen Guide*, by Denise Thornton, 2011.
31. *Living Green: The Ultimate Teen Guide*, by Kathlyn Gay, 2012.
32. *Social Networking: The Ultimate Teen Guide*, by Jenna Obee, 2012.
33. *Sports: The Ultimate Teen Guide*, by Gail Fay, 2013.
34. *Adopted, Revised Edition*, by Suzanne Buckingham Slade, 2013.
35. *Bigotry and Intolerance: The Ultimate Teen Guide*, by Kathlyn Gay, 2013.
36. *Substance Abuse: The Ultimate Teen Guide*, by Sheri Bestor, 2013.
37. *LGBTQ Families: The Ultimate Teen Guide*, by Eva Apelqvist, 2013.
38. *Bullying: The Ultimate Teen Guide*, by Mathangi Subramanian, 2014.
39. *Eating Disorders: The Ultimate Teen Guide*, by Jessica R. Greene, 2014.
40. *Speech and Language Challenges: The Ultimate Teen Guide*, by Marlene Targ Brill, 2014.
41. *Divorce: The Ultimate Teen Guide*, by Kathlyn Gay, 2014.
42. *Depression: The Ultimate Teen Guide*, by Tina P. Schwartz, 2014.
43. *Creativity: The Ultimate Teen Guide*, by Aryna M. Ryan, 2015.
44. *Shyness: The Ultimate Teen Guide*, by Bernardo J. Carducci Ph.D and Lisa Kaiser, 2015.
45. *Food Allergies: The Ultimate Teen Guide*, by Jessica Reino, 2015.
46. *Self-Injury: The Ultimate Teen Guide*, by Judy Dodge Cummings, 2015.
47. *Activism: The Ultimate Teen Guide*, by Kathlyn Gay, 2016.
48. *Pregnancy and Parenting: The Ultimate Teen Guide*, by Jessica Akin, 2016.
49. *Chronic Illnesses, Syndromes, and Rare Disorders: The Ultimate Teen Guide*, by Marlene Targ Brill, 2016.

50. *Autism Spectrum Disorder: The Ultimate Teen Guide*, by Francis Tabone, 2016.
51. *Sexual Assault: The Ultimate Teen Guide*, by Olivia Ghafoerkhan, 2016.
52. *Epilepsy: The Ultimate Teen Guide, Second Edition*, by Kathlyn Gay, 2017
53. *Sexual Decisions: The Ultimate Teen Guide, Second Edition*, by L. Kris Gowen, 2017
54. *Comics, Graphic Novels, and Manga: The Ultimate Teen Guide*, by Randall Bonser, 2017

COMICS, GRAPHIC NOVELS, AND MANGA

THE ULTIMATE TEEN GUIDE

RANDALL BONSER

IT HAPPENED TO ME, NO. 54

ROWMAN & LITTLEFIELD
Lanham • Boulder • New York • London

Published by Rowman & Littlefield
A wholly owned subsidiary of The Rowman & Littlefield Publishing Group, Inc.
4501 Forbes Boulevard, Suite 200, Lanham, Maryland 20706
www.rowman.com

Unit A, Whitacre Mews, 26-34 Stannary Street, London SE11 4AB

British Library Cataloguing in Publication Information Available

Library of Congress Cataloging-in-Publication Data

Names: Bonser, Randall, author.
Title: Comics, graphic novels, and manga : the ultimate teen guide / Randall Bonser.
Description: Lanham, Maryland : Rowman & Littlefield, 2017. | Series: It happened to me |
    Includes bibliographical references and index.
Identifiers: LCCN 2016058686 (print) | LCCN 2016058701 (ebook) | ISBN 9781442268395
    (hardback : alk. paper) | ISBN 9781442268401 (electronic)
Subjects: LCSH: Comic books, strips, etc.—History and criticism—Juvenile literature. |
    Graphic novels—History and criticism—Juvenile literature. | Graphic novels in education.
Classification: LCC PN6710 .B64 2017 (print) | LCC PN6710 (ebook) | DDC 741.5/9—dc23
LC record available at https://lccn.loc.gov/2016058686

Printed in the United States of America

To Benita, Sophia, and Zachary, my inspirations.

Contents

Acknowledgments

Thank you to Gene Luen Yang, who not only taught me about comics and graphic novels but also graciously let me use his work—you are the Man of Steel! Thanks also to the numerous authors and artists who let us use their work—you are true heroes. I hope this book leads to lots more sales of your work. A big round of applause to Chris Burns, who provided the illustrations for this book—you rock! (Check out Chris's YouTube channel for art tutorials.)

I would like to thank the librarians who helped me do the research for this book, especially Marge from the Tyrone Public Library. Big thanks to Kristi Romo for surveying her English classes for quotes for this book and her wisdom about using comics in the classroom. Thanks to Jodell Sadler for planting the seeds for this book and Arlene Hirschfelder for her guidance and encouragement. I appreciate Swati Avasthi, Gene Luen Yang, and Beau L'Amour for letting me interview them for this book.

Thanks most of all to my family, who encouraged me, and to God, who gives me strength.

Introduction

When I was seven, I received my first comic book. It wasn't Superman or any other superhero. It was an Illustrated Classics retelling of *Ivanhoe*. I learned about knights and chivalry. I went on to read about *The Three Musketeers* and *Dr. Jekyll and Mr. Hyde*. I had no idea these were books of fiction written centuries ago; I just thought they were great stories with cool pictures! In middle school (we called it junior high back then) a friend of mine introduced me to Spider-Man and Batman comics. But you had to go to the grocery store or a newsstand to buy them, so I only read them sporadically.

The fact that you're reading this book means that you either love comic books, graphic novels, and manga, or you want to learn more about them. If you already love them, there will be a lot of new information for you in this book, because you probably have confined yourself to reading a certain genre or type of comic literature. You'll find a ton of other options in this book that will interest you. Love superhero comics? Cool, but how about trying a detective or horror comic? Love memoir comics? Great, maybe a nonfiction or journalistic comic would interest you. Are you a manga freak and look down your nose at Western-style comics? I believe you'll be able to find something that will change your mind.

If you are interested in comics and graphic storytelling but don't have a lot of experience, don't worry. If you're not sure where to start, join the club! You will find a doorway into comics through this book. You'll learn about the history of comics, as well as how to read them. You'll learn about different genres of graphic storytelling and some of the differences between Japanese manga and Western-style comics. You can even learn how to produce your own comic books!

Readers of all skill levels will notice that there *a lot* of reviews and summaries of comic books and manga included in almost every chapter. That's because when I go to pick out a story, I like to know a little bit about the story so that I can make a choice that suits my interest. I believe a lot of readers are that way. So I've introduced or summarized over ninety comics, graphic novels, and manga in this volume. They range from murder mysteries to horror stories to real-life dramas of heartbreak and love. The maturity level of the books ranges from middle school stories about girls at roller derby camp to horror books that appeal to older teens and young adults. Because readers of this book will come from a variety of backgrounds, ages, and maturity levels, I've noted the books on the mature end of the scale with a written caution. Those are books with disturbing violence or higher than PG level sexual content or innuendo. Other books that are clearly aimed at adults I've left out altogether.

When I was researching this book, I had to read a lot of graphic novels. I know, I know, the painful research I had to do! What a hard life! Actually, I loved writing this book because I love graphic stories. The how-to sections I've tried to put into practice in my own life as I practice writing graphic novel scripts. Many of the illustrations in this book were created by Chris Burns, a talented teen artist who loves comics and manga. You can check out Chris's YouTube channel for art tutorials and more information.

Here's how the book is arranged:

- Chapter 1 discusses the history of comics, but the world is changing so fast that every few years brings another revolution in how people access and read comics.
- Chapter 2 explains how to read and understand graphic storytelling, because the medium uses its own visual vocabulary to relate meaning.
- Chapter 3 goes more into detail about the largest genre of Western comics, the superhero comic. I explore the history of some of the major superhero publishers and franchises, explain how the genre has become more diverse and inclusive, and give suggestions on where to get on board if you want to get into superhero comics.
- Chapter 4 traces the development of graphic novels as serious literature beyond the superhero genre. I discuss some of the groundbreaking graphic novels and how they helped develop the industry we know today. Plus, there are a bunch of reviews of great graphic novels to get you started on the more "serious" stories.
- Chapter 5 lists some graphic novels and comics that are changing the way we think about comics by using the medium in a way no one ever thought of before. Comics journalism? You bet. History? Memoir? Hybrid prose/graphic novels? I've reviewed some of the best and most popular of these gene busters.
- Chapter 6 gives a brief introduction to Japanese manga, how it differs from Western comics, and some suggestions about where to start. Plus, you'll be interested in the reviews so that you can choose a great story for yourself.
- Chapter 7 is as much for your English teacher or media center specialist as it is for you. In this section you'll learn why graphic novels should be included in the school curriculum. You'll learn why a multimodal medium—meaning a presentation that uses several different modes, or types, of art—produces an entirely different experience than prose or film.
- Chapter 8 is a reference guide for anyone who wants to create her or his own comic books. With suggestions on story creation, scripting, finding

an artist, and distribution, this chapter should be a good starting point for someone with the creative vision to put a comic together.

You'll notice a lot of teen quotes about comics and graphic novels. Some of these have been provided by TeenInk.com, which is an online community for teen expression. I encourage you to visit the site and even write your own essays (possibly about this book?). Other quotes come from several English classes that graciously agreed to let me survey them on their opinions about graphic stories they've read.

Well, there you go. I hope you enjoy reading this book as much as I enjoyed writing it. Now up, up, and away!

SEQUENTIAL ART FROM CAVE DRAWINGS TO ZOMBIE COMICS

Comics and graphic novels have become popular all over the world. On every continent, readers are choosing to read books with pictures and words, set in an arrangement that tells a story. In Japan, one-third of the books published are manga, the Japanese form of comics.[1] Here in the United States, comics sales have risen nearly 30 percent in just the last five years, according to Diamond Comic Distributors, from 73.8 million copies to 98 million copies.[2] The influence of comic books can be seen on every television channel and every summer in a string of blockbuster movies based on comics characters. Digital comics have made purchasing and reading comics so easy; all you have to do is log on to your tablet or computer.

Librarians, too, are enthusiastic about comic books and graphic novels. They note how graphic stories are some of the hottest properties they possess, and they are ordering more and more for readers. Mike Pawuk, of the Cuyahoga County Public Library in Ohio, reported in an article for *Publishers Weekly* that the number of graphic novels checked out rivals those of popular prose teen books. In 2011, graphic novels made up about 10 percent of his collection but 35 percent of his circulation—and the number grows every year.[3] Manga, too, has become wildly popular here in the United States, although it has been popular in Japan for half a century.

But comics have not always enjoyed such popularity. In the 1950s, a code was introduced that severely limited the subject matter of comics in the United States. That's because the colorful books were seen as entertainment purely for children, so authorities tried to regulate the content of those books. Graphic novels and comics have outgrown the regulation of the 1950s, and readers of any age or interest can find well-written comics both in print and increasingly online.

This begs the question What exactly do we mean by *comics*?

Figure 1.1. Comics readers are everywhere! *Photo courtesy of Ababsolutum/istock*

"'Comic books are for kids.' 'You need to grow up and stop reading comics.' Believe it or not, I've heard both of those statements in my life. I grew up with comic books and a lot of pop culture. Marvel, DC, Star Wars, you name it. I love all of those things and then some. I haven't shrunk from showing it."—Ayinde R., Owing Mills, Maryland[a]

Comics: A Definition

Most people think they can define comics, but in reality, comics are difficult to pin down! Are signs with graphic images comics? Are words drawn in artistic ways comics? How about cave drawings?

Part of the problem is the word *comics* itself. The word sometimes refers to a particular medium within the broader definition—comic books. Comic books are those serial stories that are told with pictures and words in short books. But comic books are only one niche within the world of comics, which includes graphic novels, manga, instructional manuals, and many other types of literature.

The first useful definition of comics comes from comics legend Will Eisner, who defines the medium in *Comics and Sequential Art* as "sequential art," meaning pictures or illustrations that, when put together, tell a story.[4] That seems right—art put in sequential order to tell a story. But wouldn't that include three-dimensional art like sculpture? What if you put four sculptures in a row to tell a story; is that comics? While Eisner performed a noble service by trying to define comics, his definition is a little broad.

Enter Scott McCloud, a comics creator who fell in love with comics as a young boy and tried for years to express to others why the medium held such promise. His book *Understanding Comics* (written as a comic book with panels, illustrations, and dialogue, thus embodying the ideas he discusses) has become a classic reference on the history of comics, how to understand the tools used, and a hint as to the medium's potential. He defines comics as "juxtaposed pictorial and other images in deliberate sequence, intended to convey information and/or to produce an aesthetic response in the viewer."[5] McCloud also clarifies that *comics*, when referred to as a broad medium, is properly used in the singular. So I'll be saying things like, "Comics is" rather than "Comics are." It sounds strange at first, but you'll get used to it.

This definition is pretty dense, so let's pull it apart a little bit. *Juxtaposed* means the panels come one after the other in a linear fashion on the page—as opposed to film panels, which might be called comics, except that they occupy the same space on the screen. To be comics, they need to be juxtaposed as opposed to occupying the same space. *Pictorial and other images* just means that, yes, comics involves illustrated visual art, but it also includes words, designs, boxes, and other types of images to help tell the story. The deliberate sequence means that the images are not random; they are carefully placed to either tell a story or elicit a response. *Conveying information and producing a response in the reader* implies the intent of comics—to educate someone via instructional graphics or to tell a story to produce an aesthetic response.

McCloud's definition of comics is probably the most widely accepted version, although others have tried in different ways to define the medium. The bottom line is that comics is a broad field that encompasses many different types of material, but it must include the elements he alludes to in his definition—until someone breaks the rules and stretches the boundaries, of course!

The History of Comics

Scholars have not reached a consensus about the earliest comics. Some early art forms contain a few of the elements of modern comics but are missing others. For some scholars, the earliest comics are cave paintings because some seem to be telling stories of hunts or other animal-centered events (for example, see figure 1.2). But most cave drawings contain only one event per picture—or no event at all—so they cannot be considered sequential.

Figure 1.2. Cave drawings may be the first comics. *Photo courtesy of Chris Rogers/istock*

Egyptian hieroglyphics are sometimes included in the history of comics. That's because the images are sequential and tell a discernable story. Critics argue that the pictures in the hieroglyphics are more like the letters of a written language because they denote sounds instead of objects.[6] Although the letters of a written language may be graphic, they don't fit the definition of comics.

Egyptian tomb paintings (like those in figure 1.3), however, do seem to contain all the elements of comics. These stylized paintings are meant to be read in a certain direction and tell a story. Although it is not segmented with panels, the scenes are separated by action and time.

A column in Rome called Trajan's Column, completed in 113 AD, tells the story of the Romans conquering the Dacians in the decade prior. The column is ninety-eight-feet high with a twelve-foot diameter. The story of the conquest spirals around the column in a sequential form. Of course, because the art is carved as opposed to illustrated, some historians exclude it from the history of comics. Perhaps it could be called sequential sculpture rather than comics.

The next major step in comics history can be seen in the Bayeux Tapestry, the 230-foot-long tapestry that tells the story of the Norman conquest of England in 1066. This celebrated artwork uses pictures and Latin commentary in sequence. The events of the conquest can be read from left to right, with fifty clearly delineated scenes that note very specific details. For instance, in one scene, the army becomes mired in quicksand and several soldiers are rescued. Around this time,

Figure 1.3. Egyptian tomb painting. *Illustration courtesy of Hibrida13/istock*

some stained-glass windows were created in European cathedrals that told stories graphically. These were mostly scenes from the Bible or from the lives of Christian saints.

Ancient Aztec and Mayan codices (the plural of codex, which refers to ancient books made of long sheets of paper or papyrus) contain sequential art that Scott McCloud and others label comics. These long panels tell stories of battles and daily life, as well as religious rituals of the Aztec and Mayan people. Unfortunately, many of these codices were destroyed by the European explorers who made their way to the new world in the sixteenth century.

Japanese scrolls (figure 1.4) from the twelfth century have also been discussed in the history of comics. We will discuss these scrolls in chapter 6 on Japanese manga.

Figure 1.4. Artist rendering of Japanese scroll animal. *Illustration by Chris Burns*

Game Changer

The game changer in comics was the invention of the printing press. Now people did not have to travel to the artwork to see the graphic story unfold—the story came to them.

In the Middle Ages in Europe, various books were printed with illustrations that might fall into the realm of comics—including Bibles with extended graphics, religious tracts, and so on. Most people could still not read or write, so illustrated Bibles (figure 1.5) and stained glass windows had to be not only beautiful, but tell stories as well.

In the early 1700s, William Hogarth, a visual artist, painted a series of pictures called *A Harlot's Progress*, then another called *A Rake's Progress*, both of which were published as sequential art in book form. But the first publication that resembles modern-style comics was by Rudolphe Töpffer in the mid-1800s. His satirical stories used cartoonish pictures and panel borders to tell the stories (for a similar style, see figure 1.6). These stories also featured the first interdependent combination of words and pictures in Europe.[7] Although Töpffer's publications were merely hobbies for him, the medium caught the interest of many people. British magazines began employing this kind of art throughout the rest of the century.

Eventually, comics came to America. In 1889, New York newspaper publisher Joseph Pulitzer published a full page of black-and-white humorous illustrations in his newspaper *The World*, calling it *The World's Funny Side*. Pulitzer is also

Figure 1.5. Biblical art helped people remember stories. *Illustration courtesy of Linda Steward/ istock*

Phillp (of England and Spain) hears of his wife's death.

Figure 1.6. A cartoon done in Victorian style similar to Töpffer's. *Illustration courtesy of Andrew_Howe/istock*

credited with popularizing the first modern-style comic character, the Yellow Kid, in R. F. Outcault's *Hogan's Alley*. This single panel cartoon, which appeared in 1895 after Pulitzer acquired a color printing press, focused on the humorous exploits of a group of young hooligans. The Yellow Kid remained one of the most popular characters in the early twentieth century.[8] Outcault is even more famous for creating a strip called *Buster Brown*, which lent its name to a line of shoes a few years later.

Across town, William Randolph Hearst, a rival newspaper mogul, saw the popularity of Pulitzer's funny pages and began publishing his own comics to increase readership. He hired away most of Pulitzer's cartoon creators and in 1896

Figure 1.7. Kids have loved comics for over one hundred years. *Photo courtesy of 2thirds-photo/istock*

came out with his own funny pages called *American Humorist*, an eight-page color comic supplement in the Sunday edition of the *New York Journal*. R. F. Outcault had switched papers by then, and the first of many legal battles over who owns the rights to comics characters and stories ensued. As a result, readers of both papers got to enjoy stories about the Yellow Kid.[9]

As the nineteenth century turned into the twentieth century, newspapers all over the country began publishing comics. These cartoon panels, which had not yet received the stigma of being children's fare, became very popular. In fact, without the space restrictions that came in the middle of the twentieth century, newspapers published full pages of colorful comics that helped them compete against their cross-town rivals. Cartoons such as *Bringing Up Father* by George McManus, *Krazy Kat* by George Herriman, *The Katzenjammer Kids* by Rudolph Dirks, *Gasoline Alley* by Frank King, and many others made cartoon characters household names.

Comic strips in the first half of the twentieth century migrated from pure humor and hijinks to other genres. Winsor McCay was a visionary who believed that the fantasy genre was a natural fit for a daily newspaper comic strip. His strip, *Little Nemo in Slumberland*, became very popular, and his artwork has been lauded far and wide. McCay's *Dreams of a Rarebit Fiend* and *Little Sammy Sneeze*

European Influence on American Comic Strips

In 1897, readers of the comics section in the *New York Journal* were introduced to the Katzenjammers, a German immigrant family with two prankster sons, Hans and Fritz. *The Katzenjammer Kids* enjoyed immediate popularity and stayed in the public eye for many years. Creator Rudolph Dirks (1877–1968) was born in Heide, Schleswig-Holstein, in Germany, and immigrated to the United States as a seven-year-old boy.

The main characters in his comic strip were Hans and Fritz, fun-loving boys reminiscent of two other pranksters in German comics: Max and Moritz, from a picture story by Wilhelm Busch called "Max und Moritz."

Dirks is hailed as a pioneer in comics illustration. He is among the first to write out the characters' words in speech balloons. His characters also spoke in dialect, having not learned proper English yet. Although Hans and Fritz were often clever enough to fool the adults, they almost always ended up receiving spankings for their bad behavior. Looking at the early comics today is a little shocking—many people would be uncomfortable with the level of corporal punishment demonstrated in the strips.

were also fantasy comics, although neither reached the popularity of *Little Nemo*. Fantasy strips like McCay's helped pave the way for science fiction comic books, although the strips didn't always follow a continuous story line.

Action/adventure comics were another matter. These stories were serialized for years, gathering avid readers of all ages. *Buck Rogers* by Philip Francis Nowlan; *Mandrake the Magician* and *The Phantom*, both by Lee Falk; and *Tarzan*, adapted from the Edgar Rice Burroughs novel, became popular in the first half of the twentieth century. Mandrake, who could hypnotize people and perform other magic tricks while fighting villains, and the Phantom, a costumed crime fighter based in a fictional African country, have been credited with igniting the imaginations of superhero creators in the following decades. The comic strips were followed by novels, radio shows, television series, and movies, providing the blueprint for the multimedia platforms of many comics characters to follow.

Little Orphan Annie, created by Harold Gray, was a serial comic strip that became popular in the 1920s and was published until 2010, enjoying an eighty-six-year run. A cross between a family drama and an adventure strip, *Annie* has been made into numerous films and even spawned the famous musical play *Annie*. In one of Annie's origin stories, Gray took a male version of the character—Little Orphan Otto—to Captain Joe Patterson, famous head of the *Chicago Tribune* comics syndicate. "The kid looks like a pansy to me," Patterson is said to have growled. "Put a skirt on him and we'll call it 'Little Orphan Annie.'"[10] In another version, Gray met an orphan who impressed him with her self-reliance, and he wrote the character as a girl from the beginning. Another factor in his decision, according to this version of the story, was that "at the time, some 40 strips were using boys as the main characters; only three were using girls. I chose Annie for mine, and made her an orphan so she'd have no family, no tangling alliances, but the freedom to go where she pleased."[11]

Comic Strips Become Comic Books

In 1933 the Eastern Color Printing Company gave birth to the age of modern comic books when the company collected a number of popular newspaper comic strips and put them together into a tabloid-sized magazine called *Famous Funnies*. At first the publication was printed as a giveaway for Kinney Shoe Store and other clients.[12] Soon the books became hot sellers at newsstands as stand-alone items. Existing newspaper comic strips made up the majority of the comics, but original material began to appear after the first few issues. *Famous Funnies* was published until 1955.

Another publishing company took notice of the success of Eastern's new comic books: National Allied Publications, which later became DC Comics. In 1935, National published *New Fun Comics*, a regularly published comic book that contained original material. The publication did not sell well, and National had a difficult time paying its writers. The constant staff turnover offered opportunities to new writers with new material. For instance, two teenagers from Ohio, Jerry Siegel and Joe Shuster, wrote a number of features for the publisher, including "Dr. Occult" and "Federal Men." Another of their projects was rejected over and over, a superhero story featuring Superman. Forced to take on new partners for the sake of capital, National changed its name to Detective Comics, Inc., which was commonly referred to as DC Comics.

In 1938, DC Comics introduced another title to its list of books: *Action Comics*. This new book featured the aforementioned "Superman," written by Siegel and Shuster. *Action Comics* #1 is arguably the most important comic book in the industry's history, according to historians Randy Duncan, Matthew J. Smith, and

> "Everyone needs a hero. It is second nature to look up to a role model and model your life after certain people or to have aspiring dreams to transform into a 'somebody' from a 'nobody.' . . . Decade after decade, these superheroes never seem to age. They are the sweet escape from the harsh reality to the 'good ol' days.' Motivation, determination, and perseverance — these constitute the imperative characteristics of a superhero. Unhindered by a strong moral code, they always put service above self. Attentive and punctual, they appear in the nick of time when trouble begins to lurk. To protect their family members and friends, they live two distinct lives."—Heajin Y., Phoenix, Arizona[b]

Paul Levitz, authors of *The Power of Comics: History, Form, and Culture*: "Superman . . . single-handedly established the identity of the American comic book."[13] Within a few years, *Action Comics* and its spin-off *Superman* were each selling over a million copies a month. The era of superheroes was born. We'll talk more about this in chapter 3.

But other types of comics were selling, too. Adventure, romance, and horror all became popular in these early years. By the summer of 1941 more than ten million comic books were being sold every month by twenty-nine different comic book publishers. Compare that number to January 2015, when the top three hundred titles, published by a handful of publishers, sold a total of 6.8 million copies.[14]

Comics during the War Years

As the world went to war at the end of the 1930s, some comic strip writers began to use their platform to encourage patriotism. This trend could be seen very clearly in superhero comic books such as *Captain America*, created by Joe Simon and Jack Kirby, which made its debut in 1941 with a cover that featured the hero punching Adolf Hitler. That first issue sold nearly one million copies.

Many adults remember reading a series of comic book adaptions of classic novels such as *Moby Dick*, *Ivanhoe*, and *Frankenstein*. These titles, and many more, were part of a series begun in 1941 called Classic Comics, later changed to Classics Illustrated. The first title in the series was *The Three Musketeers*, an adaption of the novel by Alexandre Dumas. Although the books were largely scorned

> "It dawned on me that to be considered a great superhero, superpowers are not required. You just need a body of people in need who are looking for someone to pull them through the hardest of times. Like Batman was to the people of Gotham. Batman will always be the greatest superhero in my book. His ability to fight crime and win while being powerless is truly iconic and inspiring. While he may just be a comic book character, his message to fight for what you believe in, even if you are just an everyday person, echoes in the extraordinary actions of ordinary people."—Lauren P., East Setauket, New York[c]

by teachers, many people the age of your parents and grandparents credit this series with introducing them to the great literary classics of centuries past. Many works of literature are still adapted to graphic novels today, some of which will be discussed in chapter 4.

Comic Books Branch Out

By 1947, circulation of almost all superhero comic books was declining. Compared with the war against the Nazis, the fight against fictional local villains seemed too mundane for the audience. Publishers began to look at other genres for inspiration: funny animals, romance, westerns, crime dramas, and horror.[15] Funny animal comics such as Walt Disney's *Donald Duck*, written by Carl Barks, gathered a loyal readership that lasted for many years.

The romance genre (like the one in figure 1.8), which had been represented by the *Archie* comics in the early 1940s, took off at the end of the decade and by 1950 accounted for a full quarter of the comic book market.[16] The romance genre really got kick-started when the team of Jack Kirby and Joe Simon—who had cut their teeth on superhero comics such as *Captain America*—produced *Young Romance* #1 in 1947.

Western comics took off after World War II as well. While they had been around since the late 1930s, they reached a new level in the late 1940s when a spate of cowboy movies were released. In 1948, the comic book *Hopalong Cassidy* was selling over eight million copies for publisher Fawcett. Other publishers saw the success of Fawcett's title and began producing their own. In 1951 DC even converted *All-Star Comics* into *All-Star Western* to take advantage of the fad.

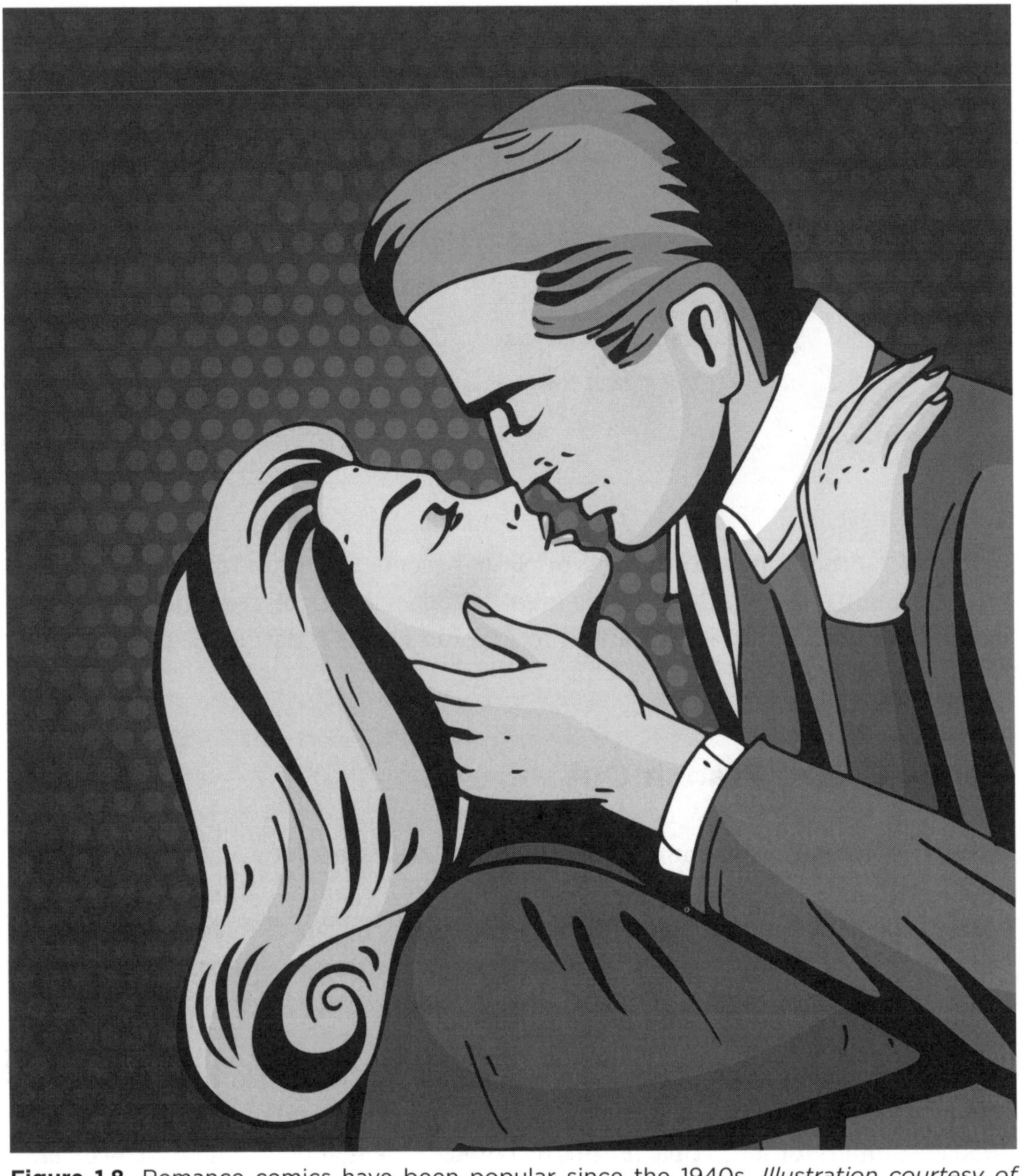

Figure 1.8. Romance comics have been popular since the 1940s. *Illustration courtesy of Sapunkele/istock*

Westerns continued to sell well during the 1950s as adventuresome cowboys took over the fledgling television industry. Dell Comics, in particular, capitalized on the western craze on television, publishing *Gunsmoke* in 1956 and then *Maverick* in 1958. The next year they added *Bat Masterson* and *Rawhide*. By 1959, westerns accounted for eleven of the top twenty programs on television, and the related comic books flew off the shelves. By the early 1960s, however, the sales of western comic books were in decline.

Crime Does Pay

As superhero stories declined in the 1940s, crime stories were headed in the opposite direction. The series *Crime Does Not Pay*, created by Lev Gleason Publications, had been published since 1942 with moderate success. But by 1948 *Crime Does Not Pay* was selling at a brisk 1.5 million copies per month. Seeing this success, other publishers began jumping on the bandwagon. The ten crime titles in 1947 were joined by twenty-three new crime titles in 1948, many of which employed the word *crime* or *criminal* as the first word in the title.[17] You may have heard of the detective Dick Tracy, who wore a long yellow trench coat—he got

Will Eisner, Godfather of Comics

The most prestigious award given to a comic or graphic novel of distinction is the Eisner Award. The award is named after Will Eisner, who labored in the business for more than sixty-five years, working tirelessly to bring graphic storytelling the notoriety it deserved. He has been called the "grandmaster" and "godfather" of American comics even though he never wrote or illustrated any DC or Marvel superhero.[d]

William Erwin Eisner was born on March 6, 1917, in Brooklyn, New York. He grew up in the crowded tenements that would later become the setting for one of his breakthrough works, *A Contract with God*. Eisner attended DeWitt Clinton High School in the Bronx, the same school that several other comics legends attended, including Bob Kane and Stan Lee. He published his first cartoons in the school paper.

In the late 1930s, Eisner formed one of the first comics production shops, called the Eisner-Iger Studio. The group specialized in providing comics features to comic book and newspaper publishers who had no in-house art staff. The studio produced the first successful female action hero in comics in 1938, when it produced *Sheena, Queen of the Jungle*.[e]

In 1940 Eisner debuted *The Spirit*, a masked crime fighter with no special powers. The writing was crisp and the strip featured great artwork. Historian Arie Kaplan says, "Many critics now say that *The Spirit*, a unique mix of bravura, derring-do, and tongue-in-cheek slapstick that ran until 1952, was one of the first attempts at the 'action-comedy' genre in comics form, inspiring later efforts such as Stan Lee and Jack Kirby's *Fantastic Four*."[f] Jack Kirby had actually worked for Eisner back in the days of the production studio. Some of the characters in the early strips perpetuated negative racial stereotypes, but in typical Eisner fashion, as he became aware of his mistakes, he changed and improved his representations.

Among Will Eisner's many contributions to the world of comics, he is credited with popularizing the notion of a *graphic novel*. He was not the first to use those words, but he brought the term to the attention of many readers with his 1978 book *A Contract with God*. The word *novel* is a little bit misleading, as the book is actually a collection of short stories. The setting for the stories is the Bronx in the early years of the twentieth century. The protagonist in the title story, Frimme Hersh, is a devout Jewish man who sees the good in the world until his daughter passes away due to a sudden illness. If you've ever asked the age-old question, "Why do bad things happen to good people?" this story will resonate with you.

Another major contribution to the comics industry came in the form of Eisner's book *Comics and Sequential Art*, which Scott McCloud claims was "the first book to examine the art-form of comics." McCloud goes on to say, "Will Eisner's work has been an inspiration to me, and to thousands of artists, for many years."[g] That was Eisner's legacy—believing that comics could be more than children's stories. "It occurred to me very early on that his medium had greater potential," Eisner said in an interview a few years before his death in 2005. "That it was more of a literary medium than anybody else thought."[h] Thanks to his efforts and excellence through the years, graphic storytelling truly has begun to fulfill that potential.

his comics start in 1948, along with many other crime dramas. As competition in this segment rose, so did the intensity of the stories. Writers included increasing amounts of violence and gory images to attract readers.[18] The backlash from parents and other authorities in the mid-1950s that led to the Comics Code Authority (more on this later in this chapter) resulted in more sanitized stories in this genre. These scrubbed stories with their tame art stopped pulling in readers, and by the end of the 1950s the crime genre of comic books had virtually disappeared.

Horror Comics Cause a Panic

As the 1940s were ending, comic publisher Entertaining Comics (EC) had been following the trends of the day, with titles such as *Crime Patrol* and *Saddle Justice*. In 1950 EC publisher William Gaines shook up the comic book industry when he launched several horror lines: *The Vault of Horror*, *The Haunt of Fear*, *Weird Science*, *Weird Fantasy*, *Crime SuspenStories*, *Two-Fisted Tales*, and *Crypt of Terror* (later renamed *Tales from the Crypt*).

The new horror stories were intelligently written and handsomely illustrated. Historian E. B. Boatner explains why the stories attracted so much attention:

> EC horror opened new vistas of death from sources previously unimagined by the reader. Victims were serial-sectioned by giant machines, eaten by ghouls, devoured by rats—from inside and out—pecked by pigeons, stuffed down disposals, skewered on swords, buried alive, dismembered and used as baseball equipment, hung as living clappers in huge bells, made into sausage and soap, dissolved, southern-fried, hacked by maniacs in Santa Claus suits, and offed in unusually high percentages by their wives or husbands.[19]

Although the other comic publishers followed suit and produced some horror titles to try and keep up, none achieved quite the ferocity and gore of the EC titles.

Until the advent of horror comics, educators and other community leaders did not pay much attention to the effect of comic books on the morality of children. They were seen as amusing, harmless time wasters. Although some educators had spoken out about comics' lack of educational content, no one really worried about their influence. All that changed with the popularity of horror comics. In 1954, soon after the EC titles began selling by the millions every month, a psychiatrist named Frederic Wertham produced a book that changed the comic book industry for several decades.

In *Seduction of the Innocent: The Influence of Comic Books on Today's Youth*, Wertham laid out his argument that comic books were undermining the morality of American youth. He described experiments that supposedly proved that comic books were contributing to the rise of vandalism and bad behavior by American children. In recent decades researchers have shown that Wertham's experiments were poorly designed and the data suspect, but this revelation came fifty years too late. Educators, parents, religious leaders, and politicians spoke out against the scourge of comics. In actuality, the book probably wouldn't have influenced many people because very few people read it, but *Ladies Home Journal* published an excerpt that reached a broad audience of a very important demographic—moms.

In 1954 a Senate subcommittee was created to investigate juvenile delinquency in the United States. During their discussion on the deleterious effect of comic books on America's youth, the subcommittee called on Dr. Wertham to testify as an expert witness. The committee found him to be very persuasive. The lawmakers also called comic book publishers to testify, including William Gaines of EC. While most of the other publishers admitted that the content of comic books had gotten out of hand, Gaines remained defiant. When one senator confronted him with one of his own covers showing a man with a bloody ax in one hand holding the severed head of a woman in the other, Gaines commented that the cover would only be in bad taste if the man were "holding the head a little higher so that the blood could be seen dripping from it."[20] As you might guess, this answer did not go over well with the senators.

In response to the increasing pressure from educators and the media, comic book publishers established the Comics Code Authority (CCA). This self-regulation stipulated that "all scenes of horror, excessive bloodshed, gory or gruesome crimes, depravity, lust, sadism, masochism shall not be permitted"[21] (see the approval stamp in figure 1.9). The words *horror* and *terror* were not even permitted in the title. EC lasted a few more years with titles like *Aces High* and *Psychoanalysis*, but their business truly had depended on the shock of their horror comics. The public outcry provided an opportunity for some of the publishers that were not putting out objectionable material, such as Archie and DC, to get ahead, but the industry fell on hard times in the second half of the 1950s. And not just because of the Comics Code.

Comic book numbers fell in the second half of the 1950s because of the rise of one momentous invention: television. By the end of the decade, nearly 90 percent of American households had at least one TV. It will come as no surprise that reading in general declined, including comic book reading. Shows like *Gunsmoke*, *Zorro*, and *Robin Hood* were capturing the attention of kids all over the country—and they were free of charge. Many of the popular comic book titles in the late 1950s came directly from TV or movies, such as *The Adventures of Jerry Lewis*, a famous actor and comedian from that era.

Superheroes Save the Day

With the tarnishing of the comic industry's reputation in the mid-1950s, publishers were looking for a genre that would pass the censors and still sell books. Superheroes—except the Big Three, Superman, Batman, and Wonder Woman—had pretty much all gone into retirement at the end of the 1940s. Atlas, another large publisher, attempted to revive Captain America in 1954 with the title *Captain America . . . Commie Smasher*. Cap lasted three issues, as did the Sub-Mariner and

Figure 1.9. The Comics Code Authority symbol was self-imposed by the comics publishers to reassure parents. *Comics Code Authority Seal of Approval is Trademark & Copyright 2017 Comic Book Legal Defense Fund. Used with permission.*

the Human Torch. Although not terribly profitable, the seeds of an idea—returning to the superheroes of the past—had been planted.

In 1955, DC tried to revive the superhero genre as well, introducing their first new character in years: Martian Manhunter, featured in *Detective Comics*. But to really revive the genre, they needed to put a new spin on an old character. In 1956, in *Showcase* #4, DC revived the Flash, which became an instant success. This Flash, Barry Allen, had similar powers to his predecessor, but a completely new identity and look. By the end of the decade the DC team, led by legendary editor Julius "Julie" Schwartz, resurrected Green Lantern as well. Both characters were firmly set in modern times, using modern science to inform their stories and adventures. The story of this superhero renaissance is discussed more fully in chapter 3.

Becoming Marvel-ous

If you've been paying attention to popular culture—and who hasn't?—you've noticed that most of the biggest movies in the past ten years have featured comic book characters. And most of those characters have been from the so-called Marvel universe. That just means that the characters have been adapted from the Marvel line of comics characters. But if you've noticed in our discussion of the history of comics so far, Marvel hasn't even come up yet by the end of the 1950s. That's because Marvel was called Atlas at that time, and it was struggling to stay afloat. At the end of 1958, Atlas had one employee—Stan Lee—and according to legend, he was considering quitting the business altogether.

Comic book history notes 1961 as a momentous year. That is the year that Atlas—now Marvel—published *The Fantastic Four* #1. Various stories have circulated about Marvel coming up with the idea to start its own "team" of superheroes. Some stories say Marvel owner Martin Goodman had been playing golf with DC publisher Jack Liebowitz when Liebowitz told him of the success of DC's team comic *Justice League* (recently changed from *Justice Society of America*). According to this story, Goodman went straightaway to Lee and told him to write a book about competing superheroes. Whether that story is true or not, Goodman certainly would have noted the success of *Justice League* by 1961. Through the years, comic book companies have famously jumped on hot trends, imitating anything the public seems to be buying.

However it happened, *The Fantastic Four* changed the industry and began Marvel on a path that has made it the leader of superhero comics to this day. The appeal of *The Fantastic Four* was immediate, with their bickering, their lifelike personalities, and their relatively young characters. Stan Lee famously said, "The characters would be the kind of characters I could personally relate to: They'd be flesh and blood, they'd have their faults and foibles, they'd be fallible and feisty, and—most important of all—inside their colorful, costumed booties they have feet of clay."[22]

Along with the legendary Jack Kirby, Lee put out one flawed hero after another: the volatile Bruce Banner becomes a raging monster in *The Incredible Hulk*; a frail doctor is transformed into the Mighty Thor in the pages of *Journey into Mystery*. But perhaps the most important hit of all came when Lee teamed up with Steve Ditko to tell the story of nerdy teenager Peter Parker, who becomes the Amazing Spider-Man in *Amazing Fantasy* #15. The problems Peter Parker faced both in and out of his costume resonated with readers and helped launch an entire line of superheroes that continue to thrive today: Iron Man, a revamped Captain America, the X-Men, Doctor Strange, Daredevil, and more. It took Marvel a decade, but by the mid-1970s, the company had overtaken DC as the dominant comic book publisher in America.

Expansion and Maturation of the Comic Book

The 1960s was a time of tremendous change around the world, especially in the United States. This change in music and the arts, in the rise of the middle class, in the reach of the news media, in the ability to travel around the world, and in many other areas of life brought about a shift in attitudes, especially in those under twenty-five years of age. Civil rights marches, the murder of President Kennedy, the presence of news reports during the controversial Vietnam War, the hippie movement, riots in many big cities—all resulted in a change in attitude

"The Vietnam War caused America to fall from its unwavering optimism into a state of knowing maturity. Once the young hot shot country going out to save the world, we grew up in an instant becoming old, tired, and depressed. Not only did the country lose its hope, the superheroes did too. Once the beacons of American heroism, they became the beacon of America's imperfections and wrong intent. Growing up was wretched for America and for its superheroes.

"The superheroes of the 1960s, the silver age of comic books, became increasingly separate from their golden age forefathers; one main aspect of their change was how they attained their powers. Superheroes were now getting their powers from freak accidents. The accidents typically involved atomic radiation exposure. These accidents symbolized the fear that people had about the use of the atom bomb in the Vietnam War. At that time, no one was quite sure of the effect that nuclear substance had on human anatomy."—Olivia R., La Jolla, California[i] toward authority. This change was reflected in comics as well as on television and in movies and music.

Chapter 3 tells the story of how superhero comics became more relevant to comics readers—with Green Lantern and Green Arrow becoming aware of social inequities and crime; with Captain American renouncing his citizenship after discovering the Watergate scandal; with Lois Lane learning firsthand how it feels to be a racial minority; and with Spider-Man experiencing the trauma of drug abuse in a very close friend. In fact, Marvel ran issues 96–98 of *The Amazing Spider-Man* (May–July 1971) without the CCA seal, since the Code administrator refused to grant code approval due to the subject of drug addiction. The books sold well, and the CCA was forever weakened. Marvel's *Doctor Strange* was also a sign of the times, with its surrealistic illustrations and adventures in magical dimensions. In fact, many people at the time saw a connection between Doctor Strange stories and their experience of visions on psychedelic drugs.[23]

The two main comics publishers, DC and Marvel, had built an audience over the past decade that was loyal to comics but looking for something even more countercultural. EC's humor publication, *Mad*, which fell outside of the CCA regulations due to its magazine format, was skewering political figures and hacking away at the foundational beliefs of the older generation. By the early 1970s, *Mad* magazine was selling 2.5 million copies per issue.[24] Hungry to express their own satires and political viewpoints, college students around the country began writing and publishing their own comics via their student-run school newspapers. Their content, art styles, and even the distribution channels were a form of rebellion for these students. As the authors of *The Power of Comics* put it, "These convention-defying, politically charged, and independently produced comics became known an underground comix."[25] As the "underground" began to thrive in the 1960s, the comic book publishers in New York—DC and Marvel—became known as the "mainstream."

One of the first and most widely circulated student publications appeared in the University of Texas newspaper the *Texas Ranger*. Graduate student Gilbert Shelton, who took over as editor in 1962, included his own superhero parody called *Wonder Wart-Hog*, one of the first underground comix to become a national hit. When a new editor phased out Wonder Wart-Hog, Shelton and several of his art mates created their own short-lived underground publication *THE Austin Iconoclastic Newsletter* (which became known simply as *THE*). The first issue of THE, which was only four pages long, ran a page-long comic called "The Adventures of J" by Frank Stack. Although it is never stated outright, J is clearly meant to be Jesus, due to the biblical clothes and the fact that in one adventure J turns water into wine. After *THE* folded, Shelton collected a number of the J strips, put them together, and convinced a friend to run off fifty copies on the law school library photocopier. This homemade comic book, *The Adventures of Jesus*, is considered by many to be the very first underground comic book. Shelton's own *Fabulous Furry Freak Brothers* would become famous in the underground comix world as well.

Many other edgy, obscene, antigovernment, and frequently violent comics were published in college humor magazines and underground newspapers throughout the 1960s. A number of these papers formed the Underground Press Syndicate and gave aspiring cartoonists their start.

One such up-and-coming cartoonist was Robert Crumb. Crumb had been making homemade comic books since he was a child. In 1967 the Philadelphia-based underground newspaper *Yarrowstalks* published several of his strips. Soon the *East Village Other* in New York began to publish Crumb's strips. Emboldened by his growing popularity, Crumb put together a book of his work, including a page of light-hearted "Keep on Truckin'" images that quickly found their way into popular culture.

The book was published as *Zap Comix* #1, after which Crumb and his wife famously walked around the streets of San Francisco selling copies of *Zap* out of a baby carriage. Hippies and other countercultural fans bought the books in record stores and "head shops" (stores where drug paraphernalia were sold), leading to further *Zap* creations. By the end of 1968 Robert Crumb was a national celebrity. His artwork was so popular that rock-and-roll legends such as the Rolling Stones and Janice Joplin asked him to illustrate their album covers.

By 1973 the underground comix industry was flourishing, providing a visible alternative to the mainstream comics publishers. According to *The Power of Comics*, "At the peak of the underground phenomenon in 1973, there were over 300 comix titles in print, with nearly as many people referring to themselves as underground cartoonists, and the average book sold 40,000 copies."[26] Although the art in these books was often less refined than mainstream comics, the books gained a reputation for being more sophisticated, due to their critiques of politics, religion, and social customs of the day.

The theme that tied all these underground comix together was their defiance toward authority—not just the government, but the CCA, which the authors flaunted with violent, sexually explicit material. It was a time of experimentation and unbridled freedom of expression. This freedom of expression bled into mainstream comic books of the day, bringing the worlds of the mainstream and underground comics closer together.

By the mid-1970s, a number of trends in the comic book industry conspired to weaken the strength of the underground comix movement. In the 1973 Supreme Court ruling *Miller v. California*, the court ruled that obscenity itself was not protected by the First Amendment right of free speech. By the court's new standard, many underground comix could be prosecuted as obscene material. At the same time, the head shops that sold underground comix alongside drug paraphernalia were being forced out of business in many communities. Perhaps most importantly, the antiauthority writers and readers of undergrounds were, well, growing up. It's fine to read rebellious comic books when you're at college with Mom and Dad paying the bills, but eventually you get a job—with a mortgage to pay and kids to raise. The underground publishers began to see their books as a means to an income rather than a means to subvert the out-of-touch authorities. All these factors led to a gradual weakening of the underground movement. Many of the writers and publishers joined the mainstream publishers or sought to go mainstream with their presses.

1970s Trends

Marvel and DC had been adapting their superhero comics to the reality of teens' lives since the mid-1960s. But other trends brought about a burst of creativity in the early 1970s. When Hollywood began producing martial arts films featuring Bruce Lee and other worldwide fighting stars, the comic book publishers followed. Marvel produced several martial arts comics, including *The Hands of Shang-Chi: Master of Kung Fu*, written by Steve Englehart with art by Jim Starlin, which debuted in 1973. Shang-Chi has been part of the Avengers and has teamed up with numerous Marvel characters, including Spider-Man and the X-Men. Over at DC, Dennis O'Neil and Jim Berry created the character Richard Dragon, who became the star of the 1975 series *Richard Dragon, Kung Fu Fighter*.

Another trend that gained traction in the 1970s was sword-and-sorcery games and novels. Marvel capitalized on the craze by licensing a pulp-novel character from the 1930s created by author Robert E. Howard: Conan the Barbarian. The first issue of *Conan the Barbarian* comic book, written by Roy Thomas with art by Barry Smith, came out in 1970 and was an instant hit. The series ran for over twenty years, finally ending in 1993. Conan was one of Marvel's biggest sellers in the 1970s.

Horror comics came back strong in the 1970s as well. This is not surprising after the independent and underground publishers had been thumbing their noses at the CCA for almost a decade. Even the mainstream publishers had begun to disregard the CCA, which had loosened its standards in 1971 to allow for the inclusion of monsters, ghosts, and ghouls, as long as they were handled in a literary and tasteful way. Marvel's best known horror comics in the early 1970s included *The Tomb of Dracula*, which featured a team of vampire hunters, and *Werewolf by Night* by Gerry Conway and Mike Ploog, both published in 1972.

One of the most important horror characters to come along in the 1970s was DC Comics' Swamp Thing. Debuting in *The House of Secrets* #92 in 1971, Swamp Thing was created by Len Wein and Bernie Wrightson. The green monster would headline his own series a few years later, only to be canceled by the end of the 1970s. In the 1980s, DC would hire rookie writer Alan Moore to resurrect and rework the Swamp Thing legend, to great success. Historians consider *The Saga of the Swamp Thing* one of the most influential series of the 1980s.[27]

Worlds Collide: Mid-1970s

Superhero comics, although experiencing a decline from the previous decade, were still the most popular comic genre of the 1970s. Early in the decade, comics legend Jack Kirby left Marvel for DC. Some label this exodus as the end of the Silver Age and the beginning of the Bronze Age of comics. At DC, Kirby conceived Fourth World, a widely ranging story line that incorporated four different series. While the run of Fourth World did not last very long by comics standards, the idea of integrating multiple titles and heroes would be a regular feature in years to come.

Another leap forward in the superhero saga would occur at Marvel in 1975 when Len Wein and Dave Cockrum attempted to relaunch the X-Men series in *Giant-Size X-Men*. Eschewing many of the old X-Men characters (who had disappeared on a mission), the creators built a multinational, multiethnic cast to draw in nontraditional comic book readers. The new team includes, among others, Sunfire, a Japanese man; Storm, an African woman; Thunderbird, a Native American (who, unfortunately, lasted just two missions before he was killed); and Colossus, a Russian teenager. A new creative team took over X-Men soon thereafter: writer Chris Claremont and illustrator John Byrne. Claremont and Byrne formed one of the most highly regarded collaborations in the history of comics, and by the end of the 1970s *X-Men* was at the top of the sales charts. This position of popularity would last for more than three decades.[28] One of the major factors in the series' popularity was an emphasis on the characters as misunderstood outcasts facing a harsh world that hated them no matter what they accomplished—a feeling that many teenagers can relate to.

In 1979, due to a shrinking audience and distribution problems, DC began to experiment with the concept of a limited series that would last only for a specified number of issues. The first was *The World of Krypton*, written by Paul Kupperberg with art by Howard Chaykin and Murphy Anderson. The series told the story of the final days of Superman's home planet, Krypton. Audiences liked the limited series, and both DC and Marvel would use the concept many times in years to come.

Independent comics, which had evolved and matured from the rough underground comix of the 1960s and early 1970s, changed the comics industry in important ways in the 1970s and 1980s. An independent publisher is any of

> ## ! Best Selling Comic
>
> *X-Men* #91, the 1991 spinoff series premier that Chris Claremont wrote with Jim Lee, is the best-selling comic book of all time, according to *Guinness World Records*. In 2015, Claremont and his X-Men collaborator for many years, John Byrne, were entered into the Will Eisner Award Hall of Fame.

the new publishers who tried to compete with the big mainstream publishers of the day, which included DC, Marvel, and Archie, among others. Many of these independently published comic books were written by mainstream writers and illustrators, but with the intent to own the rights to their own work.

Several of the new mainstream series that would become popular in the 1980s and 1990s began as minicomics or Newave comics during this time. Art Spiegelman, Jessica Able, Craig Thompson, Adrian Tomine, and other now-famous creators produced independent series in small, inexpensive formats that were later picked up by mainstream publishers. You may have seen the many volumes of *Elfquest* in the graphic novel section of bookstores. That series, created by Wendy and Richard Pini, was published independently starting in 1978. Science fiction and fantasy, helped in no small part by the popularity of a little film called *Star Wars*, were very popular in the latter half of the 1970s.

Independent publishing became quite popular with comic artists for a variety of reasons. Most importantly, artists got to keep the rights to their work, which was not the case at the large mainstream publishers. The famous fight between DC and *Superman* creators Jerry Siegel and Joe Shuster had never been satisfactorily resolved, and creators were not anxious to hand over the rights to their work no matter how much money they were making. Another reason these artists liked the independent publishers was that they were offered royalties on their work, another practice not being followed by the big publishers. Fortunately, the presence of the independents applied good pressure on the mainstream giants, which eventually resulted in much-needed changes to the financial and creative practices of the established publishers.

Comics Shops Take Over

For almost a half century, mainstream comics had been sold at newsstands. Few comics were sold by subscription, and even fewer bookstores were interested in providing these "kids' stories" to customers. The newsstand system was haphazard at best. Bundles of mixed titles were delivered to drugstores, grocery stores, and newsstands, and were put out in no particular order. Followers of specific stories might or might not find the next issue they were seeking when it came out. Large numbers of unsold comics were returned to distributors. The system needed fixing if the market was going to grow. Enter high school teacher Phil Seuling.

Seuling was a comic book fan who conceived of a better distribution system. He negotiated a deal with comic book publishers whereby they would provide a deep discount for the books on the condition that unsold books would not be returned to them. Seuling knew that fans who had been frustrated in their efforts to follow their stories at the newsstand would appreciate his system of getting them their books every month through specialty stores. His new enterprise, called Sea Gate Distribution Company, provided the precise mix of titles that the growing number of specialty comics shops wanted. These comics shops served diverse populations, which they were able to target directly and with regularity. From fewer than two hundred comics stores in 1974, the comics specialty retail network grew to approximately three thousand stores by the mid-1980s.[29]

The mainstream publishers embraced the new distribution system, called the Direct Market System, because it was much more precise than the newsstands of the past. Plus, they didn't have to take back any unsold books. While still selling their titles at newsstands, DC and Marvel both began to shift their focus to this new Direct Market world. Independent publishers also took advantage of the new specialty comics shops, providing invaluable exposure for countless small and local creations. By the way, local comics shops still provide a forum for newcomers who want to produce hard copies of their work (more about this in chapter 8).

Distribution companies—the intermediary between the publishers and the sellers—have come and gone over the years. As Direct Market became the model for reaching readers, the importance of these distributors grew. A retailer named Steve Geppi started Diamond Comic Distributors in 1982 as the model was just taking hold. After buying up several of his rivals in the 1980s and 1990s, Diamond gained a near monopoly on the distribution of comic books in the United States. The digital revolution has weakened its hold on the industry slightly, but even now if you want a wide distribution of your (printed) comics, you'll have to go through Diamond.

Three Books Change the World

The year 1986 was a momentous year for comics. Well, more precisely, for graphic novels. Many comics scholars (yes, that is an actual thing) point to that year as the period in which comics began to be taken seriously by the public at large. In that year, three serious graphic novels were published that raised the standard for comics, after which they were recognized as literature for the first time.

Art Spiegelman had been producing underground comics for several decades. His comic anthologies *Arcade: The Comics Revue* and, a few years later, *Raw* had been groundbreaking independent magazines in the 1970s and early 1980s. In *Raw #2*, Spiegelman had begun serializing *Maus*, which told the Holocaust stories of his parents using animals as characters. In 1986, *Maus: A Survivor's Tale* was published. The book "brought mainstream attention to the potential of comic books to tell stories other than those about superheroes."[30] *Maus* is a memoir in which the artist gets his father to talk about his past, including his time in a German concentration camp. By using animals as characters, the pathos of the story hits home, but in a less direct way. The second volume of *Maus*, published in 1992, won a Pulitzer Prize Special Award, the only graphic novel ever to win the prestigious award.

The publication of *Maus* by itself would have marked 1986 as a groundbreaking year in comics history. But that same year, DC published two of the most influential graphic novels of all time: *Batman: The Dark Knight Returns*, written by Frank Miller with art by Klaus Janson and Lynn Varley (figure 1.10), and *Watchmen*, written by Alan Moore with art by Dave Gibbons.

The Dark Knight Returns is a four-part limited series set sometime in the near future when an aging Bruce Wayne is drawn back into fighting crime out of a sense of helplessness and desperation. Truth be told, Wayne is also drawn back by the action and danger, which he has missed. The story is told in a sophisticated way that doesn't seem very comic bookish, with news reports, talk show hosts, comments from bystanders, and shifts in point of view that are a little hard to follow at some points. The topics covered range from cold war politics to the despotism of the super powerful to reflections on growing old. *The Dark Knight Returns* took the character back to its original dark, brooding ways, a welcome change from the campy television Batman of the 1970s. A classic battle with Superman, in which the Dark Knight is killed (possibly), provides a stunning conclusion to a thoughtful and groundbreaking book. Miller took on other Batman projects over the years, but none is so well remembered as *The Dark Knight Returns*.

If *Dark Knight* rebuilds a superhero, the other classic graphic novel from 1986, *Watchmen*, works to tear the superhero myth down. In *Watchmen*, Alan Moore explores the real-world consequences of costumed vigilantes roaming around doing whatever they think is right. The multilayered plots and subplots make the book very complex and the themes are meant for mature readers. Throughout the novel, graffiti-covered walls ask the central question of the novel: "Who's watching the watchers?" In other words, if the justice bringers are unjust, what is the recourse for those too weak to fight back? These heroes are out to change the world according to their own vision of what's right. *Watchmen* was published

Figure 1.10. *The Dark Knight Returns* by Frank Miller, Klaus Janson, and Lynn Varley. *All DC comic artwork, its characters, and related elements are ™ & © DC Comics.*

"Batman represents the selfless Samaritan that so much of society aspires to. He fights in the name of justice, order, and due punishment. Batman is the product of the fantasies of common people who wish to make a greater difference and make a stand against people who take advantage of the weak and helpless.

"The Joker stands for anarchy, cold killers, terror, and madness. The Joker is the product of a changing society on the cusp of the birth of serial killers, the fear of people who speak and act out against the government. Joker is the great nightmare of conservative republicans. He sets out to rip the system from the ground, rock by rock, inducing panic and anarchy."—Kori E., Seattle, Washington[j]

as a monthly serial, but gained a wide audience only after it was put together as a graphic novel.

In 2005 *Time* magazine included *Watchmen* on the list of the "100 best English-language novels published since 1923" alongside great American masterworks such as William Faulkner's *The Sound and the Fury*. In the explanation of why the book made the list, the *Time* website states, "Told with ruthless psychological realism, in frugal, overlapping plotlines and gorgeous, cinematic panels with repeating motifs, *Watchmen* is a heart-pounding, heartbreaking read and a watershed in the evolution of a young medium."[31] Indeed, after *Watchmen* came out, the popularity of antiheroes skyrocketed. In the 1990s, violent heroes with troubled pasts such as the Punisher and Wolverine received their own titles and were hugely popular.

The Competition Heats Up

As *Watchmen* and *Dark Knight* show, the 1980s saw the comic book "grow up." To accommodate this more mature style of comic book and comic book reader, new publishing houses cropped up in the 1980s. One such independent publisher, Dark Horse, made its debut in 1986. In chapter 8, which concerns making your own comic books, you will read about a type of script called the Dark Horse style. In many respects it has become industry standard, which is a testament to the respect Dark Horse carries in the marketplace.

Dark Horse's first publication was an anthology called *Dark Horse Presents*, which featured a number of up-and-coming creators, including Paul Chadwick, whose character Concrete was widely admired. Dark Horse assured its place in the marketplace by investing in licensing rights to some popular movie franchises, including *Aliens*, *Predator*, and *Star Wars*. It also became the home of some mainstream giants who wanted to create new works outside of the superhero realm (and retain their rights of ownership), such as Frank Miller's *Sin City* (1991) and Mike Mignola's *Hellboy* (1993). Dark Horse largely stayed away from superhero comics, a choice that has led to a steady stream of respected works and loyal customers.

Several other independent publishers arose in the 1980s and 1990s, but none achieved the stature of Dark Horse. Valiant Comics began publishing in 1991 but had closed its doors by 1999. Another startup was Malibu Comics, which began in 1987. Although Malibu published in several genres, the most well-known was its superhero line, with titles such as *Prime*, *Mantra*, and *Ultraforce*. Marvel bought out Malibu in 1994, but the titles faded into oblivion by the end of the 1990s. Malibu's most important contribution was helping another fledgling publisher get on its feet—Image Comics.

Image Comics was founded by a group of artists who believed that the big mainstream companies were profiting from their work without giving them a fair share of the proceeds. Marvel, in particular, was selling enormous numbers of books, using the writers and artists to attract customers, but then only giving them a small portion of the proceeds. The Image founders discovered that independent comics could be lucrative, as their first few books sold like hotcakes. *Spawn* #1 by Todd McFarlane sold 1.7 million copies, an unprecedented number for an independent comic.[32] The Image offerings were so in demand that DC Comics, long the number two publisher, was feeling the heat of competition. But artists are not always good business people, and Image started getting criticized for missing deadlines and for late deliveries, which frustrated fans. Image dropped back to a distant third behind the big mainstream publishers, but they had established that creator-owned properties could be lucrative. In recent years, Image has produced several blockbusters, including *The Walking Dead* comics by Robert Kirkman and Tony Moore, which have spawned the hugely popular television series.

Vertigo Comics, which was spun off by DC, began publishing comics under its own name in 1993. According to its Facebook page, Vertigo was intended "as a venue for material of an edgier, more sophisticated nature from today's most provocative writers and artists." A number of its first publications were brought over from the DC line, such as *The Sandman*, *Swamp Thing* (figure 1.11), and *Doom Patrol*. One of the most popular lines to be introduced at Vertigo is *Fables: Legends in Exile*, which tells the stories of mythical characters such as Snow White and the Big Bad Wolf who have been driven from their homelands into ours. In 2010

Figure 1.11. *Saga of the Swamp Thing*, by Alan Moore, Stephen Bissette, and John Totleben. *All DC comic artwork, its characters, and related elements are ™ & © DC Comics.*

Vertigo announced that it would become a strictly creator-owned imprint, with all the DC lines that had originated at DC going back to the parent company.[33]

There were many other smaller publishers who produced groundbreaking graphic novels in the 1980s and 1990s, which all propelled the maturation of the comic form. One of the most important was Fantagraphic Books, which produced the popular *Love and Rockets* series by the Hernandez Brothers, and *Ghost World* by Daniel Clowes. *Ghost World*, an episodic series that focuses on the relationship between two hipster girls, was part of a move toward realistic, character-based fiction that shaped the way graphic novels are written to this day.[34]

Other 1980s Trends

Several other trends in the 1980s need to be mentioned because they are important in the development of the comics industry. The first is the "crisis" at DC, which will be discussed in more detail in chapter 3. In 1985, DC Comics celebrated its fiftieth anniversary with a twelve-issue limited series called *Crisis on Infinite Earths*. The purpose of the series was to attract new readers, of course, but the writers were also trying to clean up the continuity of the DC universe. (For the definition of the word *continuity* and several other comics terms, see "Comics Terms" on page 89.) To revitalize its aging lines, DC revamped a number of stories, including the Big Three: Superman, Batman, and Wonder Woman. A similar cleaning up and polishing was going on over at Marvel as well.

In the years that followed this crisis, both DC and Marvel would revamp, restart, revitalize, and otherwise recharge their old heroes several times, giving new readers an easy entry point into their stories. The latest restart at DC occurred in the summer of 2016 with its "Rebirth" campaign. Marvel's latest major reboot occurred a year earlier in 2015, with its "All New, All Different Marvel" stories, in which all the lines went back to issue number 1.

But back to the 1980s. The decade was one of great experimentation, both in content and in distribution models, as we have seen. In 1984, a self-published, admittedly rough, but humorous superhero parody began to attract attention at conventions and in comics shops: *Teenage Mutant Ninja Turtles* (*TMNT*) by Peter Laird. According to historians Dan Mazur and Alexander Danner in their book *Comics: A Global History, 1968 to the Present*, *TMNT* was "first self-published comic to break the barrier into mainstream success."[35] Of course you've probably seen one of the many television or movie adaptions of the turtles, a testament to the fact that a self-published series can get noticed if the story is good.

As the 1980s ended and the 1990s began, a curious trend became apparent in the comics community: a wave of nostalgia seemed to take over the industry. Numerous "year 1" books were published, and collectors began buying up rare old

Golden Age comic books. The early *Batman* and *Superman* comics were selling at astronomical prices, which made speculators (people who invest in the latest trend no matter what it is) believe that comic books made good investments. So the publishers rushed to put out new number 1 issues and gimmicks such as hologram-enhanced covers. This fueled an already growing market for comics in the early 1990s, and many people thought the comic book world was booming. Indeed, sales were up, but some of those numbers were being boosted by people hoping to turn around and resell these special issues soon after they bought them. These investors soon realized that the publishers were putting out too many books for them to ever be considered valuable (remember the law of supply and demand?).

It seems inevitable now, but speculators by and large dropped out of the market by the middle of the decade. The result was that comics specialty shops had to deal with huge stacks of unsold books. Many of these shops went out of business. Marvel suffered as well, declaring bankruptcy in 1996. Fortunately for comics lovers, the company recovered and came out of bankruptcy a leaner, wiser company. After the boom of the early 1990s, the industry had to come to terms with the fact that it was smaller as the century turned than it had been just a decade before.

The reputation of comics and graphic novels was already on the rise, but a special book from 1993 really paved the way for comics to be taken seriously—even to be studied as a legitimate art form. That book was *Understanding Comics* by Scott McCloud. You will read more about this book in chapter 2. McCloud was not the first to argue that comics should be considered a serious art form, but he spoke so eloquently about the meaning and tools of comics, and he reached such a wide audience, that his opinions sparked the first true in-depth conversation about the potential of comics in mainstream audiences. McCloud built on the discussion in subsequent books such as *Making Comics*, as well as masterful graphic fiction pieces such as *The Sculptor*.

The Trend toward Ethnic Comics

The mainstream publishers had created a handful of black characters by the 1990s, but they were normally part of teams, like Storm in the X-Men, or were identified with *Black* in their name, like the Black Panther or DC's 1970s hero Black Lightning. Because there were so few minorities in general, readers unconsciously saw them as representing entire races and groups of people. This bothered some industry professionals, including an editor at Marvel named Dwayne McDuffie. He and a small group of African American comics pros decided to form their own company to write and promote stories with black characters and superheroes.

Milestone Media published its first book in 1993 and quickly became "the most successful black-owned comic book publisher in American history" according to historian Arie Kaplan.[36] Although it lasted only five years, the company changed the perception of heroes of color and proved that black characters could lead to financial success. Milestone made waves with a lot of its stories, but one in particular produced controversy. In the popular series *Icon*, the creators included a story line in which the fifteen-year-old sidekick named Raquel Ervin (a.k.a. Rocket) becomes pregnant. Her contemplation on whether to keep the baby or have an abortion sparked strong feelings on both sides of the issue. But Milestone had crossed a barrier no other mainstream publisher had crossed. The publisher's decision to employ DC to distribute its comics led to some in the African American community to call company leaders "Uncle Toms."[37]

There were other black comics creators in the 1990s, although some of them decided not to distribute their work via the usual routes. In 1990 two brothers—Dawud Anyabwile (formerly known as David Sims) and Guy Sims—produced a comic called *Brotherman* and distributed it at the NYC Black Expo in 1990. Because *Brotherman* was well written, had excellent art, and realistically portrayed urban life without the typical stereotypes, the series gathered attention from readers and other artists. Although the series only ran until 1996, the comic gave inspiration to many writers and artists who had until that time not seen very many characters in comics who looked like them. In addition, the brothers' business model, in which they produced and distributed the comics themselves—thereby keeping the proceeds within the community—inspired other individual creators to distribute their own works.

Another example of a minority-created work in the 1990s is *Tribal Force*, by Jon Proudstar with art by Ryan Huna Smith, which ran for one issue in 1996. After receiving rave reviews for the realistic stories and all–Native American cast, the publisher went bankrupt. Instead of sticking with the project, the creatives on the team went their separate ways. Although Proudstar received offers from mainstream publishers to secure the rights to the series, the writer (and actor) elected to keep the rights until he could produce the series again.[38] In 2012, a group of Native American artists made another attempt to produce comics by and about Native Americans: INC Comics, later renamed Native Realities Press, produced *Tales of the Mighty Code Talkers* among other stories.

Graphic Novels Take Over

People who study comics have noted the rise of the graphic novel. You may be too young to remember when most comic books were sold as individual stories. Many are still sold that way, but more and more comics are being combined and

Comics by and for Girls

There is a stubborn misconception still hanging around that comic books are for adolescent boys. And while that demographic certainly does still love superhero comics, more stories are being written by women targeting girls, with engaging female characters, than ever before.

Early comics targeted to girls were either female superheroes such as Wonder Woman—who in her early years always seemed to be pining for the first man she ever met, Steve Trevor—or romance books. In recent years, comics publishers have come to understand that female readers like action, humor, horror—pretty much everything male readers like! One great example of an adventure comic geared toward girls is *Lumberjanes*, volume 1: *Beware the Kitten Holy*, written by Noelle Stevenson and Grace Ellis, with art by Brooke Allen, colors by Maarta Laiho, and lettering by Aubrey Aiese (noticeably all female creators, a relatively rare occurrence in comics until recently).

This tale takes place at a summer camp where the Lumberjanes are seeking to earn as many badges as possible. Almost immediately the intrepid friends—who truly come in all shapes, sizes, and skin colors—are beset by fierce three-eyed foxes. The adventure just gets weirder from there, as the campers get lured underground into a maze full of traps that must be solved by courage, brains, and quick action. Despite getting yelled at by their straight-laced camp counselor, the girls solve the puzzle put forth by the mysterious foxes: "Beware the kitten holy." Along the way they meet other mysterious creatures, like Yeti wearing headphones and a camp of boys who may or may not be in on an evil plot. With great art and even greater humor, *Lumberjanes* proves that comics targeted toward girls are making quite an impact on the market—because they aren't just being read by girls.[k]

"Comics are now even bigger than ever. Fans flocked to the 'Marvel's The Avengers,' making it the first film to gross over $200 million in its opening weekend. Never in all of human history has that opening ever been achieved. It's insane to think that comics would ever get to this point, isn't it? At one point, we saw comics as more of a kid's thing."—Ayinde R., Owing Mills, Maryland[1]

sold in larger volumes. These larger books allow readers to consume an entire story without waiting for each month's installment. They are also easier to stock and sell at big bookstores.

Graphic novels have been around for decades. The term has come to mean any work of sequential art longer than a regular comic book. While the term *novel* would seem to imply that these books are all fiction, that is not really the case. Graphic novels include memoir, history, journalism—almost any type of book composed of sequential art, as you will see in chapter 5. When comics legend Will Eisner's *A Contract with God* came out in 1978, the term *graphic novel* really caught on. That's because the tone of the book was somewhat dark, and it dealt with very serious subject matter—even though it used sequential art.

As the 1980s turned into the 1990s, graphic novels began to be taken more seriously, and the large chain bookstores such as Barnes & Noble and Borders dedicated valuable shelf space to house the growing collection. The 1990s were also the era when interest in Japanese manga began to grow among Western comics readers. So bookstores combined the comic books, graphic novels, and manga into one colorful section. Although the Internet was alive and well in the 1990s, it was not developed into the e-commerce giant that it is today. Amazon.com did not go public until 1997, so when people wanted to buy a graphic novel, they went to a brick-and-mortar bookstore.

Although superhero comics continued to dominate the comics market in the 1990s and 2000s, more "serious" graphic novels, such as *Fun Home: A Family Tragicomic* by Alison Bechdel, were published as well. Bechdel's book looks back at growing up in the funeral home business and the author's coming to terms with her homosexuality in college. A lot of these more serious books were put out by independent publishers such as Image Comics and Dark Horse. So although the independents made up only around 30 percent of the market, their content pushed the boundaries of comics more than the mainstream publishers, who were content to stick with their money-making superheroes.

Some of Image Comics' most ground-breaking works of the period were Eric Shanower's *Age of Bronze,* a retelling of the historical siege of Troy, and *Powers* by Brian Michael Bendis with art by Michael Avon Oeming, a detective series in which the cops investigate incidents among people with superhuman abilities. And, of course, *The Walking Dead* franchise was published by Image Comics starting in 2003.

Dark Horse's most acclaimed works have also been outside the superhero genre. Two of its most well-known books were written by Frank Miller: *Sin City* in 1991 and the historical drama *300* in 1998. Both of these were adapted into successful movies as well. Mike Mignola's *Hellboy* is another Dark Horse title that has achieved success as both a comic and a series of movies. A number of *Star Wars* adaptions have helped Dark Horse finance some if its lesser known and more experimental stories.

In the first decade of the 2000s, graphic novels gained wide acceptance. Too many have been published since 2000 to mention here—a testament to the increasing number being created—but several graphic novels have made their way into high school and college classrooms because of the quality of their storytelling and the importance of their themes. In 2003 Pantheon Books published the groundbreaking *Persepolis* by Marjane Satrapi. The book had first been published in France (in French) a few years earlier. *Persepolis* tells the story of Satrapi's growing up in Iran in the 1970s when the society was experiencing dramatic cultural changes. High school teachers assign the book for its historical education as well as its sophisticated storytelling. The book is reviewed in more detail in chapter 5.

Another book that has found its way into classrooms is Craig Thompson's *Blankets*, published by Top Shelf in 2003. *Blankets* combines beautiful prose with innovative graphic techniques to portray emotional changes in the character—Thompson himself—as he works through the trials of his teen years in snowy Wisconsin. The book is used in classrooms to explore themes of love, the loss of religious faith, and how graphic storytelling has matured into an effective way to tell a story.

In 2007, a graphic novel called *American Born Chinese*, by Gene Luen Yang, won the respected Michael L. Printz Award for Young Adult literature. Normally reserved for prose books, the award showed that graphic novels were starting to be considered mainstream literature. *American Born Chinese* tells three different interweaving stories that shine light on what it feels like to be an Asian American student growing up in a majority white country. The book also is used in many high school classroom discussions.

The Digital Revolution

The computer changed the world in the 1970s and 1980s. The Internet changed it again in the 1990s and 2000s. Before these revolutionary developments, comic

"Raise your hand: who heard of the 'Guardians of the Galaxy' before the movie came out? Now look at them: household names alongside the Avengers. I believe that it's because these aren't just drawings on a piece of paper. They are ideals to strive towards. They show us the best of what we can become."—Ayinde R., Owing Mills, Maryland[m]

books were written and drawn by hand, with colors laboriously separated, then sent to large presses that needed to produce huge quantities to make any money for a publisher. People had to go out and buy these books at a store. After the comic was read, it sat around collecting dust. It seems very exhausting and old-fashioned, doesn't it?

Now creators can write, draw, and color their creations on a computer in a fraction of the time it used to take. Digital presses can work color magic without all the laborious hand separations of the past. Internet distribution sites can get the comics to readers without going through the old distributors or sitting in the comics shops. Readers can go to their computer or tablet and download a comic book instantly without ever leaving home. According to the authors of *The Power of Comics*, these changes have caused a monumental shift in the comics industry, including "an increasing fractionalization of all media," meaning that media of all kinds are looking for small, interested niches, not the broad viewership of the past. All of these changes result in "an explosion of self-expression, and an era where a more diverse range of creative voices are speaking out in many media forms."[39] When Amazon bought Comixology in 2014, it was a sign that digital comics are the future.

Although the golden age of superhero comics ended in the 1950s, I believe we are living in the golden age of comics right now. Many stories with realistic characters and everyday subjects—topics that nobody would dream of telling in a comic forty years ago—are making their way into print. Even superhero stories are written with amazing complexity and stunningly beautiful art. A mind-boggling number of comics that deal with interesting and complex themes are available in the both brick-and-mortar bookstores and online. In addition, comics from other countries have been translated and published here in the United States, so you can discover stories told from many different perspectives, in many different styles. Because the consciousness of the reading public has been raised to a level where diversity is paramount, all the comics publishers—including the mainstream publishers—are creating diverse characters who inhabit interesting worlds just around the corner.

HOW TO READ AND ENJOY COMICS

Is reading a comic or graphic novel easier than reading a prose novel? You just look at the pictures and read the words, right? Well, sort of. As it turns out, comics creators take great care in communicating to readers, in both words and illustrations. Knowing more about their tools will help you better understand what you're reading and fully enjoy their nuances.

When you read prose, you are decoding symbols. When you see the word *elephant* you picture a large gray animal with a long nose, even though there is no actual animal in front of you. When you look at the words *drank from the pond* you picture it sucking water from a small body of water. Readers take little squiggly black lines and turn these symbols into mental images. Try and decode this:

$$\& \$ @ 9 k ($$

What is your mental picture? Probably nothing, since you are not able to decode what the originator (me, the author of this book) wanted to convey. Words on a page are just symbols. Our brain has to work to corral the symbols and decode them into a meaningful message.

We decode symbols all the time: on maps, on walls, in instruction booklets, even peoples' body gestures have a meaning that we are required to interpret without being told. We call all of these decoding activities "reading." We read textbooks, maps, messages on phones, peoples' facial expressions. Reading is simply learning to take symbols, or *icons* as comics theorist Scott McCloud calls them, and turn them into mental pictures.[1]

This chapter owes a debt of gratitude to Scott McCloud, whose 1993 book *Understanding Comics* is still the most widely read and frequently quoted book on how to understand and create comics. He discusses why sequential art is such a powerful medium with its combination of written words and sequential visual art. If you've read any comics or graphic novels, you no doubt agree that the medium is enjoyable and powerful.

Where does this power come from? And how do we perceive the meaning the author intends with so few written words?

The Language of Comics

In his book *The Visual Language of Comics*, researcher and illustrator Neil Cohn quotes several comics legends as they compare comics to a language. Among others, he quotes legendary Jack Kirby, who says, "I've been writing all along and I've been doing it in pictures." He also quotes famous cartoonist Chris Ware, who says, "Comics are not a genre, but a developing language."[2]

Cohn then proceeds to say that these comics legends are wrong. He makes the claim that comics is actually not a language in and of itself; rather, comics is a social convention and cultural product that is written in a *visual* language of sequential images. (Comics also uses written language to convey meaning, but we'll get to that in a little while.) So the language of comics is visual language. Other social conventions use visual language: road signs, instruction manuals, and the cave paintings mentioned in chapter 1. None of these are considered comics, but they share certain rules that govern visual language.

"I love comics and graphic novels because it's more than a book. That might sound obvious, but it's true. So much can happen on one page, it's quite remarkable. In a book, you might read dialogue and have it brush by you without a second thought. But in a graphic novel, you get a facial expression with the comment. You get an action with the comment. It's possible to get background info just by the text itself, or, you can get a portrait of a starry night sky overlooking some mountains that takes up a couple pages by itself. It's moments like these that make comics and graphic novels so special. They encompass so much in each frame. A picture truly does speak one-thousand words, but then you add words to that picture, and you get something truly magnificent. Now I know I'm talking about comic books as a form of art, but in order to master it, you have to treat it like art. And for all of us comic book readers, it truly is an art form. It's the combination of the author and the illustrator. It's the merging of ideas to make this symphony of mass chaos and order."—Zachary B., Tyrone, Georgia[a]

Like spoken language, visual language has a grammar and a vocabulary—a set of rules that governs its meaning. As expressed in comics, visual language has been developing for a century and a half. In that amount of time, comics' visual language has gathered many rules and conventions. We're going to discuss a number of those conventions in this chapter so that as you read comics, graphic novels, and manga you can more deeply appreciate how the authors and illustrators are getting their stories across. You will never read a comic the same way again!

The book *The Graphic Novel: An Introduction* includes a beautiful statement about the vocabulary and potential of comics:

> The possible vocabulary of comics is, by definition, unlimited, the tactility of an experience told in pictures outside the boundaries of words, and the rhythm of how these drawings "feel" when read is where the real art resides. . . . Comics are an art of pure composition, carefully constructed like music, but constructed into a whole architecture, a page-by-page pattern, brought to life and "performed" by the reader—a colorful piece of sheet music waiting to be read.[3]

So let's learn to "read" comics in a new way.

The Power of Symbols

The idea of symbols is important in this discussion. These symbols individually don't mean that much:

s " t ! B " a

But put them together on the page of a book like this

"Bats!"

and suddenly a whole host of meanings suggest themselves. Showing some bats flying toward you in a frame can add another layer of experience (figure 2.1).

The symbols in comics don't stop with words and pictures, however. Even a straight line is a symbol in a graphic story. By itself, a line doesn't produce a lot of reaction on a reader's part, and neither does a box, for that matter. But start putting boxes next to each other, with human figures in them, and suddenly your brain starts to interpret a story.

Figure 2.1. Seeing bats is different than reading about bats. That's the power of graphic storytelling. *Illustration by Chris Burns*

The boxes in figure 2.2 have no words telling you what's happening, and yet you probably created a story. The subjects in the two boxes may have nothing to do with each other, but your mind is already filling in the story. That's because comics uses a well-defined language, a visual vocabulary if you will, to tell stories. From your experience, you know a lot of the conventions of this visual language, so you immediately participate in the action by imagining a scenario.

Will Eisner has been called the "godfather of modern comics."[4] That's because he was one of the first writer-artists to take the medium seriously back in the middle of the twentieth century. He also wrote serious books about comics that have helped define the medium and lead others to create their own. He wrote the book, literally. Eisner talks about the language of comics:

The format of comics presents montage of both word and image, and the reader is thus required to exercise both visual and verbal interpretive skills. The regimens of art (e.g., perspective, symmetry, line) and the

Figure 2.2. Now you start to imagine a story. *Illustration by Chris Burns*

regimens of literature (e.g., grammar, plot, syntax) become superimposed upon each other.[5]

That's why we don't just "look" at a comic or graphic novel; we correctly describe it as "reading," even if the page has no written words. A prose novel uses nouns, verbs, adjectives, prepositions, and other types of words—plus punctuation marks—to provide meaning. We consider all these things together to make up the "vocabulary" of prose. But what is the vocabulary of comics?

A Box Is a Box . . . or Is It?

Graphic novels, comics, and manga use many different elements to tell their stories:

- Panels
- Lettering
- Dialogue balloons and captions
- Gutters
- Camera distance and shot placement
- Motion lines
- Sound effects
- Standard gestures
- Color palettes
- Page turns
- Sequence structure

All of these devices, or symbols, deserve an explanation so that as you read a graphic novel you'll more fully appreciate the storytelling.

Panel

Prose stories use sentences, paragraphs, and chapters to capture the story and propel it through time. These small chunks accumulate to become more than the sum of their parts. Although many comics also use words and sentences, most comics utilize a completely unique graphic element to capture their stories and propel them through time: panels. These frames (although they are not always squares or even visible to the reader) are the building blocks of comics.

At its most basic, a panel is simply a means of capturing a moment in a story. Many times the panel is a box, akin to a photograph or a frame of film. But a comic panel is special: it isn't confined to a fraction of a second like a photograph, and it does not combine with many similar frames to try and imitate real time like film. A comic panel is carefully chosen by the creator to illustrate the most important moment of a sequence. Neil Cohn, author of *The Visual Language of Comics*, describes it this way:

> The way a scene is "windowed" by a panel can impact the clarity of a sequence. . . . [P]anels have several ways to depict the same scene, solely by modulating the amount of information that they show. This selection of how to present a scene demonstrates panels' roles as attention units.[6]

The time contained in a frame, as we will see in a following section, is elastic and depends on a number of elements within the frame.

So technically, a panel is just a frame containing a moment in a story. But when we talk about panels, it's not just the box around the action; it's everything inside as well. The brain doesn't consciously register all the individual elements, because it is trying to add up all the pieces into a coherent whole. Just like when you're reading a prose story, you don't say, "There's the subject, there's the verb, there's the direct object." Well-written sentences don't point out their components; they just come together to tell a flowing story. Same with comics—each panel uses a variety of elements to communicate effectively.

Most fundamental to the panel are the lines that make up the border. That may seem obvious, but the appearance of the lines and the shape of the panel can be changed to add a layer of meaning to the story. A typical panel is a square or rectangle, the size of which is determined by the number of characters, the action taking place, and the words spoken. But what if a panel had wavy lines instead of straight? The most common use of a panel like that is a flashback—a shift in time to the past or to a memory of something that has already happened. Oftentimes the writer doesn't even have to reference that it's a flashback; the reader just understands that she is now seeing a scene from the past.

Sometimes the lines of a box are straight, but the panel is unevenly shaped, like a rhombus or another shape. This is often done during chaotic action, when the lives of the protagonists are in danger or something surprising is occurring. The atypical shape reveals that life is being thrown out of balance and the reader is asked to join the characters as they pursue balance and a restoration of harmony.

The space ship panels in figure 2.3 show a scene drawn by teen artist Chris Burns, who has provided a number of the illustrations in this chapter. Notice the irregularly shaped second panel. As the space ship is fired on, the panel shape adds tension by breaking the regular rectangular format. When you start to notice details like this, you realize how many elements are involved in how we read comics.

An absence of lines around a panel can be used as a communication tool as well. This technique is often used to draw attention to a certain event or setting. Sometimes this is an important moment of enlightenment or decision making. At other times, the artist wants to establish a mood. The absence of panel borders forces the reader to slow down as time seems to stop for a moment. You may remember the story about Milestone Media's series *Icon* from chapter 1. The series is famous for featuring a pregnant fifteen-year-old heroine named Raquel Ervin (a.k.a. Rocket). In *Icon* #7, Raquel talks with a doctor at a clinic about her options. After Raquel asks, "What if I don't want the baby?" the panels drop away; she and the doctor appear in a borderless region—even the background scenery has disappeared.

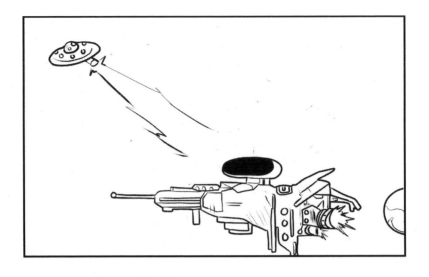

Figure 2.3. Changing the panel shape causes tension. *Illustration by Chris Burns*

Here's what one commentator wrote about the effect of that borderless panel:

It seems as though the doctor and Raquel have slipped out of place, without the other panels' clearly defined borders. . . . What happened in the intervening "nonpanel," and why did it take place, on the page, in a way that seemed not to have taken place at all in the setting of the story, literally outside of its framing? Raquel and her doctor recruit the reader in a new conversation at the moment they appear out of panel, when they break the legal framework around their situation.[7]

This technique can also be used to imply unlimited space, such as a character looking to the sky and seeing an ocean of stars that seem to "bleed" off the page without any barrier. These scenes without any border set a tone or mood that stays with the reader even after a return to the more traditional panels and a re-start of the story's time sequence.

There really aren't any hard and fast rules for how panels are supposed to be used. Creators arrange them in many different styles and shapes to involve the reader as much as possible without being confusing. Because comics is a visual medium, the more the arrangement of the panels involves a reader's other senses (even if only in her or his imagination), the more vivid the story will be.

Sequence of Panels

Most people have learned how to follow the panels on a page. The traditional pattern in the Western Hemisphere is left to right, top to bottom (see figure 2.4).

Contemporary writers play with this traditional format by including distinctive panel shapes and juxtaposing them in arrangements that require more work and involvement on the reader's part. For instance, many artists are using a two-page spread as one wide page, putting panels left to right across the entire spread. This has the effect of speeding up the pace of reading, which works well for action sequences. However, this can be annoying sometimes because a slice of the art is inevitably lost in the center crease of the spine. Artists get around this by putting important objects to the left or right of this dead space, even though the panel encompasses it.

How do you know when to read down the left-hand page and when to read across a whole spread? The most common way an illustrator lets you know to read across is to stretch a panel across the center crease where the pages come together. Most of the time, the rightmost panel on the top tier of the left page will be self-contained with a tiny bit of margin between it and the center crease. That means read down to the second tier on the left page. But if the panel crosses the center line, the entire spread should be read like one long horizontal page. This spread layout usually is reserved for momentous occasions.

Sometimes comics creators will attempt to achieve a special effect by using an unconventional panel flow. In *The Shadow Hero*, Gene Luen Yang uses a circular arrangement in one scene (figure 2.5) so the readers end up at the place they started. The effect is that readers feel the frustration of the gunmen—no matter how hard they try, the hero is invulnerable to their bullets.

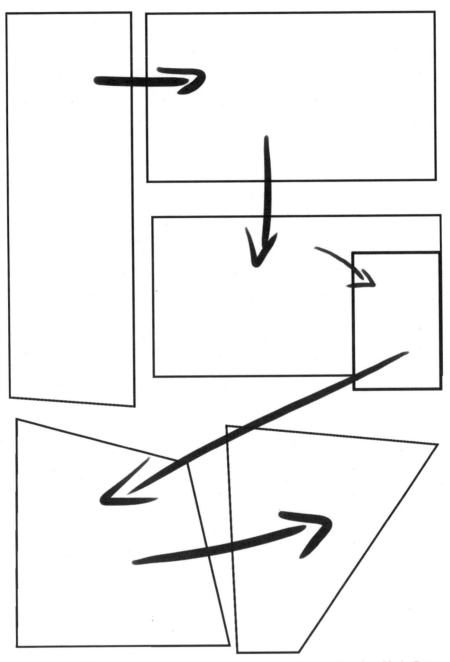

Figure 2.4. Western comics panel reading flow. *Illustration by Chris Burns*

The danger of laying out panels in a nontraditional order is that the reader may get confused or frustrated. The last thing you want as a comics creator is to drive your reader out of the story. But it's exciting when authors tell stories in new ways; in most cases, the extra effort is worth it.

Writer Neil Gaiman and the artists who worked on *The Sandman: Preludes and Nocturnes* use a lot of unusual panel shapes in this volume. They also make the reader work by bending tiers of panels from one corner to another, sometimes read-

Figure 2.5. Circular panel flow from *The Shadow Hero* by Gene Luen Yang. *From THE SHADOW HERO © 2014 by Gene Luen Yang. Illustrations © 2014 by Sonny Liew. Reprinted by permission of First Second, an imprint of Roaring Brook Press, a division of Holtzbrinck Publishing Holdings Limited Partnership. All Rights Reserved.*

ing up, sometimes down. These arrangements give a dreamlike quality to the work, which is appropriate for the main character—Morpheus, the King of Dreams.

Chapter 6 gives an introduction to Japanese manga, but generally manga is read top to bottom, just like Western comics. However, if you try reading a Japanese comic from left to right, you're going to be really confused. That's because Japanese is read right to left, so manga is also read from right to left (figure 2.6 shows how to read manga). Meaning you start from what we would consider the back and work forward! It takes a minute to get used to, but it's not hard to pick up. Most books are labeled at the beginning to help new Western readers.

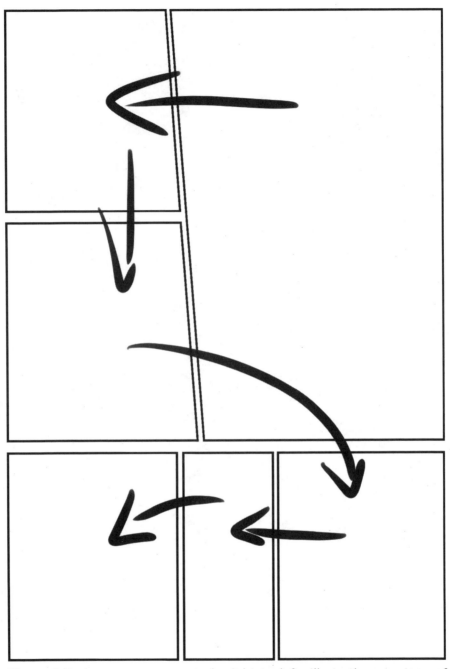

Figure 2.6. Japanese manga reads right to left. *Illustration courtesy of Chris Burns*

Dialogue Balloons and Captions

In chapter 1, we talked about the father of modern comics, Rodolphe Töpffer. In these comics the description of the action takes place below the scene in the form of a caption. We still include captions in our comics today, but normally they appear in a box within the comic panel. Captions can range from simple exposition—"Meanwhile, in Detroit . . ."—to first-person thoughts from a character: "I knew I was in trouble when I heard her laugh." Normally caption boxes are rectangular to separate them from dialogue.

Dialogue in comics is typically portrayed in oval boxes called word balloons or word bubbles (see figure 2.7). Most of these have a hook or arrow pointing to the speaker. The balloon shapes are not cast in stone; plenty of artists play with them. In the groundbreaking *The Dark Knight Returns*, Frank Miller's masterpiece from 1986, all the established notions concerning captions and word balloons get tossed out the window. He even has a lot of captions below or above the frame—a throwback to old Mr. Töpffer's original style!

Most panels have one or at most two dialogue balloons. This is done for a variety of reasons, but the most relevant is that dialogue starts the clock ticking on the time within the frame. Ostensibly, a frame is a snapshot in time because the characters are static and unmoving. But as they speak, time begins to pass. A response from another person is more time elapsing, with the characters still stuck in that one position. So to keep the reader's brain from rebelling at this conflict, authors try and minimize the dialogue within any single panel. Of course, as with any other rule, comics creators regularly throw this guideline out the window, as author Brian Michael Bendis does in *Ultimate Spider-Man* #9 (from the graphic novel, published in 2015). After Miles (as Spider-Man) subdues the Ringer, he has a long conversation with the police captain:

SM: So, uh, listen, this guy with the rings.
PC: The Ringer.
SM: Yeah.
PC: I know all about The Ringer. You the one that knocked him unconscious?
SM: Accidentally.
PC: Well, good for you, kid. You get the key to the city.
SM: Really?
PC: No. Tell me the truth, is this going to be a thing?
SM: What?
PC: You. Are you going to be hopping and bopping around my neck of the woods . . . ?

All this dialogue is in *one panel*. It takes up the whole page, but it is still one panel. Actually, that is not even the whole dialogue; there are more lines before this excerpt and then it goes on after this exchange. So you can see that the "one exchange per panel" rule is more like a guideline that is occasionally broken to achieve a specific effect.

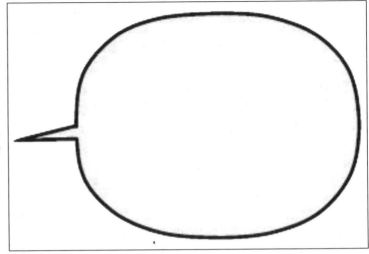

Figure 2.7. A word balloon is a visual tool to specify spoken words. *Illustration courtesy of Chris Burns*

Another type of word balloon is the thought bubble (or thought balloon). Many times these are shaped like a cloud and attached to the character through a line of bubbles. Most contemporary graphic novels don't use thought bubbles anymore, opting instead for some sort of caption from the POV of one of the characters. Thought balloons are more common in graphic novels geared toward middle grade readers such as Raina Telgemeier's *Smile*. They work with this age group because the younger protagonists don't have the same kind of filters as older teens or adults. Unlike thought captions, characters' thought balloons are addressed to themselves, not the reader. Some authors of middle grade novels use thought balloons to jump around into various characters' heads. This increases tension but can disorient the reader if not used sparingly.

The graphic novel adaptions of the Artemis Fowl series use "thought captions" to great effect as the POV changes from teen mastermind Artemis to fairy crime fighter Holly Short. The trick with thought captions is to provide enough information to push the action or characterization forward without becoming exposition-heavy. If we had wanted to read a prose book, we would have done it—so it's best when creators keep it to a minimum.

Lettering

In comics, lettering is an actual job. That's because even the shape and texture of the lettering conveys meaning beyond the actual words on the page. Maybe you've seen this type of onomatopoeia in a comic book, especially if you read superhero comics:

Boom!

Figure 2.8. That's more like it! *Illustration courtesy of Chris Burns*

If you saw this word, in this font, in a comic, you'd think the publishers did not take advantage of the power of lettering as an element of visual vocabulary. You'd say, "Make the word *look* like the sound! Or have the artist draw it out so that my brain can 'hear' the sound!" This is what most creators do when they work to convey the idea of that sound. Even though comics is a visual medium, creators do all they can to involve a reader's other senses.

Figure 2.8 is more what the word demands, right? The right type of lettering can add to the sensuality of a panel. Lettering can boost the emotional power of words to suggest love, anger, depression, fear, sarcasm, or any other emotion. Lettering styles can also help establish a physical setting, suggesting ice, fire, lightning, wind, rain, blazing heat, or a host of other environments. Look at figure 2.9; you can almost feel the dampness of the words rising from the page.

When I looked outside...

Figure 2.9. The letter art communicates by itself. *Illustration courtesy of Chris Burns*

There is a scene in the graphic novel *Blankets* in which the creator, Craig Thompson, really uses the power of lettering as another layer of communication. The main character is in his girlfriend's room about to read his Bible. The caption at the top of the page is lettered in a script that could be described as handwritten and casual. As the main character reads a story from the Bible, the font changes to a more formal looking font with serifs (the little decorative lines at the beginning and end of letters in more formal looking fonts), as if the words come straight from the Book (which they do).

This change in lettering style adds a layer to the story. The words from the Bible look strict, straight, proper. Readers almost feel like they should sit up straight when they read them. This contributes to the character's view that the church puts unwelcome restrictions on his actions. By contrast, the character's own words come across as relaxed and intimate, drawing us to the boy as if we're talking with a friend. That's the power of lettering at work.

The Gutter

You may think of a gutter as a metal trough running around the roof of your house, but there is another kind of gutter; it's one of the most powerful tools in graphic storytelling. The blank space between panels in a comic book is called the gutter. Every page contains multiple gutters (unless it has only one panel, of course). These spaces may appear to be devoid of information but nothing could be further from the truth.

To demonstrate the power of the gutter as part of comics vocabulary, I want you to think about all the things you *can't* see right now. There's a lot, right? When you look around you in your home or at your school, you only see a very small slice of life. You can't see what's happening with kids your age in Iceland or Tanzania (unless you're reading this in Iceland or Tanzania, which would be awesome!). You believe those countries exist, but you can only imagine from movies or pictures what is happening there at this moment. In truth, you can't even see what is behind that person sitting in the far row of your classroom, or what's under that counter in the kitchen; you must use your imagination to interpret what is there. This is how comics mastermind Scott McCloud introduces the idea of gutters—by making readers understand how much their mind fills in the blanks of what they can't see.

Comics are like life in the sense that they offer only a limited slice of any story. Because each frame freezes one moment of a story, a lot is left to the imagination. At first it seems like the curse of comics, but that very limitation leads to a stunning amount of reader involvement—which is the secret of comics' worldwide popularity. Sean Tulien, a comics author and editor, explains it this way: "The absence of length and content is not a shortcoming of the comics genre—it gives rise to more artful omission that immerses the reader in the narrative while keeping the beats and scenes fast and flowing."[8]

We sometimes compare comics to film because they share a visual vocabulary (frames, shot placement, gestures, and so on). But whereas films try to capture all the action within a scene in "real time," comics capture action one static moment at a time. Because of this limitation, the reader must sign an imaginary contract that he will use his imagination to fill in the missing pieces of the story. No other media has this type of push-pull, giving us selected images while demanding a high degree of reader imagination. That's the magic of comics. "The comics reader fills each gutter based on her own experiences; she paints the canvas of white space with her personality and perspectives. And the more personal a reading experience is, the more immersive it becomes," says Tulien.[9]

What do you believe happens in the series of two panels in figure 2.10? The teen artist, Chris Burns, hasn't given you the answer; he has forced you to use your imagination. Has a player on the opposing team hit a fly ball? Or is a bird doing some business and it is falling on the boy's head? Only the reader knows. That magic space between the panels—in which the reader is complicit in whatever happens in the story—is why the gutters are so crucial to any graphic story. Mc-Cloud calls this important act of imagination by the reader "closure." He writes in *Understanding Comics*, "Every act committed to paper by the comics artist is aided and abetted by a silent accomplice. An equal partner in crime known as the reader. . . . From the tossing of a baseball to the death of a planet, the reader's deliberate, voluntary closure is comics' primary means of simulating time and motion."[10]

McCloud points out that our minds engage in closure many times every day: when we see only a portion of a neon sign and instantly figure out what the rest of the sign says; when we figure out what is about to happen in a movie as an embracing couple falls out of the frame; or when we see the toe of a shoe sticking out from a corner and figure out a sibling is about to try and scare us. We rely on closure to make sense of a world where we see only a sliver of what's happening.

Closure helps us put the story together in a comic, although we can see only a series of frozen moments. Closure also keeps us in a comic scene, even when there is no background provided or very minimal detail. In fact, McCloud makes the argument that the fewer visual details provided, the more readers see themselves in a comic.[11] When too much detail is provided, readers' brains see the adventures of a distinct person. By contrast, when the figures are drawn with almost no details—such as the characters in Charles Schulz's *Charlie Brown* comics—readers identify closely with the characters.

So when I said earlier that comics is very much a contract between the artist and the reader, the mechanism by which this occurs is closure. Readers willingly

Figure 2.10. What happens in the gutter? *Illustration courtesy of Chris Burns*

employ their own brain—informed by their own experiences—as tools for the storyteller, who has to choose his moments carefully. Readers' participation in the experience allows them to connect all the frozen moments into a connected, unified, flowing reality.

Figure 2.11 is a page from the book *Yummy* by G. Neri, with illustrations by Randy DuBurke. What do you think is happening in the series of panels at the

Figure 2.11. What happens in the gutter? *From YUMMY, published by Lee & Low Books, Inc. © 2010 by G. Neri. Illustrations © 2010 by Randy DuBurke. Reprinted by permission. All Rights Reserved.*

bottom of the page? Does the boy rob the man who just took out money from the ATM? Although the author never states what happens in that final panel, the reader has a pretty good idea that a crime has taken place. That shows the power of a gutter on a comics page.

Camera Distance or Shot

Because comics has a number of aspects in common with film, we often borrow film terminology when trying to explain a comics technique. One of these borrowed phrases is *camera shot* or *camera angle*. Although graphic novels are normally drawn, not photographed, the panels give the impression that the reader is viewing the action through a lens. Where the artist chooses to locate his imaginary camera is very important.

We will delve into "psychic distance" more fully in chapter 8, where we discuss writing techniques for budding creatives. For now, we can highlight some of the different shots so that as you read a graphic novel, you will be aware of what the author and illustrator are trying to communicate. The basic shots are similar to those a cinematographer must choose:

- *Close-up*—the camera is very near one character's face, so that every detail of an expression can be seen. An "extreme close-up" is obviously even closer than that—a nose or the words on a coffee cup or a spider resting on a finger.
- *Medium shot*—the camera is a few steps away from the character, allowing some background and one or two other characters to be in focus. This is the most common camera shot used in American comics. If no directions are given in a script, an illustrator will assume the author intends a medium shot in a particular panel.
- *Long shot*—the camera is backed up a moderate distance from the characters, so that the environment or background takes center stage (e.g., an entire classroom).
- *Establishing shot*—the camera is outside of the action area in a wide, panoramic view, showing the location of the scene, normally without any of the characters in view. Establishing shots are often accompanied by caption boxes to kick-start the dialogue in a scene before we actually see the characters themselves.

These decisions about camera distance are not made lightly. All of these shot decisions come with a list of advantages, as well as a corresponding list of disadvantages. A wider shot allows more characters or scenery elements to be included in the frame; the disadvantage is that each person or scenic item will be drawn with

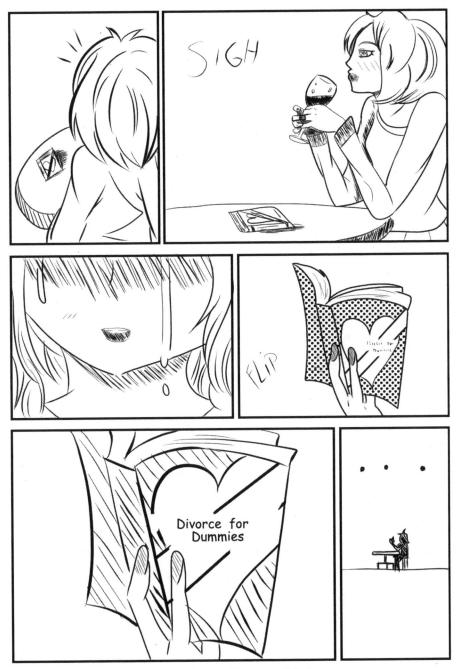

Figure 2.12. Close-ups can be very effective. This is a manga sequence, so read right to left. *Illustration courtesy of Chris Burns*

less detail. A close-up allows lots of detail for the character being illustrated, but the reader can't see anyone else's reaction. Figure 2.12 shows a manga sequence with close-ups.

As with the opening shot in a film, the first panel of a comic book or section is usually an establishing shot, sometimes called a "splash page." Will Eisner says that the first panel—indeed, the entire first page—is a "launching pad for the narrative and for most stories it establishes a frame of reference. . . . It sets a climate."[12] The disadvantage of a very wide establishing shot is that the reader can't see any characters. Reading a caption can help, as the reader uses closure to figure out who is speaking and why the characters are located in that place.

In addition to the camera distance, illustrators have to decide on camera angle. As with distance, each decision about angle comes with advantages and disadvantages. Comics creators frequently use straight-on angles as characters talk to each other, similar to a lot of film shots. This is comfortable territory for a reader, but too much of this angle can get tedious—especially since the characters in graphic novels don't actually move. A bird's eye view of the action can be used for a change of pace, allowing the reader to see things the characters themselves cannot see; the downside is that facial reactions will be lost. Sometimes a close-up of a hand or some other element in the scene is very powerful, such as one interesting basketball sequence in *Nothing Can Possibly Go Wrong* by Prudence Shen and Faith Erin Hicks. The main character's hand is drawn elevating above his opponents' hands, sinking shot after shot. The reader gets the feeling of total athletic supremacy, that the guy cannot miss.

Camera angle and shot placement are closely related to point of view, as we will see in a moment.

Point of View

The point of view, or POV, in a story is "the perspective from which a book is narrated. . . . Point of view is used to show readers in whose mind and through whose eyes they are seeing the world of the story."[13] In both prose and graphic novels, readers search immediately for the story's POV. You know the three POV choices from English class:

1. *First person:* "I turn the corner and see a shadow. I run."
2. *Second person:* "You turn the corner and see a shadow. You run."
3. *Third person:* "Monique turns the corner and sees a shadow. She runs."

On the very first page of a novel, the reader is asking, "If the story is in first person, who is speaking? If the POV is third person, who is the narrator? Is the narrator going to stay close to the main character or omnisciently wander into the heads of multiple characters?" If the reader has to search too hard, or the author has not made it clear right away, the reader can get discouraged.

Most graphic novels establish a POV immediately by visual and prose clues. Some, however, hide the POV for a little while to provide background information. This is especially true if the book is part of a series; the writer can't assume that the reader has read the first installments. The creators of the graphic novel version of *Artemis Fowl: The Arctic Incident*, adapted by Eoin Colfer and Andrew Donkin with art by Giovanni Rigano, employ a delayed POV. In the first section, the reader doesn't meet either character who will eventually tell the story in first person. Fortunately, the section is labeled as a prologue so the reader doesn't get too confused.

Graphic novels lend themselves very well to first person POV. This provides an emotional bond between the main character and the reader. First person also feels very intimate, especially when the story is told in the present tense. The reader sees the character's thoughts as they occur in real time, so there is very little filter present to buffer the reader. This creates an immediacy that can stimulate the senses and stir the emotions of the reader quickly. The recent *Ms. Marvel* comics, starring Kamala Khan, are written in first person present: "So, I'm pretty sure I just got shot," she says in a caption box in issue 4.

First person past tense, by contrast, feels less immediate and more reflective. The narrator has had time to process what has happened, so the story feels more like a memoir than an action movie. First person past tense is often addressed directly to the reader, either as a confessional or as a lesson to be learned. This kind of first person past tense can be seen in *Wonder Woman: Spirit of Truth*. In a caption, Wonder Woman addresses the reader from an older, wiser perspective: "With that she turned and ran. The girl had seen me only as an unwelcome intrusion into her world. A bizarre creature every bit as threatening as the tank that nearly killed her." There is an intimacy here, but the past tense is characterized more by a distancing than a drawing close.

In Bryan O'Malley's *Scott Pilgrim vs. The World*, the POV is close third person. This means that the main character, Scott, never addresses the reader directly, although the "camera" follows him closely. Because it's "close" the POV never switches to another character and after a while, it feels like first person. Most of the story unfolds visually or in dialogue, but once in a while the narrator addresses the reader directly in the form of a caption for information or flashback purposes: "Scott's last haircut / 431 days ago / 3 hrs before breakup with last girlfriend / (blames breakup largely on haircut)."

Third person omniscient can be interesting, but this POV is not as popular for graphic novels because it's more difficult to pull off in the limited space. Because the narrator is omniscient, the reader can eavesdrop into the thoughts of several characters. This "head hopping" can be interesting but must be done carefully so the reader is not confused. *Justice League of America*, written by Brad Meltzer and illustrated by Ed Benes, is written in third person omniscient. The reader gets into the heads of Wonder Woman, Batman, and Superman as they try and decide whom to invite to the crime-fighting party. The technique gives a variety of perspectives but can also be confusing at times.

The opening spread of G. Neri's *Yummy* illustrates how the POV of a graphic novel can help set the tone or mood of the story. The main character has illustrated himself right into some of his city's most famous stories (with Al Capone, Michael Jordan, and Oprah Winfrey, among others), which gives us a feeling of closeness with the character as he tells his story. This will be important as the narrator delves into an emotionally draining tale of crime and lost youth.

Knowing how the author and artist establish the POV helps in understanding and enjoyment of a graphic story.

Motion Lines, Sound Effects, and Standard Gestures

Almost all graphic stories require the depiction of action or movement—a slap in the face, a car trip, a speeding spaceship, a dinner plate dropped on the floor. So what can a creator do when an action scene is required? In film, it's easy—just line up a bunch of frames to trick the eye into seeing a continuous action. Comics artists, on the other hand, freeze each action into a static frame. From the earliest days of comics, creators have wrestled with the problem of how to simulate motion in a satisfying and believable way.

At first, comics creators tried to draw multiple images within a frame. Some even tried to simulate the blur of an image as it might appear in a photograph. Eventually the superhero artists such as Jack Kirby and Bill Everett created the quintessential motion lines that we still see today. In fact, Scott McCloud writes that Kirby's lines "became so stylized as to almost have a life and physical presence all their own!"[14] Almost every type of comic, graphic novel, and manga uses these stylized motion lines to draw the reader into the story and get the heart beating a little faster.

Linguist Neil Cohn calls these motion tools "indexical lines" and puts them in categories:

- Path lines (also called motion lines or action lines) use stylized lines to show a path of an object.
- Scopic lines depict the path from a person's eyes to an object they are looking at.
- Radial lines depict something radiating out of an object, such as heat from the sun or a funky smell from a garbage can.[15]

Figure 2.13. Car crash with traditional American motion lines. *Illustration courtesy of Chris Burns*

Interestingly, Western comics creators have in the past used different types of motion lines than those of Japanese manga creators. The typical American motion line used to be drawn entirely behind the object, showing the origination and the present location of the object (figure 2.13). This gives the impression that the reader is a motionless bystander watching the action.

By contrast, Japanese manga creators have typically drawn the moving object "statically" with streaming lines in the background of the moving object (figure 2.14). These lines appear to show both where the object has been and where it is headed. According to Cohn this gives the illusion that the reader is moving "at the same speed as the object, resulting in a blurred background."[16]

Of course, there are many exceptions to both of these typical uses. Especially as manga gets more and more popular in the United States, American artists are employing manga tools to produce special effects in their own art.

Figure 2.14. Car crash with traditional Japanese motion lines. *Illustration courtesy of Chris Burns*

Indexical lines are not just used to simulate motion, however. When you see lines emanating straight out of a character's head, as in figure 2.15, what comes to mind?

These lines have no meaning by themselves, but in association with a face looking startled, they can express extreme surprise, anger, or confusion. This, again, is not stated in words but when the reader is versed in the grammar of visual language, symbols like these help communicate to the reader.

If you can almost feel motion through the use of motion lines, you can almost hear sounds when an author includes sound effects. Artists often draw out these words in ways that involve the inner ear even more vividly, as mentioned in the section on lettering. All these techniques are an effort to involve all the senses, which makes any story more enjoyable and memorable. Look back at the first panel in figure 2.14: your eyes read the sound effects, and the inner ear hears them.

Another visual tool artists use is the standard gesture. What is happening in figure 2.16? You know the character is surprised, even without knowing the situ-

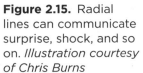

Figure 2.15. Radial lines can communicate surprise, shock, and so on. *Illustration courtesy of Chris Burns*

Figure 2.16. The gesture says it all. *Illustration courtesy of Chris Burns*

Figure 2.17. Standard gestures. *Illustration courtesy of Chris Burns*

ation he or she's in. We've been memorizing standard gestures and postures our whole lives, and comics artists tap into this data bank to communicate information. Eisner describes it this way: "The human body, the stylization of its shape, and the codifying of its emotionally produced gestures and expressive postures are accumulated and stored in the memory, forming a non-verbal vocabulary of gesture."[17]

Many artists try not to be too obvious with this vocabulary of gesture, for the same reason you are told to stay away from clichés in your English classes. Standard gestures persist, however, because they are a type of visual shorthand—they give so much information to the reader so quickly. What do you think are the emotions being expressed in figure 2.17?

"Comics at first were all about truth and justice. But now, things have changed. Characters tackle more mature subjects, while still having the same-lightheartedness that kids love. Take for instance, Captain America and Iron Man. Two icons of Marvel Comics. They both stood for heroism and truth, always working together. Then, you have 'Civil War': a story that divided the two heroes. It touches on dividing friendships and the ramifications that come from that. It's not afraid to go the extra mile and deal with very difficult topics that most other mediums wouldn't."—Ayinde R., Owing Mills, Maryland[b]

In film or television, these attitudes or emotions would go through many intermediate gestures to convey their meaning. In visual art, the artist must choose one solitary instant to move the story forward. This body language is mostly undetectable to readers, but if you look closely you will be able to recognize this vocabulary of gesture.

In many cases, a character's body language helps the reader interpret the dialogue of the panel. Look again at the gestures in figure 2.17. How would this line of dialogue be interpreted by each of the characters: "Nothing can stop me now!"

Color Palette

Early comic strips and comic books used a four-color system on cheap newsprint. Shapes and colors needed to be bold because of the nature of the technology. That's why a lot of early superheroes were created in bold, primary colors—think Superman's apple-red *S* over a lemon-yellow background on a lake-blue shirt—that could transcend the limitations of the printing press.

As technology progressed, artists were able to use more subtle designs and colors that seemed more lifelike and less garish. Artists also began experimenting with more imaginative forms and colors so that color actually became part of the vocabulary of comics beyond the use of words and shapes. As McCloud says in *Understanding Comics*,

> Suddenly it seemed possible for color to take on a central role. Colors could express a dominant mood. Tones and modelling could add depth. Whole scenes could be virtually about color! Color as sensation, color as environment . . . [w]hen used well, color in comics can—like comics itself—amount to far more than the sum of its parts.[18]

Authors and artists choose color palettes that they believe will best tell their story. In addition, colors can change in various sections of a story based on the mood that needs to be set. Illustrators will often use a neutral or sepia-colored background to signify a flashback. Abrupt changes in color can change the reader's mood instantly, without any need for exposition in a caption box.

An example of an abrupt color change can be seen in the 2012 restart of *Aquaman* by Geoff Johns, illustrated by Ivan Reis. The first two pages are comprised of narrow, vertical panels that reach from the top of the page to the bottom, giving the impression of great depth. The colors are deep gray and black, with forms appearing in fluorescent blue as ravenous sea creatures escape from a trench that has long been closed. The colors help readers imagine how dark and cold it must be at that depth in the ocean. Then, suddenly, on the next page, the sun is shining and the panels are awash in color, as if we have come up for air. This change is meant to have a visceral effect on the reader.

In the graphic novel adaption of Ray Bradbury's *Fahrenheit 451*, the color palette is predictably hot—orange, yellow, and red—giving the impression that the pages themselves are hot to the touch. Interestingly, this changes as the main character, Montag, becomes more aware. The hot colors give way to cooler, more soothing colors, which changes the mood.

A good number of comics that you read—especially from publishers not named Marvel or DC—will have no color at all. Because of the cost of reproducing color pages, many comics start out as black and white. *Bone*, the ultra-popular comic series from the 1990s, started out in black and white. Now the publisher has produced a color version that adds a whole new dimension to the story.

In general, when a comic lacks color, the words and ideas are more prominent. When a story is in color, the art itself takes a more central role, although those stories still contain important ideas. Color comics can seem more real than black and white, but do not neglect great stories just because they lack color. Much of Japanese manga is in black and white, and the stories these books contain can be very compelling.

Page Turns

Many teens can still recall their favorite picture books. Part of the magic of picture books is the suspense of the page turn. Do you remember Grover's frantic pleas in Sesame Street's *The Monster at the End of This Book*? He begs the reader on the right-hand side of each spread, "Please don't turn the page!" Of course, the reader gleefully turns the page to see if the monster will indeed appear.

Page turns are also part of the magic of comics. Done well, a mini-cliffhanger at the bottom of the right page in a spread can add suspense to a story. Like most well-written comics, the book *Runaways*, volume 1, by Brian K. Vaughan and Adrian Alphona, contains a number of these dramatic page turns. One especially good one comes near the end when the teens have let their parents know that they have figured out the grownups' lies. As the parents discuss how to deal with this new threat, one of the fathers asks, "How could they all betray us like this?" Then in the last frame, in the lower right-hand corner of the right-hand page, another mom holds a note in her hands and says, "I'm not so sure that all of them have." It's a stunning moment—you *have* to turn the page to find out who the mole is in the teens' gang!

Time in Comics

As readers progress through a comic, they probably don't stop to ask why the writer chose each specific moment that has been captured in the panel. Using closure, they connect the moments together to form a flowing story in their minds. But the idea of time in comics is amorphous and irregular, which is one of the things that makes comics so difficult to write but enjoyable to read.

Think about how you sense time in real life: it feels very flexible. When you are young, you are barely, if ever, aware of time. Moms are constantly saying, "Let's go, you're so slow." That's because young children have a fluid conception of time. When they get hungry they eat; when the sun gets hot they play in the house; when it gets dark they go to bed; other than that, it's pretty much play time all day! As you get older, you sense time ticking at the pace of events. A basketball game seems to fly by because there is action in every moment. A boring history lecture, on the other hand, seems to last about two days because there are no signposts to mark progress. Besides sitting and looking at the hands of a clock, we experience time by common events: classes last fifty-five minutes; doing dishes lasts fifteen minutes; a slap in the face is a few seconds; a movie lasts two hours.

Films, like comics, must portray time somehow. The frames in a film come quickly in sequence—twenty-four per second—in order to simulate real time. The viewer's eye is willingly tricked into seeing a lifelike time sequence. Filmmakers can play with this idea by slowing down or speeding up a scene to produce a heightened effect. But in general, time in film feels analogous to real life.

Comics writers don't have the luxury of imitating real time. This is both a blessing and a curse. Creators have to choose which moments, and how many of them, to highlight on a page so that the story will flow in a way that best tells the story. Creators also have a variety of tools to employ as they seek to give the reader an impression of time passing. The beauty of comics is that a whole book can illustrate a very short time, or a hundred years can pass in the span of one page. Our minds willingly travel at the speed of the comic when it is well done.

Time in a comic is influenced by a number of factors. Obviously, the time that elapses in a graphic novel is the summation of all the individual spreads, and each spread is the addition of all the panels on those two pages. But the magic of time happens at the level of the panel. In figure 2.18, how much time is elapsing?

Figure 2.18. No time passes in this snapshot, right? *Illustration courtesy of Chris Burns*

The action seems pretty linear and instantaneous, right? Maybe one second has elapsed. How about in figure 2.19?

Figure 2.19. Now this panel takes up some time. *Illustration courtesy of Chris Burns*

Now the scene takes at least seven seconds, even though it contains the same action and the same number of characters. What makes it feel like more time has elapsed?

In short, action and dialogue have added time to a scene that originally seemed more like a photograph than a panel from a comic. Our brains are trained to see a photograph as a snapshot in time. In comics, that perception is manipulated using actions and dialogue. In figure 2.19 the speed lines beneath the cork indicate duration of an action, which stretches out the time sequence. Some artists use ordinary sequences like a dripping faucet, the countdown of a rocket, or the rhythm of an at-bat in a baseball game to simulate the passage of time.

Dialogue slows the action down even more, adding another chunk of time into the scene in figure 2.19. In fact, dialogue is the most common tool in anchoring a story in time. In a lecture given at Hamline University where he teaches, Gene Luen Yang, author of *American Born Chinese*, *The Shadow Hero*, and many other books, says as a general rule that only one dialogue balloon should be included in a panel, or one statement and one response. Any more than that becomes cumbersome and gives the reader a chance to say, "Hey, this is too much time spent in this one frozen moment." That's why the scene from *The Ultimate Spider-Man* I mentioned earlier is so mind-bending. All that dialogue, taking all that time, and yet the characters don't move a millimeter.

You've probably heard the term *willing suspension of disbelief* in an English class. It just means that the audience or readers willingly put aside their logical objections about the limitations of a medium so that they can enjoy the story. We know there is no such thing as magic or residential wizard schools, and yet, through a willing suspension of disbelief, we enjoy J. K. Rowling's Harry Potter books because we love the characters and plots. In the same way, Miles Morales's story (in the earlier example) is so compelling, we willingly set aside our reaction of, "Hey, these characters are talking but they're standing still." In fact, our brains do the job of animating the characters for the artist in the absence of any actual movement.

Other tools authors use to convey time in a comic include frame shape and number of frames on a page. How much time do you think is going by when you look at the man sitting on the bench in figure 2.20? No time at all, right? Your brain probably sees it like a snapshot. But what happens when we elongate the frame horizontally?

Figure 2.21 feels completely different, doesn't it? The story here has been transformed by the shape of the panel, which implies a long duration of time. In addition, the caption gives it an almost timeless quality, making it seem as if a lengthy amount of time is passing.

The number of panels on a page is another tool authors use to help set the pace of a story. In general, readers read faster when there are fewer panels on the page. A lot of smaller panels require more concentration, and the reader slows down to absorb all the details. Larger panels require less work, and the reader reads them at a faster pace, especially if they contain action. Action panels tend to fly by as the reader gets caught up in the story.

Figure 2.20. No time passes here, right? *Illustration courtesy of Chris Burns*

Figure 2.21. The longer frame gives the impression of time passing. *Illustration courtesy of Chris Burns*

Be aware, as you read graphic novels, of how the author and artist are manipulating the time in a story—and how it affects your enjoyment or participation in the story.

Visual Style

Beyond all the tools and symbols that comics authors use, the very style of the art is an integral part of the storytelling. Jan Baetens and Hugo Frey, authors of *The Graphic Novel: An Introduction* (which I quoted earlier in the chapter), have this to say about art style: "In short, drawing style becomes an absolutely central notion in the structure of any graphic novel."[19] They describe a type of scale, in which art can be placed between two extreme positions—

the highly subjective style in which the personal expression of the author takes all priority over the representation itself (what matters at the subjective pole is the personal way something is drawn, not the object of the representation) and the decidedly objective style (in which the object of the representation is the highest priority, at the expense of the personal expression of the author who wants to stay as neutral and invisible as possible).[20]

So as you read graphic stories, note how the *subjectivity* or the *objectivity* of the art is impacting the storytelling.

More Than the Sum

How often have you heard the phrase, "Slow down!" Well, it's really important with comics. Graphic novels use many different elements of visual grammar to tell their stories, and being aware of them helps deepen your understanding of the text. However, graphic novels are more than the sum of their parts. Now that you know some of the tools used by graphic storytellers, stop thinking about them; because unless your brain combines all the elements together you won't appreciate the beauty of the story.

We use the phrase *more than the sum of its parts* to describe sports teams. A tall girl might be a good athlete, but unless there is another player who can handle the basketball with skill, the center on a basketball team isn't going to score many points. Graphic novels work the same way—that wide shot of the old house has very little meaning without the caption, the specific color palette, the foreboding shape of the panel, the sound effects of the wind whistling through the trees, and the placement of the image on the page. As comics researchers Frances Gateward and John Jennings say in their book of essays on comics, "Comics, when created by a skillful and informed hand, can speak with the power of words and text combined. This power is many times more potent than either mediation can achieve on its own."[21]

THE EVOLUTION OF AMERICAN SUPERHERO COMICS

We love our superheroes. From earliest recorded history, poets and storytellers have created tales of brave, bold, clever women and men who battled evil and freed their lands from invaders. Our own preoccupation with superheroes should come as no surprise, even in our increasingly technological society. Superheroes go about getting the justice that we rarely see in real life. Their extranormal abilities—whether super strength, blazing speed, mind reading (telepathy), shape-shifting, flight, matter or energy manipulation (telekinesis), underwater

Figure 3.1. Super Teen! *Illustration courtesy of Chris Burns*

"Superheroes give us the opportunity to jump out of our own lives and fantasize about being someone else, someone with power, someone that can make a difference. Superheroes might not be logical in their super abilities, but they embody the moral desire to do the right thing, and they symbolize the good in all of us. This is how superheroes have impacted American society, by giving people something more than themselves to believe in."—Stephen W., Evansville, Indiana[a]

breathing, Teflon-tough skin, supersmarts (like our Super Teen in figure 3.1), or any other power you can dream up—allow us to imagine the power and control we've always wanted for ourselves.

Thousands of years ago, the tales of superheroes were told by bards around a campfire or in a marble amphitheater. Today we see our mythical saviors in movies and in comic books. The trouble with movies is that only a few are made each year, and the film format can incorporate only a few incidents within its time frame. So early in the twentieth century, writers turned to another medium for their stories: comic books. Once seen as useless amusement for preteen boys, comic book superhero stories have turned into a multibillion-dollar industry (if you count the movies) that attracts readers young and old, male and female, human and extraterrestrial.

It won't be possible to trace every twist and turn in the superhero comics market in this chapter, but I will hit some of the highlights and give a good overview of how the industry has changed. If you're already into superhero comics, you may not see your lesser-known favorite discussed here because of space constraints. But I will tackle the rise and fall of some of the major superheroes. So, as one famous character famously said, "Up, up, and away!"

A Super Start

Since the early twentieth century, American authors had been writing stories with heroic figures such as Zorro, Doc Savage, the Shadow, and the Spider.[1] Some of these appeared in books, others on the radio or as daily strips in newspaper "funny pages." In the 1930s, publishers began to collect newspaper strips and bundle them together in short books called comic books. And then in 1938, a comic book was published that would change the world and usher in an age of superheroes that is still going strong today. That was the month that DC published *Action Comics* #1. This was the world's first introduction to Superman, a character created by two eighteen-year-olds in Cleveland, Ohio.

Restarts Sell Big

Comics publishers start over every few years with new number 1 issues utilizing new writers and artists. Sometimes this is to clean up an unruly history that has gotten too muddled to understand. Sometimes it's just a publicity stunt to attract new readers. Whatever the reason, it works. In the summer of 2016, DC revamped and restarted all their major series, calling it Rebirth. Although they have been second to Marvel in numbers of books sold for years, that month they dominated the sales charts with eighteen of the top twenty titles. Notice how many of the top twenty sold in July 2016 are number 1, 2, or 3.

1. *Justice League* #1 (DC)
2. *Justice League Rebirth* #1 (DC)
3. *Batman* #2 (DC)
4. *Civil War* #3 (Marvel)
5. *Batman* #3 (DC)
6. *Nightwing Rebirth* #1 (DC)
7. *Civil War* #4 (Marvel)
8. *New Super-Man* #1 (DC)
9. *Nightwing* #1 (DC)
10. *Hal Jordan and the Green Lantern Corps Rebirth* #1 (DC)
11. *Hal Jordan and the Green Lantern Corps* #1 (DC)
12. *Wonder Woman* #2 (DC)
13. *Flash* #2 (DC)
14. *Titans* #1 (DC)
15. *Superman* #2 (DC)
16. *Detective Comics* #936 (DC)
17. *Batgirl and the Birds of Prey Rebirth* #1 (DC)
18. *Superman* #3 (DC)
19. *Flash* #3 (DC)
20. *Batgirl* #1 (DC)[b]

Jerry Siegel and Joe Shuster were friends who worked on the school paper at Glenville High School in Cleveland, Ohio. They had been writing and drawing comics for the school newspaper and had even sold a few strips to various publishers. The pair approached publishers with the original Superman—who initially was a villain—but were rejected.[2] Finally, after five years of refining, the pair finally succeeded in selling the idea to National Allied Publications—later called DC (for Detective Comics). Superman was an instant hit.

> "Superman is an all-powerful being who can move planets and do the impossible. Yes, he isn't supposed to be relatable. He is never meant to lose. His story is one of a god living among men. It's about doing the right thing."—Ayinde R., Owing Mills, Maryland[c]

Why was the story of Superman so resonant with people in 1938? There were many reasons. First, the country was still mired in the struggle of the Great Depression. People were looking for a hero, as they do in all times of great need. But more than that, the American people were still very conscious that they were a country of immigrants. Superman was the last survivor (at least that had been revealed) of the planet Krypton. He had been separated from his parents and was being raised in an alien environment. Many people—including Siegel and Shuster, children of European Jewish immigrants—felt that sense of loss mixed with new hope.[3]

The Man of Steel flew off the pages of the magazine and into the public imagination. The first issue introduced readers to the smart and sassy Lois Lane, and featured Superman fighting a mob of gangsters. Many early comics in the late 1930s and early 1940s pitched the superhero against local thugs, who more often than not have abducted the hero's love interest. It became clear after a few issues, however, that the Man of Steel was not going to break a sweat fighting local tough guys, so the writers began creating larger, more colorful villains. These evildoers—such as Lex Luthor, "the mad scientist who plots to dominate the earth" (*Superman* #4, 1940)—came to be known as supervillains, due to the grand scale of their diabolical schemes.[4]

Seeing the success of Superman, his publishers quickly created another superhero who would remain in the public's imagination for many decades: the Batman. After the Caped Crusader came the Flash, Hawkman, Green Lantern, the Atom, and Wonder Woman, just to name a few.[5] A rival publisher called Timely (later to become Marvel) launched several superheroes of its own, including Sub-Mariner, the Human Torch, and Captain America.

Superman has come a long way. He was briefly married to Lois Lane in 1955 before that story was revealed to be a dream (this is a favorite gimmick for introducing bizarre or misleading stories). From the beginning he could leap great distances—one-eighth of a mile—according to the early comics, but somewhere along the way he gained the power of flight. As with all superhero abilities, later writers came along and explained their origins for more skeptical readers. Superman's ability to fly was attributed to Earth's relatively weaker gravitational pull as compared to Krytpon, Superman's home world. His Kryptonian cells also get supercharged in the presence of a yellow star, which Earth conveniently revolves around.[6]

Most early superheroes had some power—Green Lantern has his magic ring, Captain America has superhuman strength, Wonder Woman has unnatural strength and beauty gifted from the Greek gods. But not all superheroes were conceived with these powers. Most famously, the Batman debuted without any extra powers. From the beginning the Batman used his natural strength, crime-solving mind, and technological gadgets to subdue criminals. This humanness has contributed to the timeless appeal of Batman, who is still one of the comic world's most popular superheroes. As one teen noted on TeenInk.com, an online community for teen expression,

> "Batman and Superman . . . have both had an enormous impact on me through their major films, comic books, cartoon series and action figures. Even though the characters are fictional, they have become real to me, and I look up to them as the heroes they are in the comic books and movies."—Stephen W., Evansville, Indiana[d]

> Batman will always be the greatest superhero in my book. His ability to fight crime and win while being powerless is truly iconic and inspiring. While he may just be a comic book character, his message to fight for what you believe in, even if you are just an everyday person, echoes in the extraordinary actions of ordinary people.[7]

The Golden Age

Historians divide the superhero comics into four rough ages: Golden, Silver, Bronze, and Modern. There isn't strict agreement when one era changes into another, but the comics of each time period share certain storytelling traits that make it helpful to group them together. I'm going to give you a brief overview of these eras and a few of the characteristics that define them.

We've already discussed the beginning of the Golden Age, which was started in 1938 with the introduction of Superman, and ended in the mid-1950s with DC's relaunch of *The Flash*. Superhero comics flourished before and during World War II, when readers enjoyed reading about their heroes saving the day against despicable foreign enemies such as the Nazis. Unfortunately, comics creators also developed unfair racial stereotypes, especially concerning Japanese people. During this era, supervillains were one-dimensional and easy to hate, as they were mainly gangsters or enemy superspies.

By the early 1950s, readers had grown tired of superheroes and many dropped by the wayside in favor of western comics, science fiction stories, romances, even horror comics. The crime and horror comics were so disturbing to some adults that the appearance of the book *Seduction of the Innocent: The Influence of Comic Books on Today's Youth* by Dr. Frederic Wertham changed the industry. In the book, Dr. Wertham claimed he had done scientific studies that proved that comic books were turning America's teens into delinquents. The science was later found to be largely fake,[8] but the effect of his book was immediate and drastic. Committees were formed to study the effects of comics. The U.S. Senate even held hearings on comic books.

To avoid any further intrusion by the government, the comics publishers got together and created their own Comics Code Authority (CCA). The CCA prohibited the depiction of violence and gore, and the words *terror* and *horror* could not be used in titles. Sexual content was also restricted, even what we would consider mild innuendo today. Depictions of drug abuse were likewise banned. Books that did not have the stamped CCA seal (figure 3.2) were not sold through many distributors, so most of the comics publishers knuckled under and lived by the restrictive guidelines.

Because the CCA severely limited the popular genres of comics at the time, DC decided it was time to return to superheroes. Superman, Batman, and Wonder Woman were among only a handful of characters who survived from the Golden Age, and each had dedicated readers. But in 1956, DC reinvented the Flash, and the Silver Age of comics was ushered in.

The Silver Age

The Flash had been cancelled in 1949, but he was updated for a more savvy audience and launched in *Showcase* #4 (September 1956).[9] The new Flash was police scientist Barry Allen, who gained his super speed after being caught in a spill of toxic chemicals during a lightning storm. With an update to his look and love life, the Flash was instantly popular and inspired several other reintroductions of retired superheroes: Green Lantern, Hawkman, and the Atom, to name a few.

Figure 3.2. *Comics Code Authority Seal of Approval is Trademark & Copyright 2017 Comic Book Legal Defense Fund. Used with Permission.*

One of the characteristics of the Silver Age is that many of the old characters were reintroduced with a less fantastical, more science fiction story line.[10] For instance, in the 1940s Green Lantern's Hal Jordan finds a magic lantern that gives him mystical powers. In the late 1950s, Hal's story is rewritten so that he receives a power battery that charges a ring. This battery, which Hal calls a Green Lantern, comes from an alien who crash-lands on earth. This makes him a member of the Green Lantern Corps, an elite crime-fighting force that is responsible for the entire galaxy.

> "The heroes come to life and truly save us. When America needed a soldier, Captain America punched Hitler in the face. When nerds needed a mascot, Bruce Banner and Peter Parker strapped on their lab goggles."—Emma S., Plymouth, Minnesota[e]

As their heroes gained a following, the editors at DC decided to put them all together in a winning combination called the Justice League of America (JLA). The League was a reinvention of the old Justice Society, but "society" was seen as too quaint and elitist.[11] In 1960, the JLA debuted in *The Brave and the Bold* #28, and soon became a bestselling title. Initial members were Green Lantern, the Flash, Martian Manhunter, Wonder Woman, and Aquaman. Superman and Batman were also among the initial members of the JLA, but played mostly supporting roles.

At that time, rival Marvel did not have a group of superheroes to compete with DC's Justice League. That would change in 1961 when Marvel debuted *The Fantastic Four*. This series, written by Marvel's legendary Stan Lee, has an interesting genesis. The story goes that Marvel's publisher, and Lee's boss, Martin Goodman, had been out playing golf with a bigwig at DC. This DC insider confided to Goodman that *Justice League of America* was flying off the shelves. Returning to the Marvel offices, Goodman told Lee to create their own version of the Justice League. The trouble was that Marvel didn't have a stable of hot-selling superheroes to choose from, as DC did. As hard as it is to believe today, Marvel wasn't publishing any superhero comics at the time.

So Stan Lee did what you do when your teacher asks you to do something crazy—he made something up. Lee created a quartet of superheroes called the Fantastic Four: Mr. Fantastic, Invisible Girl, Human Torch, and the Thing.[12] Typical of the Silver Age, these heroes were a little more lifelike than the one-dimensional, uncomplicated crime fighters of the Golden Age. For example, the Fantastic Four, while friends, bickered with one another in a way that seemed very true to life. The Thing also struggled with anger toward his fellow heroes, reflecting an obsession with personal psychology that permeated the middle decades of the twentieth century. *The Fantastic Four* was instantly popular, and inspired even more teams at Marvel—the Avengers and eventually X-Men.

The 1960s ushered in what some have called the Marvel Age of comics, because Marvel introduced some major characters during this decade, most notably Spider-Man, the Hulk, Thor, and Iron Man. You will recognize these characters as the inner core of the Avengers, whose recent movies defined what a successful superhero movie could be.

Stan Lee, Comics Marvel

No doubt you've seen the old man who always makes a cameo appearance in the Marvel superhero movies, Stan Lee. You've probably also heard that he created many of the superheroes that exist today: the Fantastic Four, Spider-Man, the Hulk, Iron Man, and many more. But did you know that Stan Lee had worked at Marvel (it was called Timely back then) for more than twenty years before he created those blockbuster characters in the 1960s?[f]

Stan Lee, born Stanley Lieber in 1922, had been hired in 1939 as an editorial assistant. Lee had always dreamed of writing the great American novel. In 1941 Lee took over the writing of *Captain America*. After World War II, as Marvel's superheroes lost their readership, Lee worked on western comics, romances, even horror comics to make ends meet.

During a time in which he thought of leaving comic books, Lee's wife encouraged him to concentrate on—and treat seriously—the medium that had occupied his time for so long.[g] Soon thereafter he wrote *The Fantastic Four* with legendary Marvel artist Jack Kirby. Then came *The Hulk*, then *Spider-Man*, and the rest is history. Stan Lee has been writing comics for more than seventy years, penning a bestseller called *Romeo and Juliet: The War* in 2012—at age ninety![h] Lee is credited with some of comics' most innovative traditions, such as getting rid of the sidekick, making superheroes more human, and dealing with tough social issues within the story line.[i]

Generally speaking, writers in the Golden Age of comics had tried to steer clear of controversial issues. Silver Age writers changed all that.

Superheroes in the 1960s began to question their own values, as well as the values of the culture in which they lived. Comic books began to feature stories about entry into the Vietnam War, protests on college campuses, drug abuse, and race relations. The first black superhero to be featured in a comic book debuted in 1966, as the Fantastic Four are trapped in Wakanda, home of the Black Panther. Several female superheroes also made their debuts in the 1960s, including Invisible Girl from the Fantastic Four, and Jean Grey, a founding member of the X-Men. I will talk more about how comics have become more inclusive later in the chapter.

The Silver Age of comics ended sometime around 1970. That was the year comics legend Jack Kirby left Marvel Comics to join DC. Some people prefer to say the Silver Age ended in 1973 when Spider-Man's girlfriend, Gwen Stacy, was killed (*Amazing Spider-Man* #121). Modern readers are somewhat used to characters dying in comics today (many of whom miraculously come back at a later date), but in the 1970s, that was a monumental event. Imaginary story lines had featured deaths before, but this time a major character really, truly died. It was a heartbreaking moment for many readers and a turning point in superhero comic writing.[13]

The Bronze Age

Whatever date you choose for the beginning of the Bronze Age, comics story lines became even grittier than they had been in the exploratory era of the late 1960s. DC led the way into the Bronze Age with a series of *Green Lantern/Green Arrow* comics, the so-called relevancy series written by Denny O'Neil and Neal Adams—both men in their twenties at the time.

Jack Kirby, Trend-Setting Illustrator

Jack Kirby, born Jacob Kurtzberg in 1917, is the artist who designed and drew much of the Marvel universe in the 1960s. He created or co-created the Fantastic Four, the Hulk, Thor, the X-Men, the Avengers, the Black Panther, and others.

Although he is most famous for his contribution at Marvel in the 1960s, Kirby had been working in animation and comics since the mid-1930s. In the 1940s, he and business partner Joe Simon created the instant hit *Captain America*, as well as the romance comic book *Young Romance*.[j]

Kirby's art has come to epitomize American comics, with its energy and movement. "By the time he was in his mid-twenties, he inspired scads of imitators with his rousing, dynamic cartooning style, which conveyed movement and conflict with a violent intensity, smashing though panel borders and assaulting the page."[k]

Kirby didn't just do artwork. He and writer-editor Stan Lee developed a way of working in which Lee would provide a basic outline, then give Kirby tremendous freedom to create the story visually. When the art was done, Lee would go back and fill in the dialogue. This has become known as the Marvel style of writing comics.[l]

This series introduced issues that were on the minds of young Americans, especially those on college campuses.[14] DC had dealt with racism and civil rights to a certain extent in the 1960s, most notably when Lois Lane became an African American for a day to understand the plight of Metropolis's black community. But this treatment did not come across as seriously as the treatment in *Green Lantern* #76 in April 1970. In this issue, Green Lantern punishes a group of poor people who are fighting against injustice. Green Arrow, who is more in tune with what's going on in the community, lets Green Lantern know he's fighting for the wrong side. Particularly effective are the panels in which an older black man confronts Green Lantern:

I been readin' about you, how you work for the blue skins . . . and how on a planet someplace you helped out the orange skins . . . and you done considerable for the purple skins! Only there's skins you never bothered with—! . . . the black skins! I want to know . . . how come?! Answer me that, Mr. Green Lantern!" (*Green Lantern* #76, April 1970)

The relevant comics also confronted an issue on the minds of many young people at the time—drug abuse. This was in direct conflict with the CCA, which prohibited any mention of drug use. In *Green Lantern* #85, September 1971, the greens are horrified to discover that Green Arrow's former sidekick Speedy is addicted to heroin. In the same year, Marvel released a *Spider-Man* story line in which Peter Parker's friend Harry Osborn struggles with drug addiction. This was the beginning of the end for the CCA, which relaxed its guidelines—as long as drug use was shown as destructive.

"Probably every person that has ever seen or read about a superhero has imagined himself or herself in that role. People have pretended to possess incredible and amazing super powers, and with these powers they see themselves soaring across the city skyline, swooping down to stop a robbery or save a kitten stuck in a tree. Using that tremendous power, they would be able to avert natural disasters and save the innocent bystanders from certain destruction. But even if nobody has any of these supernatural abilities, there could still be superheroes because most of what it takes to be a superhero is the will to step up and do the right thing when no one else is willing to."—Stephen W., Evansville, Indiana[m]

Even Captain America was not immune to questioning his own actions and intentions. In the mid-1970s, Cap became so disenchanted with the corruption in American politics (remember Watergate from your U.S. history class?) that he briefly abandoned his roots and became Nomad, a man without allegiance to any specific country.[15]

The Modern Age?

By 1980, the Bronze Age of comics had ended and the Modern Age had begun. Personally, I think "modern age" is misleading. The comics world in 1980 was much different than it is today with our proliferation of niche heroes and digital reading devices. A better way to talk about the evolution of superheroes in this period would be by decade, so that is how I will continue the discussion.

The 1980s were monumental in superhero comics. After writing more relevant and inclusive characters in the 1970s, the industry went through a downturn. Many kids and college students stopped reading comics. The comics publishers knew they had to write something captivating to save the industry.

One of the major events from the 1980s was the *Crisis on Infinite Earths* at DC. This series was promoted as a celebration of DC's fiftieth anniversary, but the company took the opportunity to clean up a lot of conflicting story lines in the DC universe. Until the *Crisis* story line, many characters had inconsistent, even conflicting histories. For instance, Superman was originally written as the sole survivor of the planet Krypton. Subsequent stories, however, revealed that he had a cousin from his home planet, Supergirl, and many Kryptonians survived in a bottled-up city called Kandor. Worse yet, different versions of DC's major characters existed on parallel worlds and would occasionally meet up in one of the planes of existence.[16] There was Earth-1, where the Silver Age heroes existed; Earth-2, where the Golden Age versions lived; Earth-3, where evil versions of American superheroes existed . . . you get the idea.

Writer Marv Wolfman and illustrator George Perez set out to unify the concurrent versions of DC's superheroes. The plotline in this twelve-issue series is complicated, but suffice it to say that the villain Anti-Monitor is seeking to destroy all the parallel earths on which all these conflicting superheroes lived. At the end of the series, the DC universe is a very different place. The multiple-earths paradigm that had existed for decades was gone. Earths 1, 2, 3, S, C, and all others were merged into one earth with a completely rebooted continuity. After *Crisis*, only one version of each superhero remained.[17] DC tried to replicate this idea of rewriting history in an ongoing series several more times in the years to follow, but none were as groundbreaking as the original *Crisis*.

Comics Terms

Anyone who's followed a specific character, especially a superhero, in comics has heard terms such as *crossover* that they don't quite understand. Here is a list of common comics terms with brief definitions.

Continuity: This refers to the past events contained in that character's backstory. On a larger scale, it also refers to the events that have taken place in the larger universe in which the character is placed, such as the Marvel and DC universes. When the continuity gets too muddled, the publisher will create an event to simplify or codify the story.

Crossover: This is a story in which one or more characters appear prominently in a series that normally features other characters. Crossovers can be both internal or between universes, although they normally stay within the same publisher. At its most basic, a crossover can refer simply to a character making a guest appearance, but normally, a crossover is a multi-issue occurrence, often part of an event.[n]

Event: This is a crossover story on a generally larger scale than normal. Often events include many characters from a shared universe coming together. These often affect stories for months at a time. They are big promotional occurrences.

Retcon: Short for *retroactive continuity*, retcon is when a past event in a shared universe or a character's past is suddenly changed retroactively. This can be done to add new elements to an existing story that allows for future stories. Or it can be an update; for example, Tony Stark was originally wounded in Vietnam but Marvel retconned this and now he was hurt in Afghanistan.[o]

Marvel published a similarly inclusive world-altering event in the mid-1980s, named *Secret Wars*. In the series, a cosmic entity named the Beyonder takes many of Marvel's biggest heroes and villains and pits them against each other in a weapons-stocked arena called Battleworld. More of a toy-selling gimmick than a story-driven series, *Secret Wars* nevertheless changed several of Marvel's characters. Most notably, Spider-Man begins to sport an all-black costume, later revealed to be an alien symbiote.[18]

Marvel's *Uncanny X-Men* should be mentioned in the context of the 1980s because this series, written by Chris Claremont, was groundbreaking in many ways and defined the X-Men for decades to come. Claremont took a comic that had been in the shadows and turned it into the highest-selling comic book on the market. He seemed to be able to tap into the marginalization felt by many people in American society and bring it out in the mutants on the page. The series became so popular that the movie *X-Men* (released in 2000) is seen by many as the first successful movie franchise based on the Marvel universe.[19]

Game Changers of the 1980s

Although Marvel comics had outsold DC comics in the first half of the 1980s, DC produced a handful of titles that not only flew off the shelves but also redefined the comics industry. The most famous written about one of the Big Three (Superman, Batman, Wonder Woman) was *Batman: The Dark Knight Returns* (DKR). Written by Frank Miller, DKR weaved the tensions of the Cold War into an engaging story line. Notable in this story was the presence of a female Robin, as well as a knock-down, drag-out fight to the (apparent) death between Batman and Superman, who is sent by the U.S. government to destroy the masked vigilante. DKR was printed in a perfect-bound format rather than comic book style, and the collected graphic novel is still a popular seller to this day.

But the really groundbreaking book that changed the way comics are viewed was *Watchmen* by Alan Moore and Dave Gibbons. Released in twelve issues in 1986, and then as a graphic novel in 1987, *Watchmen* was written in an entirely different way than superhero stories of the past. The tale unfolded in a strict nine-panel-per-page layout, with prose sections interspersed—newspaper clippings, letters, and so on—that shed more light on the characters' backgrounds. The story explores what life might be like if there were real costumed vigilantes in society fighting crime. Most of the characters in the story have no special powers, except Dr. Manhattan, whose rearranged atoms make him almost godlike (although without any sense of morality). Set as a counterpoint to the story is a comic book story-within-the-story that tells of the unfortunate adventures of a shipwrecked man trying to make his way back home from a deserted island. The complex story and mature themes garnered instant attention and has been much copied since it was published in 1986.

Both *The Dark Knight Returns* and *Watchmen* put graphic novels—even those with superheroes—on the literary map. The books can be found in most libraries and bookstores to this day. More importantly, the books opened the door for other graphic novelists who wanted to be taken seriously as writers and artists.

The biggest event in superhero comics in the 1990s was the death of Superman. The graphic novel that contains the entire story (still available today) says on the cover, "The best-selling graphic novel of all time." In the story, Superman fights the most powerful menace he has ever faced—Doomsday. The final battle takes place outside of the *Daily Planet*. Each of these final twenty-two pages contains only one panel. In the end, Superman defeats the destructive alien but, in the process, dies of wounds he has received. Fittingly, he dies in the arms of his longtime love, Lois Lane.

The death of Superman led to a hugely popular mystery as to which, if any, of four supermen might emerge to take the original's place: John Henry Irons (a.k.a. the Man of Steel); a cyborg named the Man of Tomorrow; the Metropolis Kid, a teenaged Superman clone; and the alien Last Son of Krypton. Of course, we know today that the real Superman was returned—he was too valuable a commodity and too loved by readers to abolish!

The first decade of the 2000s saw tremendous growth in the industry. All of the comics companies produced stories that reflected on, and responded to, the attacks that occurred on September 11, 2001. It became clear that Americans still wanted to turn to their superheroes for comfort after hard times.

Although Marvel had declared bankruptcy in the 1990s,[20] the success of the Spider-Man movies in the early 2000s, as well as blockbusters featuring Iron Man, the Hulk, and the Avengers, led to a resurgence of Marvel's superheroes in the first two decades of this century. *Guardians of the Galaxy*, which had been around for decades, also enjoyed a renaissance thanks to the 2014 movie.

In 2011, after many confusing crossover and reboot events, the brass at DC decided that their multiverse had truly become too confusing—again. They wanted a genuine restart that would be accessible to younger readers, as well as

"Yes, these heroes have it all. In addition, they are the only people who can pull off wearing tights. This is all part of the package that includes a secret headquarters overflowing with advanced gadgets and a unique way of transportation (i.e., 'Batmobile,' superhuman ability to fly and web-shooters)."—Heajin Y., Phoenix, Arizona[p] people who had been introduced to their characters in movies. Their *New 52*, published beginning in 2011, started everything from scratch. After a crossover story called *Flashpoint*, all DC titles were cancelled and started back up with brand new number 1 issues. Batman, Superman, Wonder Woman, Aquaman, and many others received new starts. Superman, in particular, has gone through changes in this decade, in which he has lost many of his powers and discovered new ones. In 2016, DC once again launched an event and a restart to pull in new customers. They called the event Rebirth, and their sales data in the first few months were amazing—it was a genuine surge in interest for the long-running second-largest comics publisher. If you're looking to start reading any of these characters, these are good places to start.

Around the same time, Marvel made its universe more accessible to new readers by launching Marvel NOW! Their biggest hitters were relaunched with number 1 issues, including *X-Men*, *Captain America*, *Fantastic Four*, *The Hulk*, *Iron Man*, and others. Marvel's *Secret Wars* of 2015 was another event that featured many new versions of established characters and paved the way for a new generation of readers. Then in 2016 the Civil War event, along with the corresponding Marvel movie of the same title, became very popular. The sales on these titles, including digital sales, provided evidence that new starts will gain new readers.

The new digital comics world is helping younger readers get connected with older characters, as well as colorful newer characters such as She-Hulk, Spider-Gwen, Deadpool, and Harley Quinn.

Diversity in Superhero Comics

In the 1930s and 1940s, just about all superheroes were white men: Superman, Captain America, Batman, Aquaman, Green Lantern, the Flash—the list goes on. That homogenous casting has changed, as you can tell from almost any issue of any comic. One major change is the number of female superheroes. We've come a long way from Wonder Woman standing alone with all those guys.

Female Superheroes Take Charge

Comics publishers for many years assumed that a vast majority of their readers were adolescent boys. Studies have shown just the opposite. In 2014, market research showed that the percentage of female readers may be as high as 47 percent.[21] Ask people who attend one of the Comic-Con conventions around the country, and they will tell you the same thing: there are as many women attend-

"An interesting case study is Wonder Woman, and how the comic book industry has portrayed a woman who's modus operandi is being a strong female character. However, her symbolism has changed over the years as well as how her creators have handled her character, the values she promotes, and what it really means to be the most powerful woman alive."—Caroline A., Syosset, New York[q]

ing as men. Comics publishers have taken notice and are working hard to bring in more female superheroes that their fans can relate to.

The first widely recognized female superhero was Wonder Woman, debuting in 1941 in *All-Star Comics* #8. Although she is described as having "a hundred times the agility and strength of our best male athletes," she is pretty much defined by her physical beauty. The comments of people who see her walking down the street in her first public appearance define her allure:

Female character:

"The hussy! She has no clothes on!"

Male characters:

"Boy! Whatta honey!"
"Aw . . . I'll bet it's some sort o' publicity stunt for a new movin' pitcher."
"If it is, they certainly go to extreme lengths to attract the public eye!"
"Well, they certainly attracted my eye!" (*Sensation Comics* #1, January 1942)

Although Wonder Woman roams the globe vanquishing ruthless enemies, her first series of episodes all end with her disguised as Diana Prince and pining away that she can't win the heart of her love, Captain Steve Trevor.

Created by William Moulton Marston (a.k.a. Charles Moulton), the inventor of the lie detector, the Amazon Princess was created as a role model for girls. Teens today who read the old 1940s comics might not agree with that statement, since Diana seems somewhat demure and subservient. In her early years, Wonder Woman's origin story revealed that she was made of clay by her mother, Hippolyte, Queen of the Amazons. This story was rewritten in the twenty-first century to reveal that Diana was actually the product of a tryst between Hippolyte and Zeus, thus accounting for her superhuman strength.

Contemporary portrayals of Wonder Woman have evolved along with the changing role of women in the last seventy-five years. Once a nurse who pined after a wounded pilot, the Amazon princess now plays in a rock band and regularly stars as one of the leaders of the Justice League. In *JLA: A League of One* (2000), Wonder Woman shows how far she's come by defeating all her colleagues on the Justice League—including Superman—and saving the world all by herself.

Although there were a good many female characters in romance comic books during the early years, there were very few genuine superheroines. Most of the female characters in superhero comics were love interests of male superheroes or victims caught up in the villains' schemes. Often a captured female character gave the male superhero a reason to fight.

In the 1960s, as societal attitudes toward women began to change, female superheroes emerged—albeit slowly. The Fantastic Four's Susan Storm, initially called Invisible Girl—changed to Invisible Woman in the 1980s—appeared in 1961. Although she played a mostly supportive role to the male leaders on the team, her character represented a step forward. The only female member of the original X-Men, Jean "Marvel Girl" Grey appeared in 1963, with the power of telekinesis (the ability to move objects with the power of the mind) and later telepathy (the ability to communicate using extrasensory means). In the late 1970s, in one of the most well-known comics stories of all time, Jean Grey saves her X-Men teammates and transforms into Phoenix. This character has almost godlike powers but soon disappears from the universe (of course she returns, like most dead superheroes) after being corrupted and renamed Dark Phoenix.

The Uncanny X-Men, which was relaunched in the mid-1970s by writer Chris Claremont, introduced several strong female characters who broke stereotypes and gained a large following. Storm, debuted in 1975, could manipulate weather and fly by means of riding wind currents. She enjoyed a leadership role from the beginning and received one of the earliest female solo books. Rogue is another famous female X-Men character, introduced in 1983. She could absorb powers and memories of others, which made her particularly scary.

Since the 1990s comics have become more and more inclusive. In fact, times have changed so drastically that in 2013, Marvel introduced an all-female X-Men team composed of Storm, Rogue, Jubilee, Kitty Pride, Rachael Grey, and Psylocke. Two years later, Marvel followed that up with A-Force, an all-female replacement for the Avengers. DC also has a long-running female superhero team called Birds of Prey. These kinds of developments could not have been dreamed of in the preceding decades.

In a move that angered some old-school fans, Marvel even changed one of its oldest heroes, Thor, into a female character in 2014. As evidence that readers of comics are no longer mostly teenage boys, Marvel recently reported that the new Thor titles are outselling the old Thor by 30 percent.[22] Emboldened by the new readers and energy, Marvel has replaced another of its old white male characters with a female. First appearing in *Invincible Ironman* #7 during the summer of 2016, Riri Williams has taken over the title and garnered lots of attention as the new Ironman. The fact that the book is written by a white male raises some eyebrows, but creator Brian Michael Bendis has a long track record of writing with integrity and respect.

One of the most telling signs of change and inclusion in the superhero writing world is the new *Ms. Marvel*. Debuting in 2014, Ms. Marvel is a sixteen-year-old Pakistani American, Kamala Khan. More interesting still—she is a Muslim. Talk about a departure from the old stereotype of the white male superhero! Ms.

Fan Favorite Kelly Sue DeConnick

In a recent poll by the website ComicBookResources.com, readers were asked to vote for their favorite female superhero comics writer. Kelly Sue DeConnick edged out the legendary Gail Simone, famous for her Women in Refrigerators website and engaging superhero scripting.

DeConnick is best known for her restart of Ms. Marvel (a.k.a. Carol Danvers), who has quickly become one of Marvel's mainstay comics. But DeConnick got her start in comics with Tokyopop, adapting Japanese and Korean comics into English.[r] She wrote a few smaller assignments for Marvel before getting her first big break when she wrote a miniseries featuring Norman Osborne of *Spider-Man* fame. After a brief stint on *Supergirl* for DC, DeConnick launched *Captain Marvel* and worked on *Avengers Assemble*. She also created a revival of *Ghost* for publisher Dark Horse.

Since the introduction of *Superman*, there has been an ongoing tension in the comics industry over who owns the rights to the characters and stories. Desperate to get published, *Superman* creators Jerry Siegel and Joe Shuster sold the rights to DC before the character ever appeared in print. Siegel and Shuster were never able to get those rights back, despite numerous lawsuits. Creators like Kelly Sue DeConnick have benefitted from those early battles, having kept the rights for her series written for Image Comics—the popular *Pretty Deadly* series, as well as *Bitch Planet*, about a female prison on a distant planet.

Marvel has superstrength and the ability to morph her body into different shapes. And yet, she is very much the average high school girl, with worries about tests, boys, and disagreements with her parents.

G. Willow Wilson, the writer of the new *Ms. Marvel*, talked about the change taking place in the comics world and its readership. "People are looking for new stories," says Wilson. "Books like *Ms. Marvel* have changed industry math. They've changed the industry dogma that female characters don't sell, minority characters don't sell, new characters don't sell."[23]

The former Ms. Marvel, Carol Danvers, who became Captain Marvel in 2012 (series written by Kelly Sue DeConnick), is another strong female character. The origin story of Captain Marvel is long and convoluted, but Carol Danvers has gathered quite a following in the comics world. In fact, according to Marvel, she will be the first female to headline a Marvel universe movie.[24]

Racial Diversity in Comics

Publishers are also realizing that a stable of all white superheroes does not reflect the society we live in. So they've set out to change that. If you're interested in racially diverse superheroes, there are a lot more to choose from today than there were in the Golden and Silver Age of comics. One of the most earth-shattering decisions in recent years was casting Spider-Man as a black teenager, Miles Morales, in 2011. For a few years he existed in his own universe as Ultimate Spider-Man, but he eventually became the one and only Spider-Man in the Marvel universe.[25]

The Black Panther (a.k.a. T'Challa), king of the fictional African nation of Wakanda, is widely considered to be mainstream comics' first black superhero. He initially appeared in the *Fantastic Four* story line in 1966. Although his character seems stereotypically written to a modern audience—for instance, using the word *Black* in the moniker—the character attracted minority readers who had been ignored up until that time. Dwayne McDuffie, a famous African American comic writer who passed away in 2011, credits those old Black Panther stories for giving him his desire to get into the industry.[26] If you want to read a contemporary retelling of T'Challa's story, check out *Black Panther: Who Is the Black Panther* (2015), by Reginald Hudlin with art by John Romita Jr., which was the highest-selling superhero graphic novel in early 2016, as well as various *Avengers* stories in which he takes part.

The Falcon, Sam Wilson, is widely recognized as mainstream comics' first African American superhero. He debuted in 1969 and is still going strong today, both in comics and in the movies. He was a frequent fellow fighter in Captain America's stories in the 1970s and a member of the Avengers through the years.

Dwayne McDuffie, African American Comics Pioneer

One independent publisher in the 1990s changed the perception of African American superheroes more than any other: Milestone Media, founded by Dwayne McDuffie and a group of African American writers and illustrators. The writer/editor had grown tired of each lone minority superhero representing an entire group (because there were so few). So he and a group of industry professionals went out and started their own company. And the comics industry has never been the same.[s]

Dwayne Glenn McDuffie was born in Detroit, Michigan, in 1962. He tells the story of walking into a candy store and picking up a comic off the news-stand—and being an instant fan. In particular he remembers being impressed with the Black Panther stories: "I was fascinated with it. I didn't understand why at the time, but the reason was because I had never seen a bunch of people who looked like me and they were the heroes. They were the heroes and the villains and the streetsweepers and the doctors, and all of a sudden I could be anything, I didn't have to be a sidekick."[t]

After graduating college as an English major and attending grad school, McDuffie worked as an editor at a financial magazine—and was hating life. A friend pointed him toward Marvel, which was looking for an editor. He got the job and worked on a number of projects throughout the 1980s. The first comics series that McDuffie created (with artist Ernie Colon) was *Damage Control*, a satirical book about the cleanup crew that repairs the damage done when the superheroes and their enemies trash the city in a fight. *Damage Control* was featured in several miniseries in the late 1980s and early 1990s, but because of a perception that the series was undercutting the Marvel heroes, it was phased out.

After a few years of freelance writing, in which his most famous character was the now-black Deathlok, McDuffie and a group of friends founded Milestone, a completely minority-owned independent publishing house. They produced their first titles in 1993 and "quickly became the most successful black-owned comic book publisher in American history."[u] McDuffie and his co-owners chose DC to be their distributor, a decision that prompted criticism from other black-owned comics publishers, who accused them of "Uncle Tom-ism."[v] But McDuffie never wanted to create only African American heroes—his goal was to bring many cultures to the limelight.

However, other forces were working against the company in addition to criticism from black publishers, not least of which was the decline of the comic book industry in the mid-1990s. The company closed its doors in 1997, but not before they had produced several memorable series: *Hardware*, *Blood Syndicate*, *Icon*, and *Static*, the last of which was later developed into an animated series called *Static Shock*, for which McDuffie wrote scripts.

After Milestone, McDuffie kept busy writing, editing, and producing comics and animated programs until his death in 2011. Dwayne McDuffie will be remembered not only as a creative genius but a man who worked to bring a multicultural perspective to the comics industry.

He actually became the new Captain America in 2014 when he was handed the vibranium shield by Steve Rogers, the former Captain America.

Another black superhero who made an impact on the comics world is John Stewart as Green Lantern. Stewart appeared in 1971 in the series in which DC was discussing "relevant" subjects in *Green Lantern/Green Arrow*. At various times he has been a part of the Justice League, and he is still out and about in the universe fighting crime as one of the most popular Green Lanterns.

Other black superheroes worth checking out: Steel (John Henry Irons); Monica Rambeau (Captain Marvel/Photon/Pulsar/Spectrum); Vixen (Mari Jiwe McCabe); Batwing (David Zavimbe); Static (Virgil Hawkins); Luke Cage, who was recently reintroduced to the Avengers and his own comic book line; and many others. *This just in*: just before publication of this book, it was revealed that a fifteen-year-old African American girl named Riri Williams, a genius from MIT, will be taking over as Iron Man when Tony Stark walks away from the suit. So another high-profile superhero will be minority race—times really are (slowly) changing!

How about other ethnicities? Where are the Asian superheroes, the Hispanic superheroes? There aren't many, unfortunately. And there are more female Asian and Asian American superheroes than male, for some reason. For instance, Marvel recently came out with Silk (a.k.a. Cindy Moon), a year after the company introduced Kamala Khan as Ms. Marvel. Gene Luen Yang's *The Shadow Hero* (figure 3.3) resurrects the Green Turtle, a short-lived Chinese American hero from the 1940s. In July 2016, DC introduced a new superhero from China—Kong

Red, White, and Black

Sometimes writing comics from the perspective of a minority is criticized for being "too serious." In 2002 Marvel Comics produced a controversial retcon (retooling of an established origin story) for Captain America that echoed an incident in U.S. history that many would rather forget. The seven-issue series, called *Truth: Red, White & Black* by Robert Morales and Kyle Baker, gives the heretofore secret origins of the Super Soldier program before Steve Rogers became the super soldier. The premise is that before Dr. Reinstein, the inventor of the serum, deemed the top-secret formula safe enough to test on Rogers, he first worked out the formula's kinks on a group of unknowing black soldiers.

If this sounds vaguely familiar, it's because it is based on the real-life story of the U.S. Public Health Service conducting secret experiments on hundreds of black men with syphilis in Tuskegee, Alabama, starting in the 1930s. Like the men in the study, the black soldiers are given the serum without proper knowledge of the experiments in which they are participating. Then the soldiers are sent out into battle so that the doctor can observe the effects of the serum in action. All but one of the soldiers die in combat. The survivor, Isaiah Bradley, briefly wears the red, white, and blue uniform of Captain America on a failed rescue attempt in Germany. By the end, the imperfect serum has destroyed Bradley's brain, and he comes home with the consciousness of a child.

While many readers appreciated the series, some fans criticized it for being too negative and overtly political. One scholar theorizes that many of those who complained were unhappy with the story being told from an African American viewpoint in the predominantly white superhero universe: "[It] is readers' assumption that black equals political and that political equals bad or, at least, unentertaining. . . . [The series] inserts politics where politics ought not be, and makes comics too much like work and school and not enough like fun."[w]

Figure 3.3. *The Shadow Hero* by Gene Luen Yang and Sonny Liew is a welcome addition to the pantheon of Asian superheroes. From THE SHADOW HERO © 2014 by Gene Luen Yang. Illustrations © 2014 by Sonny Liew. Reprinted by permission of First Second, an imprint of Roaring Brook Press, a division of Holtzbrinck Publishing Holdings Limited Partnership. All Rights Reserved.

Kenan—in the *New Super-Man*, written by Gene Luen Yang with art by Victor Brogdanovic. Other Asian superheroes you may want to check out are Daken Akihiro, Jimmy Woo, Shang-Chi, Amadeus Cho, Mantis, and many others.

Hispanic/Latino/Latina superheroes have also played second fiddle for most of comics history. That, too, is changing. For Hispanic superheroes, check out White Tiger (Hector Ayala), Arana (Anya Corazon), Victor Mancha, Miss America (America Chavez), Blue Beetle (Jaime Reyes), Aztek: The Ultimate Man, and many more.

Native American superheroes are another severely underrepresented group in comics. In 1970, a character named Red Wolf appeared with the Avengers. He gained enough of a following that he received his own brief run in 1972. Lack of interest—probably as a result of poor cultural research and cheesy writing—led to Red Wolf's cancellation in 1973. Marvel reintroduced Red Wolf at the end of 2015, along with other "all new, all different" restarts. The new *Red Wolf*, written by Nathan Edmondson and illustrated by Dalibor Talajic—with cover drawn by Native artist Jeffrey Veregge—showed more cultural sensitivity, but received mixed reviews as a story. The X-Men also briefly had a Native American member in 1975, John Proudstar (a.k.a. Thunderbird), but he was quickly killed off in his second mission. Native artists have also produced their own superhero series, such as *Tales of the Mighty Code Talkers* by Arigon Starr, which follows the exploits of the first Choctaw Code Talkers in World War I. *Tribal Force* by Jon Proudstar also provides positive, nuanced portrayals of Native life.[27]

If you're looking for Arab American heroes, check out *The 99* comic book series. The series was developed by Dr. Naiof Al-Mutawa, who wanted kids to be exposed to good Arab role models. The story of *The 99* focuses on ninety-nine gemstones that contain knowledge and power from the thirteenth-century Library of Wisdom in Baghdad, Iraq. The gemstones choose worthy carriers, although each one must decide whether to use his or her power for good or evil. Most of the issues were published online only, although a few made it to print. A six-issue crossover series with the Justice League of America was published in 2010.

Diversity in Sexual Orientation

Sexual orientation is another issue being addressed by comics writers. In preceding decades, homosexual superheroes have mostly been in the shadows or "in the closet." That is changing.

The first openly gay superhero in the Marvel universe was Jean-Paul Beaubier (a.k.a. Northstar), a member of the Canadian superhero team Alpha Flight.[28] Northstar's writer, Chris Claremont, intended him to be gay in 1979 when he was introduced, but he did not "come out" until 1992. Northstar married his beau, Kyle Jinadu, in *Astonishing X-Men* #51 (2012).

Kate Kane (a.k.a. Batwoman), a relative of the first 1950s Batwoman, is a popular character who is also a lesbian. After Kate Kane was forced to leave the military due to her sexual orientation, she took up the mantle of Batwoman. Her relationship with Gotham City police officer Maggie Sawyer progressed to the point where Kane proposed to Sawyer, but the two were never married. Gossip has it that the editors at DC did not allow it to happen (they claimed later they didn't want any of their characters married, gay or otherwise), leading to the resignation of the creative team on the series.[29]

Other LGBTQ characters to check out: Apollo and Midnighter, Renee Montoya (a.k.a. the Question), Wiccan and Hulkling, Phyla-Vell and Moondragon, and many others.

Where Do I Start?

We've talked about a lot of superheroes in a lot of different times. With more time and space, I could talk about dozens more, especially those being published by independent writers and distributors—those superladies and supergentlemen have not received much attention in these pages. Maybe you're new to comics and want to start reading the books featuring one of the characters mentioned. Where do you begin? Do you go back to the first comic ever published about that person and try and collect all the books? The short answer is, no! The comics companies try to keep their storytelling fresh for each new generation of readers, so every few years they stage an event so that they can start all the stories over and gather new readers.

In the following section, I'm going to make some suggestions about where to start with several different popular characters from the Big Two—DC and Marvel. They are all graphic novels, so you won't have to track down a bunch of individual issues. Keep in mind that these are just my suggestions, but each of the books mentioned contains a story about the character's origins, plus a few of his or her best adventures.

If you're interested in Wonder Woman, don't go back to the 1940s comics, unless you're interested in the development of her story. In 2012, DC published a new Wonder Woman series that begins with the graphic novel *Wonder Woman*, volume 1: *Blood*, by Brian Azzarello, with art by Cliff Chiang and Tony Akins. It retells her origin story and launches her on all-new adventures. I've found that some of Wonder Woman's best one-off adventures can be found in *Sensation Comics*, written and illustrated by various people and collected in volumes over the past few years.

Figuring out where to start on Superman and Batman is a little more complicated. So many great comics and books have been written about those two that
you could really begin at any of the various starting points and find a great story.
For Batman, if I was to advise friends on where to start, I would tell them to read
Batman: Year One by Frank Miller and David Mazzuelli first. That graphic novel
gives a gripping account of Batman's origin story. Then move on to *Batman: The
Long Halloween* or *Batman*: *Hush*, both highly entertaining detective stories and
both written by Jeph Loeb, with art by Tim Sale and Jim Lee, respectively. Along
the way, read *The Court of Owls* by Scott Snyder with art by Greg Capullo, and
of course *The Dark Knight Returns* by Frank Miller with art by Klaus Janson and
Lynn Varley. Or you could start with DC's 2016 Rebirth series, which resets the
Batman story and opens it up to new readers.

To get started on Superman, I would recommend two: *Superman: Birthright*
by Mark Waid and Leinil Francis Yu or *Superman: Earth One* by J. Michael Strac-
zynski and Shane Davis. These two have slightly different takes on Superman's
origin story but both are great. You've also got to read *Kingdom Come* by Mark
Waid and Alex Ross, which is my favorite Superman story, although it concerns
him as an older hero. Along the way you should read *The Death of Superman* (by
a host of writers and artists), which DC claims is the single best-selling graphic
novel of all time. While we're talking about DC's Big Three, don't miss out on
the fun when they all get together in the form of the Justice League of America.
A good place to begin with the Justice League of America is *JLA*, volume 1, by
Grant Morrison, Howard Porter, and John Dell.

I am personally very partial to Aquaman, also a DC comic. There's only one
place to begin with the prince of Atlantis—*Aquaman*, volume 1: *The Trench*, written by the legendary Geoff Johns, with beautiful art by Ivan Reis and Joe Prado.
Johns's series of four graphic novels is very entertaining and is followed up by
more great stories by the very capable Jeff Parker in subsequent volumes.

Speaking of Geoff Johns (and you have to speak of him if you're talking about
some the greatest comics of all time), the best place to start reading another DC
legend—Green Lantern—is with the 2005 classic *Green Lantern: Rebirth*, written by Johns, with art by Ethan Van Sciver and Prentis Rollins (figure 3.4). This
book—which contains some of the greatest writing I've encountered in superhero
comics—retells the origins of the Green Lantern, including a much more meaningful explanation of the negative power of the color yellow.

On the Marvel side, you also have to make some tough choices about where to
begin. If you want to start on the old character of Spider-Man in a new way, pick
up *Ultimate Comics Spider-Man* #1, by Brian Michael Bendis, with art by Sara
Pichelli, Chris Samnee, and David Marquez. This graphic novel tells the story of
the new Spider-Man, Miles Morales, one of the first of the major superheroes to
be African American. He faces a fascinating assortment of villains—including his

Figure 3.4. *Green Lantern: Rebirth,* by Geoff Johns, Ethan Van Sciver, and Prentis Rollins. *All DC comic artwork, its characters and related elements are* ™ & © *DC Comics.*

uncle—and becomes an integral member of S.H.I.E.L.D. Another great Spider-Man title is *Ultimate Spider-Man: Death of Spider-Man*, also by Brian Michael Bendis, with art by Mark Bagley.

You've probably seen at least one of Marvel's *The Avengers* movies. Where to start if you want to get into the comics? Try *Avengers*, volume 1: *Avengers World*, written by Jonathan Hickman with art by Jerome Opena and Adam Kubert. This book introduces some new faces and has some big, bold adventures. Of course, if you're partial to the early Avengers comics of the Stan Lee era, as I am, check out *Avengers Epic Collection: Earth's Mightiest Heroes*, by Stan Lee, Larry Lieber, and Larry Ivie, with art by Jack Kirby, Don Heck, and Dick Ayers—it's a fun read. I am partial to everything Geoff Johns and Brian Michael Bendis have written, and they both wrote Avengers stories, so those would also be worth picking up.

Like many people, I was introduced to *Guardians of the Galaxy* via the great movie in 2015. So I looked up their comic books and started with *Guardians of the Galaxy: Cosmic Avengers*, written by Brian Michael Bendis, with art by Steve Mc-Niven and Sara Pichelli. This series, which contains several volumes, was hugely entertaining. Then I discovered that there was another, slightly older series called *Guardians of the Galaxy*, volume 1, written by Dan Abnett and Andy Lanning with art by Paul Pelletier, Brad Walker, and Wes Craig. This is also a great series. Either of the books mentioned would be a good place to join this hilarious crew in their madcap adventures.

Or there are a host of new superheroes that have joined the pantheon of comics legends. Because most of these comics are collected into larger graphic novels, they can be ordered on Amazon.com or checked out of your local library. Don't worry if the character you're interested in has been killed off or phased out . . . she or he will be back! As the minister at the funeral of Rex Mason (a.k.a. Metamorpho), said to Superman in the graphic novel *JLA*, volume 1:

> The sad fact is, normal people aren't very interested in metahuman funerals anymore, Superman. Everyone knows you people come back all the time. Heaven knows how many times I've buried the Immortal Man! I'm sure Metamorpho won't stay down for long . . . (Morrison, *JLA*, volume 1)

So have no fear, go out and conquer the world . . . of superhero comic books!

Reviews of Some Groundbreaking Superhero Comics

Let me just say before you complain that your favorite superhero book is not reviewed here, that there are *thousands* of good graphic novels featuring superheroes. I have picked out books that are unique either because they feature minority heroes or because they have deeper themes and complexity. But I apologize in advance to readers who were looking for a certain hero and I haven't written about him or her!

Superman: Kingdom Come

This book is hailed by many to be one of the great superhero graphic novels of all time. It's on most lists of "Essential Graphic Novels," along with *Watchmen* and *The Dark Knight Returns*. It is one of my personal favorite books I've ever read—not just graphic novels, but any book of any kind; it's that good. The book has gained its reputation for many reasons. One is the deeply impactful writing by Mark Waid. Each chapter begins with the narrator quoting apocalyptic verses from the book of Revelation in the Bible, which then get fulfilled in most surprising ways. The narrator is an aging pastor who receives the "gift" of being able to see the future and travel between times and dimensions. He travels with a mysterious angel named the Spectre, who can't intervene in the story because the time is not right.

Superman is retired. So is Wonder Woman and most of the Justice League. Humanity wanted newer, stronger, flashier, more violent superheroes, and the children of the first wave of heroes provided that. So the first generation washed their hands of humanity and its problems. But the new gods are out of control and care nothing about human life. Wonder Woman convinces Superman to come out of retirement and teach the new heroes how to be true heroes. Batman seems unconvinced but comes to the aid of humanity in the end. As the Justice League defeat the new heroes, Superman wonders what to do with them. He finally decides to build a giant "gulag" for the outlaw metahumans. When that powder keg blows up, the fate of the superheroes—and humanity in general—hangs in the balance. The book asks the question of why humanity is so quick to "look up in the sky" to solve its problems.

The art in this book, by Alex Ross, is just as exquisite as the story. Each panel is a painting—I don't mean that metaphorically. Each panel has been painted by a master artist and every detail seems to glow and stand out. Each panel could be framed; they are that beautiful. The story alone, and the art alone, would make this book a masterpiece but together—every comics lover needs to read this book eventually.[30]

Batman: The Dark Knight Returns

In superhero comics, pretty much every list of "The Best of All Time" seems to include one book: *Batman: The Dark Knight Returns* by Frank Miller, with art by Klaus Janson and Lynn Varley. As I was doing research for this book, I came across several college classes devoted to the study of this book as a piece of literature. That's because the story is told in a complex, layered way that engages the reader on every level. The themes are mature, demanding, frightening, and mentally stimulating. The structure is like few other comic books you will read—a utilitarian sixteen-panel-per-page format that is frequently deviated from to achieve emotional impact. Miller often violates a guideline taught to rookie writers—one narrator or point of view per page. See if you can count the number of points of view contained on the left side of the spread in figure 3.5.

I count five different points of view: panel 1 is Batman (Bruce Wayne); panel 2 is an aging Green Arrow; panel 3 is Robin; panel 5 is Superman; panel 7 is a policeman inside a tank; then panel 10 goes back to Batman. With this many people chiming in to tell the story—and we didn't even get to see the numerous reporters, politicians, analysts, talk show hosts, and other television personalities that speak on other pages—readers are forced to read carefully and slowly, just as they would a prose work of literature.

I won't bother to summarize the plot, because there are so many subplots that it would take this whole chapter. Suffice it to say that an aging Bruce Wayne decides to don the cape again and clean up Gotham City. Along the way he trains a teenage girl as Robin and deputizes a horde of former hoodlums to be his Sons of Batman. In the end, Batman feels the need to kill Superman—or come as close as anyone has ever come—so that the Man of Steel can feel what it's like to be human. Spoiler alert—at the end of the book, they hold a funeral for Bruce Wayne, who dies during his fight with Superman. Supposedly. This is one of the great books of our generation (of any medium), so I strongly suggest you take the time to read it.

Captain America: Sam Wilson, *Volume 1*: Not My Captain America

I have to hand it to Marvel Comics. They've taken a lot of risks in diversifying their superhero cast. It's paying off with tons of new, diverse readers who heretofore never saw themselves in comics before. They're taking plenty of flak, too. In a previous story line, Steve Rogers handed the famous red, white, and blue shield to Sam Wilson, essentially passing down the responsibility of being Captain America to his friend, the former Falcon. As we have seen for decades, the writers at Marvel are not afraid to tackle current issues. The team here—writer Nick Spencer, with artists Daniel Acuña and Paul Renaud—is no exception. Wilson narrates the opening of this story (from issue 1), explaining his own disillusionment with the experience so far. "Let's just be honest here,"

Figure 3.5. *Batman: The Dark Knight Returns*, by Frank Miller, Klaus Janson, and Lynn Varley. *All DC comic artwork, its characters and related elements are ™ & © DC Comics.*

he says. "This country is as divided as it's ever been. Red and blue, black and white, Republican and Democrat, North and South—feels like we're constantly at each other's throats."

Add to this disillusionment the fact that, since he has cut ties with S.H.I.E.L.D. and the U.S. government, he has basically run out of money to fight bad guys, and you have a thoroughly engrossing story. In a touching scene that shows the kind of people who do relate to this new Cap, Sam's brother—a pastor in Harlem—passes the bucket in his church to help pay the bills. But Sam has to fly coach class to and from his missions, a far cry from the cushy ride when he was an Avenger!

The villains in this first volume are interesting and, in truth, somewhat likable. The head of the Sons of the Serpent is fed up with immigrants, and he takes the border patrol into his own hands. The banter between him and the new Captain America is intelligent and witty. After being told to pack up his pickup truck, this sardonic villain replies, "Well, see, that is just a pernicious stereotype—we arrived in a minivan, sir. Do tell me—are you really so far ahead on appeasing terrorists and apologizing for our country's greatness that you have the time to come down here and flout still more of our laws?"[31] It will be an inside joke for years that this kind of dialogue was written during an election year featuring a hotly contested presidential contest.

Of special interest is Cap's crime-fighting companion, Misty Knight, a throwback butt-kicking private detective with a wicked afro. The relationship between Sam and Misty provides both romance and friction. This series also reveals who the next Falcon will be. And in a move that may be considered a sort of nose thumbing at the segment of the population that complained about a black Captain America, Marvel is putting out another Captain America (a white Cap named Steve Rogers) who turns out in the first issue to be—wait for it—a member of Hydra.

The Shadow Hero

What, you haven't heard of the superhero called the Green Turtle? That's because he was introduced in 1944 by a tiny publisher in a book called *Blazing Comics*. The Green Turtle's adventures lasted only five issues and his origin story is never introduced. He has been called the first Asian American superhero although very little is known about him. But in 2014, Gene Luen Yang and artist Sonny Liew reintroduced the Green Turtle to a modern audience in one of the best superhero graphic novels of recent years.

The Shadow Hero tells the story of nineteen-year-old Hank Chu, who takes up the mantle of the Green Turtle after his father is killed by Chinatown mobsters. In a humorous spoof on other classic superhero origins, Hank is exposed to dangerous radiation, animal bites, and a mystic before he gives up and learns to fight the old-fashioned way. As he fights the Tong of Sticks who are terrorizing the neighborhood, he meets and falls in love with a beautiful and dangerous woman—the daughter of his enemy Ten Grand. Hank, as the Green Turtle, uses his wits and a special power given him by the mythical Spirit of the Turtle—the ability to avoid getting shot by bullets (see figure 3.6)—to defeat his foe and bring justice to the neighborhood.

The art and vibe of the book make it seem like a throwback to the superhero comics of the Golden Age. But the writing is subtle and clever, giving homage to the first heroes but shedding light on the plight of Asian Americans in the United States during the 1940s when the story takes place. The characters—especially Hank's humorously stereotypical mother—are endearing and three-dimensionally conceived. Hopefully Yang and Liew will collaborate in the future to bring us more of the Green Turtle.[32]

The Unbeatable Squirrel Girl, *Volume 1:* Squirrel Power

Okay, there are some comics that are just so much fun they're hard to resist. *Squirrel Girl*, written by Ryan North, with art by Erica Henderson, is one of those tales. The story does not take itself too seriously, but is well written enough to be hilarious and entertaining. This exchange between Squirrel Girl and her squirrel pal, Tippy-Toe, while packing boxes for college, displays the humor of this volume:

> TT: You sure you don't want the squirrel army to carry these for you?
> SG: I'm sure, Tippy, but thank you. Secret identity, remember? I'm Doreen Green, completely regular college student.
> TT: Who just happens to have a tail?
> SG: Nope! Who knows how to tuck her tail into her pants . . . and who just happens to appear to have a conspicuously large and conspicuously awesome butt. (Issue 1)

Doreen is off to school to pursue a normal life when she meets a cute guy (who will actually talk to her) and her seemingly stiff roommate, Nancy Whitehead, who quickly learns her secret. Squirrel Girl meets a bad guy almost immediately when she arrives at campus—Kraven the Hunter, who is threatening her squirrel friends. But that is not the worst of it. Doreen soon learns that Galactus, the devourer of entire worlds, is on his way to Earth. Of course, none of the other superheroes will believe her, so she must take care of Galactus herself. On the moon. Using a cast-off Iron Man suit. She defeats both of these foes using a

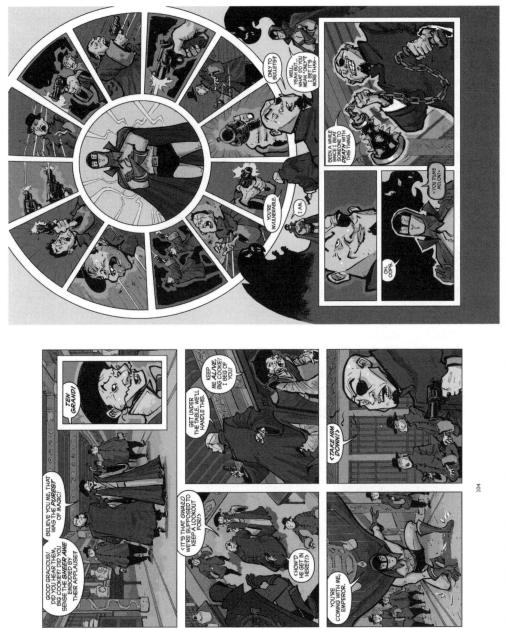

Figure 3.6. *The Shadow Hero by Gene Luen Yang. From THE SHADOW HERO © 2014 by Gene Luen Yang. Illustrations © 2014 by Sonny Liew. Reprinted by permission of First Second, an imprint of Roaring Brook Press, a division of Holtzbrinck Publishing Holdings Limited Partnership. All Rights Reserved.*

minimum of violence and a maximum of cleverness and humor. *Squirrel Girl* is a very enjoyable read with great art.[33]

Superman vs. Muhammad Ali

Shortly before this book went to publication, the world mourned the passing of one of the greatest athletes of all time, Muhammad Ali. The word *athlete* seems like the wrong word to describe this global diplomat for human rights and African American awareness; it's like calling a vintage red Maserati an automobile. The boxer who called himself "the Greatest of All Time" won a lot of fights against a lot of tough people and spoke out against injustice wherever he saw it. At times his comments did not sit well with those people in power, but Ali didn't care. He said and did what he felt was right, and millions of people loved him for it.

But could he beat Superman in a fair fight? That was the question some comics creators in the 1970s began asking. Comics superstars Neal Adams and Denny O'Neil wrote just such a story, and it proved very popular in 1978 when it came out. They created a scenario that pitted the two against each other in a bout to see who would represent Earth in a fight to decide Earth's future. But how can you stage a fair fight with a super being from Krypton? To make it fair, Superman builds a boxing ring in space around a "Kryptonian continuum disruptor" so that he can fight without superpowers. First, however, Ali must teach the Man of Steel the "sweet science." Guess who wins in a boxing match between Muhammad Ali and Superman? You can find out yourself since they have rereleased this very entertaining graphic novel. But suffice to say, the two work together to win Earth its freedom from alien enslavement. One of the highlights of this book is the cover—the crowd watching the boxing match is a who's who of the decade, filled with dignitaries, movie stars, musicians, and famous DC characters who turn out to watch the fight.[34]

Ms. Marvel, *Volume 1:* No Normal

The blurb on the front cover says it all: "This may be the most important comic published in 2014" (ComicsAlliance.com). To say that sixteen-year-old Pakistani American Kamala Khan—Marvel's first Muslim-religion hero—made a splash when she took over being Ms. Marvel in 2014 would be an understatement. The comic book community by and large loved her, not just because she represented a community rarely explored in comics, but because the stories were entertaining and had great artwork. Written with great humor and bravado by female writer G. Willow Wilson, Kamala "embiggened" herself right into the hearts of fans, new and old alike. The art by Adrian Alphona threatens to steal the show at times because he frequently uses "sight gags" to add humor, like a top hat–wearing frog at a party, humorous brand names at her friend Bruno's convenience store, and a robot chilling in a coffee shop as Kamala walks by it.

The first section of the book, predictably, explains how Kamala gets her superpowers. As she leaves a party (which she was not supposed to attend) she experiences a mist that sends her into a hallucination. She sees Captain America, Iron Man, and Captain Marvel, who confer on her odd words of encouragement and superpowers. At first she is blonde like Captain Marvel but in a wonderful symbolic move, she rejects the classic American ideal and goes back to being herself. She realizes that she is able to change her body to whatever shape she wants to meet the need at hand. In the adventures that follow, she tries to balance her newfound powers and responsibilities with old-fashioned parents, crushes on boys, homework, and a strict curfew. A team-up with Wolverine—who has lost his healing power—to fight new villain the Inventor establishes Ms. Marvel as a truly clever and powerful hero.[35]

Silk: The Life and Times of Cindy Moon

Several new characters have joined the Spider-Man universe, or Spider-Verse, as the publisher likes to call it. Cindy Moon (a.k.a. Silk) is a great addition. *Silk: The Life and Times of Cindy Moon*, is written by Robbie Thompson, with art by Stacey Lee, Annapaola Martello, and Tana Ford. Cindy Moon is an Asian American character, which helps diversify Marvel's line, although her culture is not prominent in the way that Kamala Khan's is in the new *Ms. Marvel* series.

Cindy has just been freed from ten years of seclusion—or imprisonment, depending on what you want to call it. After being bitten by the same radioactive spider that bit Peter Parker, Cindy gained similar powers—only she shoots organic webs straight out of her fingers. At the time, she was so freaked out by her new abilities that she accepted the offer to be trained by a mysterious man, who has since disappeared (maybe). When Cindy emerges from her seclusion, she finds her family missing.

In the family's place, Cindy finds a plethora of bad guys who need their butts kicked, and she is more than willing to do the job. One of these bad guys calls himself Rage and wears a dragon suit. What's wonderful about this story is that Cindy actually turns Rage, whose real name is Harris Porter, into a good guy. The really bad guy, or bad girl, is Black Cat, who tries to get Cindy to work for her. The Cat sends a troop of technologically enhanced soldiers to bring Silk in. In a team-up with Spider-Man Peter Parker (who has a major crush on her), Cindy escapes and finds out that one of the bad guys knows where her family is—just before he is killed by Black Cat. The creators do a great job of transitioning to flashbacks that reveal Cindy's story a piece at a time; these flashbacks occur in muted colors that lend a nostalgic feel to the sequences. *Silk* is a great book with beautiful art—and an exciting entrant into the larger Spider-Man story.[36]

Runaways, *Volume 1*: Pride and Joy

Imagine if you spied on one of your parents' adults-only get-togethers and found out they were a part of a secret organization of supervillains. That's what happens to a group of unsuspecting teens in *Runaways*, by Brian K. Vaughan and Adrian Alphona. This series has become super popular with teens, and with good reason. The writing is great—full of humor, adventure, romance, and tons of plot twists. The style is very Marvel (which makes sense, since Marvel is the publisher), with real teen problems that make interesting subplots to the larger adventure of foiling the evil parents. The cast is very diverse, another aspect of the story that makes it inviting.

As the story unfolds, the friends begin to manifest powers or abilities of their own. Karolina, who can fly, is from another planet; Gertrude has a genetically engineered dinosaur she can control; Molly has mutant powers; Chase has a mechanical weapon-hand; Nico, a Japanese American, can use magic. Only Alex, the de facto leader of the group, doesn't manifest any special powers or abilities of his own. But this African American young man uses his intelligence and strategic thinking to help guide the teens as they seek to prove their parents' crimes.

When the six teens—who don't especially like each other—are forced to hang out while their parents seclude themselves to cut checks for their annual "charity" meeting, boredom immediately ensues. That is, until Alex suggests the group members follow a secret passage to spy on the parents. There they see their sup-

"The story of The Runaways unfolded in front of me. In the beginning chapters, six teenagers find out their parents are super villains. Upon witnessing their parents murder a young girl, the teens run away from home and set out to take down their criminal empire. I read the entire first volume in two days. I was at a difficult time in my life, when I too felt trapped by evil parents and as powerless as the characters at the start of the story. Because of this, I thought the comics were the greatest literature ever written."—Emma S., Plymouth, Minnesota[x] posedly good parents murder a young girl in a ritual for their organization, called the Pride. When the teens, who try to gather evidence to prove their parents' guilt, are discovered, they must drop off the grid and hide until they can figure out how to take down the organization. In the closing pages of this volume, one parent discovers a note written by one of the teens confessing that he or she will act as a mole within the teens' group. So not only do you have to get future volumes because they're enjoyable; you've got to find out who is the spy![37]

Sandman, *Volume 1*: Preludes and Nocturnes

When the very best comics and graphic novels are mentioned, Neil Gaiman's *The Sandman* series is usually near the top of the list, along with *Watchmen*, *Maus*, *The Dark Knight Returns*, and other books that are classified as literature. The first book in the series, *Preludes and Nocturnes*, can be read as a stand-alone novel or as the introduction to the entire series of ten volumes (plus some additional stories written later). Is this a superhero yarn? Well, sort of. Gaiman has crafted a tale that combines mythology, superheroes, adventure, mysticism, and just plain old amazing storytelling. The art in this volume, by Sam Kieth, Mike Dringenberg, and Malcolm Jones III, is also spectacular; moody, lush, and detailed, the art is perfect for this multilayered tale.

The story opens with a group of mystics trying to capture the supernatural being, Death. Instead, they get Death's brother, Dream. While he is trapped in a mystical bubble, humanity suffers in terrible ways. When Dream escapes, he sets about recovering his stolen items that give him his power. The journey takes him to visit DC hero John Constantine, as well as to hell to try and defeat a powerful demon in a contest to retrieve his magical objects. The final story features his sister, Death, as they travel together in a very memorable story that leads to Dream recovering his will to fulfill his destiny. Eventually, if you love graphic novels and comics, your journey will lead you to Gaiman's *Sandman* series. Caution: the storytelling in these books is dense and sometimes difficult to understand; in addition, some themes are mature, so *The Sandman* series is more suited to older teens.[38]

Daredevil/Echo: Vision Quest

I want to talk briefly about one more book. *Vision Quest*, written and illustrated by David Mack, may be the most visually beautiful graphic novel I encountered in my journey of writing this book. If you are a Daredevil fan, you may be disappointed in the story line, because Daredevil barely appears. The book is really about Maya Lopez (a.k.a. Echo) finding herself after a very dark time in her life.

Actually, very little action occurs in this book. Much of it is flashback to Maya's early years with her father, who is in the employ of a man who will become very important to her destiny: Kingpin. After learning that Kingpin killed her father—and subsequently nearly killing Kingpin in a previous book—Maya embarks on a mission to find her purpose in life. She visits "the Rez" where she

Top Five Superheroes of All Time

It's kind of difficult to secure reliable sales data from the first three decades of comic books, but writers and scholars have done extensive research and come up with what they believe are the five top-selling comic book characters of all time. This information comes from a 2016 article by Kaitlin Miller for the *Sun Times National* (online).

5. *Captain America*. The first issue of *Captain America*, which featured Cap punching Hitler on the cover, sold more than one million copies. Despite being discontinued in the 1950s, the character made a comeback to appear in more than eight thousand issues that have sold over two hundred million copies.

4. *X-Men*. The X-Men hold the Guinness World Record for the best-selling single issue of a comic with 1991's *X-Men* #1, which sold 7.1 million copies. The franchise has sold more than 270 million copies in all and includes more than ten thousand issues.

3. *Spider-Man*. This Marvel mainstay first appeared in 1962 and was an instant success due to his distinct powers and everyday teen appeal. Spider-Man has sold more than 360 million comics and starred in more than eleven thousand issues. The highest-selling Spider-Man adventure is Todd McFarlane's *Spider-Man* #1, which sold 2.5 million copies in 1990.

2. *Batman*. Despite his lack of powers (or perhaps because of them) Batman has become one of the most iconic superheroes of all time. Since his debut in *Detective Comics* #27 in 1939, Batman has appeared in almost thirteen thousand issues and sold more than 460 million copies.

1. *Superman*. The superhero who effectively established the genre is also the best-selling comics hero of all time. His comics have been continuously printed since his debut in *Action Comics* in 1938. The Man of Steel has starred in almost twelve thousand issues, selling more than six hundred million copies. 1987's *Superman* #75 is the best-selling at three million.[y]

grew up, and seeks out the Chief, an old medicine man. He sends her on the vision quest of the book's title—a four-day fast in the wilderness, where she encounters various animals sacred to her people. At the end of the four days she meets Wolverine. That unlikely confrontation leads her into further self-understanding. She goes back to civilization to clean up her relationship with Daredevil, with whom she had a difficult breakup. Okay, that's about it as far as the action goes.

The aspect of this book that makes me want to review it here is the art. It's difficult to describe—you have to see it to understand its power. Every page contains a collage of paintings, pencil sketches, sign language instructions (Echo is hearing impaired), oddly shaped panels, sometimes a complete absence of panels, intricate frames and borders, splashes of color that affect mood, ornamental leaves and animal drawings, abstract symbols, newsprint words glued onto the paintings, words spelled with blocks or other objects—I can't list them all because there are so many elements that bring meaning without words. The result is a gorgeous book that sinks viscerally into your soul so that you "feel" the story in a way that prose cannot even come close to. This is a shining example of the power of the graphic medium.[39]

BEYOND SUPERHEROES: THE GRAPHIC NOVEL GROWS UP

Few of you reading this book receive a monthly comic book in the mail from one of the big mainstream publishers. This method of receiving comics, called subscription, is almost nonexistent in today's world. Most of you, also, will not go to a comic book store and buy an individual issue of your favorite series. This was the model that gained popularity in the 1980s and 1990s, but many comics shops have gone out of business. Most of you reading this don't even know where the nearest comic book store is in your area. A lot of you, however, probably have seen the giant graphic novel and manga section at the big bookstore near you. And even more of you have looked at comic strips or books on a computer or tablet your family owns.

Why did I just run through a brief history of comic book distribution? Because it highlights the enormous technological changes our world has experienced since the first comic books were produced in the 1930s. These technology changes, along with massive cultural shifts, have affected not only the distribution of comics, but the length, artistry, and subject matter of comics as well.

We are now living in the age where the graphic novel has become the focal point of comics. Even stories that begin as serial comic books are written with

"I read the page, then the next and, without even noticing, I had gone through the whole comic book. 'Now,' I thought to myself, 'I realized why my parents were so adamant on getting the bigger book, with multiple comics.' I was hooked. I couldn't help it but I was addicted."—Michael B., Plymouth, Minnesota[a]

> "It dawned on me that to be considered a great superhero, superpowers are not required. You just need a body of people in need who are looking for someone to pull them through the hardest of times. Like Batman was to the people of Gotham. Batman will always be the greatest superhero in my book. His ability to fight crime and win while being powerless is truly iconic and inspiring. While he may just be a comic book character, his message to fight for what you believe in, even if you are just an everyday person, echoes in the extraordinary actions of ordinary people."—Lauren P., East Setauket, New York[b]

the intent of putting them together into a larger graphic novel. In *The Power of Comics*, historians Randy Duncan, Matthew J. Smith, and Paul Levitz write that "sales of graphic novels have climbed in recent years." They report that in the eleven months during which their book was written (in 2013), the sales of graphic novels rose 5 percent over the prior year.[1] Since 1986 and the publication of *Watchmen*, *The Dark Knight Returns*, and *Maus* (which won the Pulitzer Prize in 1992), graphic novels have gained respect as works of literature.

More and more serious authors have written graphic stories, including authors who wrote only prose until recently—like Greg Rucka, who was a well-known novelist before he wrote for DC's *Wonder Woman* and *Superman*.

Another reason graphic novels have gained ground is that big booksellers like Barnes & Noble (and Borders before it went out of business) began to stock them in their own special section. If you look at the graphic novel/manga section of a big bookstore, it's not in the children's section—it's usually near the front of the store. A lot of the graphic novels are superhero books, but there are many others as well.

In addition, readers get to read the stories that were published in the past. Before the age of graphic novels, readers had to go to used bookstores or specialty comic shops to find individual old issues. It's easy now to read the original *Wonder Woman* or *Fantastic Four* or *Fables* in collected forms. You can get these at many libraries, bookstores, or online.

The surge in popularity of Japanese manga has also accelerated the rise of graphic novels. Here in the United States, we don't get a chance to read the weekly and monthly serials put out by Japanese publishers. But when the consolidated volumes of translated Japanese manga are published by American subsidiaries, the books fly off the shelves. The manga take up just as much room as American graphic novels—or more—on big bookstore shelves.

Top Ten Graphic Novels for Teens 2016

The Young Adult Library Services Association (a division of the American Library Association) puts together lists of great graphic novels for teens every year. We will be featuring some of those lists throughout this book. That's because librarians are great resources and advocates for graphic novels; plus, they have the power to get books into the hands of teens. So here is their list of the top ten graphic novels for teens in 2016 in alphabetical order:

- *Awkward*. Written and illustrated by Svetlana Chmakova.
- *Drowned City: Hurricane Katrina and New Orleans*. Written and illustrated by Don Brown.
- *Lumberjanes*, volumes 1 and 2. Written by Noelle Stevenson, Grace Ellis, and Shannon Watters; illustrated by Brooke Allen.
- *Ms. Marvel*, volume 2: *Generation Why*. Written by G. Willow Wilson; illustrated by Jacob Wyatt and Adrian Alphona. And *Ms. Marvel*, volume 3: *Crushed*. Written by G. Willow Wilson; illustrated by Takeshi Miyazawa and Elmo Bondoc.
- *Nimona*. Written and illustrated by Noelle Stevenson.
- *Roller Girl*. Written and illustrated by Victoria Jamieson.
- *Sacred Heart*. Written and illustrated by Liz Suburbia.
- *A Silent Voice*, volumes 1, 2, and 3. Written and illustrated by Yoshitoki Oima.
- *Trashed*. Written and illustrated by Derf Backderf.
- *The Unbeatable Squirrel Girl*, volume 1: *Squirrel Power*. Written by Ryan North; illustrated by Erica Henderson. And *The Unbeatable Squirrel Girl*, volume 2: *Squirrel, You Know It's True*. Written by Ryan North; illustrated by Erica Henderson.[c]

You can find these books at your local or school library, or buy them at an online or bricks-and-mortar bookstore.

❓ What's Your Favorite Graphic Novel?

Several English teachers (in Minnesota and Georgia) passed out surveys to their students, asking them what their favorite comic, graphic novel, or manga is. Here are some of the answers:

- *American Sniper, Things They Carry*—"I love Vietnam stories." *Tamar*—"I love spy/war" (Lucas, 18).
- *Nightwing*—"Just my favorite superhero" (Amelia, 18).
- *Superman: Transformed*—"Interesting story with a different twist on Superman's character" (Dane, 18).
- *Smile*—"It's a good story. Funny" (Taylor, 17).
- *Hana Kimi*—"It was made into a Korean drama, and I enjoyed that so I read the manga" (Kayla, 18).
- *Yu-Gi-Oh*—"I would always watch the anime as a kid" (Kayla, 18).
- *First They Killed My Father*—"I liked learning about the Cambodian culture" (Damon, 18).
- *Naruto*—"Teaches people to never give up and many more life lessons" (Crispin, 18).
- *Avengers: Infinity War*—"I get so consumed by its conflict and characterization. It's simply amazing." *Saga*—"The art style is beyond appealing as well as its sophisticated universe." *X-Men: Old Man Logan*—"The darkness of these comics contrast the usual romantic plots superhero arcs follow" (Ashlyn, 18).
- *Kitchen Princess*—"I like Romance and food and this series had both" (Destiny, 18).
- All Marvel Comics—"I love the different superheroes and the seemingly endless different powers each one contributes. My favorite is the Vision" (Austyn, 17).
- *Persepolis 2*—"It showed a side of a young culture that we've never really seen before" (Alex, 18).
- *D. Gray-man*—"[Manga] story about different people with super powers facing evil" (Alina, 18).
- *American Born Chinese*—"Colors pop out, imagery is cool" (Adom, 19).

- *Black Butler*—"Demons." *Shingeki No Kyojin*—"Characters; dislike— cliffhangers" (Tyler, 14).
- *Naruto*—humor. *Black Butler*—"The way they fight. I liked the fact that there is a 12 or 13 year old who is an earl. The fact that the butler Tanaka keeps drinking tea" (Ebed, 12).

If any of these books sound interesting to you, look them up!

Farewell, Serialization

In the book *The Graphic Novel: An Introduction*, authors Jan Baetens and Hugo Frey make the claim that we can bid "farewell to serialization." They outline four ways in which graphic novels differ from serial comic books:

1. *Form*—The authors point out that graphic novel creators tend to explore the rules and push the boundaries of form beyond the limits that comic books traditionally have followed. For instance, Will Eisner, in *A Contract with God*, the first popular graphic novel, "liked working with unframed panels, creating a more fluid dialogue between the various images on the page."[2] Also the role of the narrator is normally more pronounced than in comic books.
2. *Content*—The authors explain that graphic novel content is more "adult," not in the sense of pornographic but in the sense of "serious and too sophisticated—or simply uninteresting—for a juvenile audience."[3] They say that graphic novels also are disposed toward realism, because they include nonfiction genres such as memoir.
3. *Publication format*—graphic novels tend to adopt a format that resembles that of the traditional novel in size, cover, paper, binding, and number of pages. They are produced to look different than the infamously cheap comic books. Also, the graphic novel "prefers the one-shot formula," which allows the reader the satisfaction of finishing the story rather than being forced to seek out a follow-up at a later date.
4. *Production and distribution*—the authors stress the importance of independent publishers in the rise of the graphic novel. Although early graphic novels did not meet with great success in specialty shops and head shops (in the 1970s and early 1980s), graphic novels are now sold at all major brick-and-mortar and online bookstores.

Despite these solid differences, the authors point out that many people disagree that graphic novels and comics are fundamentally different, and caution readers not to make "too strong or sharp division between comics and the graphic novel."[4]

Graphic Novels That Shaped the Industry

The rest of this chapter is dedicated to reviews of really great graphic novels that in some way changed the way people think about this art form. These books are leading the way in changing minds about the study of comics as serious literature. They are longer than serial comic books, although they may be a compilation of serials. Because they are so well conceived, even the novels that started as serials don't read like a bunch of individual stories thrown together. In my humble opinion—and the opinion of many librarians whose reviews I've consulted—these are some of the best graphic novels for teens.

Some readers will argue that their favorite comic is not among those featured here. There could be several reasons for that:

- Some material is not quite appropriate for teens, so I may have deliberately left it out. For instance, *Watchmen* was discussed in chapter 1 from a historical standpoint, but I'm not going to review it because it has some violent and abusive references that are for mature readers only.
- Some I might have missed because they were published during the time this book was being written.
- Some I may have read but didn't think they had a wide enough appeal to include.
- Some probably just escaped my notice—there are a lot of books out there to read!

So forgive me in advance if your favorite is not here. But this is a great list for any high school or public library.

One more word about the books reviewed in this chapter. Some great ones don't appear because they are in chapter 5, which is about genre-bending comics. Those are the books that fall into more nontraditional categories. Some books defy categorization and could be in either chapter.

Maus: A Survivor's Tale

The Pulitzer Prize is considered one of the most prestigious awards in literature. Authors who win one become forever known as "Pulitzer Prize–winning author

. . ." In 1992, for the first (and only) time, a graphic novel won a Pulitzer Prize. The book was *Maus* by Art Spiegelman.

Maus tells the true story of Spiegelman's parents living in Nazi-occupied Poland and then continues their plight after they are taken to Auschwitz, the German concentration camp. *Maus* is a great example of the power of comics to tell a difficult story. In the book, the Jews are represented as mice, while the Nazi soldiers are cats. Minor characters in the book take the form of other types of animals. The author, Art Spiegelman, portrays himself as a mouse as well, as the story jumps back and forth between present day and the 1940s. The layers in the story run deep, as the author struggles to relate to his father—yet another consequence of past experiences.

Maus is brilliant and widely regarded as one of the greatest graphic novels ever written. But the book also raises questions. Is it history, since the story is true in essence? Is it historical fiction, since some the dialogue is, by necessity, invented? Where should it go in the library—under graphic novels or in nonfiction? Or should it be placed in the memoir section? Most librarians I've talked to solve this by placing it with all the other graphic novels in the nonfiction section. The attention that Maus received helped break some of the barriers that were holding comics back from being considered serious literature. Suddenly, comics authors were free to pursue genres other than superhero—other than fiction, even.

The art in *Maus* is black and white with very detailed background and textures. This detail is contrasted by the relatively featureless faces, which allows the reader

"People say comics are easy to read, but there's so much happening on one page, and you have to pay attention to all of it in order to receive the full experience. If you skim through the comic without really diving into what the comic has to offer art wise, then you aren't reading the way the author intended you to. You're getting a lackluster experience. When you really dive in and dig deep into the comics, you'll find that you'll be moved into the world of that comic. You can put yourself in that scene. If you think comics are easy to read, then you aren't reading it the right way. The backgrounds display so much information by themselves, and THEY ARE THE FREAKING BACKGROUNDS. You can't lose focus, or you'll miss that the box shape indicated a shout instead of a regular tone. Or the words were more prominent. Like I said, there's no easy comic book to read. Not when you read it the right way."—Zachary B., Tyrone, Georgia[d] to imagine himself as the character as he reads. The artist fits a lot on a page, so the effect is quick-paced and chaotic, mirroring the characters' lives. The effect is one of almost total immersion as the story is read, which allows readers to empathize with the characters in a way that they might not in a purely prose account.

In one scene, Spiegelman, in the voice of his father, tells the story of how his parents were betrayed by smugglers they thought they could trust and sent to the camp. Jagged word balloons heighten the tension, as well as irregularly shaped panels. The panels on the left side of the spread are nice and aligned, but on the bottom of the right spread, as the parents are discovered, the effect is one of loud noises, time speeding up, people crowding together, life being thrown off balance. This is not only reading about history; this is in a sense *reliving* history, putting yourself—via the imagination—in someone else's shoes.[5]

American Born Chinese

Every group has its own list of the ten or twenty or fifty best graphic novels for teens, but almost every list has *American Born Chinese* by Gene Luen Yang on it. The graphic novel has won a host of awards, perhaps the most impressive of which is the Michael L. Printz Award for the best young adult book in 2007, awarded by the American Library Association. As I've researched comics and graphic novels used in high school classrooms, this book (along with *Maus* and *Perepolis*) comes up frequently.

American Born Chinese weaves three stories together that, at first, seem unrelated. The book opens with a gorgeous splash page filled with Chinese mythical characters. The gods, goddesses, demons, and spirits are having a dinner party. Only they haven't invited the monkey king, who has worked hard to attain an impressive level of kung fu and spiritual enlightenment. When the monkey king tries to join the dinner party, he is tossed out because he is a monkey. After busting up the guests at the party, he returns home and begins to rue the fact that he is a monkey. This resentment sets the stage for tale number two, the story of Jin Wang, a Chinese American who moves to a mostly white school where he longs to fit in. Soon he meets a Taiwanese immigrant named Wei-Chen Sun, on whom Jin looks down because he is FOB (fresh off the boat). This sets up the third story, which features a blond American high school student named Danny who must endure the yearly visit by his stereotypically exaggerated cousin, Chin-Kee. When Chin-Kee is around, Danny is embarrassed and ashamed because he feels like his cousin is ruining his reputation.

I will not ruin the story by telling you how these three stories come together in the end, but Yang has written a very surprising and enlightening ending that is also funny and emotionally touching. There are many brilliant aspects to this

Figure 4.1. *American Born Chinese* by Gene Luen Yang. From AMERICAN BORN CHINESE © 2006 by Gene Luen Yang. Reprinted by permission of First Second, an imprint of Roaring Brook Press, a division of Holtzbrinck Publishing Holdings Limited Partnership. All Rights Reserved.

novel, including its beautiful art; but one of the most effective graphic storytelling techniques is how Yang develops three different worlds with varying backgrounds, colors, and characters. It's almost like being in a theater with three stages side-by-side. When the curtain comes down on one, the audience turns to the next, with its different scenery and styles. When Chin-Kee comes on stage, there is a laugh track at the bottom of the page as if he is performing in a TV sitcom, a clue to the reader that this character is exaggerated and larger than life (see figure 4.1).

Yang includes a lot of insults and stereotypes in the course of the story, which are meant to make readers uncomfortable, especially if they have ever thought or said what is represented on the page. This book not only is entertaining but also gives a sobering lesson in generalizing and stereotyping. In the end, readers walk away asking themselves if they are really being themselves, or possibly trying to be someone they are not meant to be.[6]

Roller Girl

Roller Girl, by Victoria Jamieson, might be single-handedly responsible for the resurgence of roller derby in the United States in the past five years. Okay, maybe that's an exaggeration, but it's no exaggeration when I say that this book has many, many fans. The main characters in the story are middle schoolers, but I know high schoolers who love this book because of the heartfelt emotion and exciting action in the book—not to mention the great art. Also, the author explains roller derby rules, which to a casual viewer looks like rugby on roller skates—basically incomprehensible without a tutorial.

As the story opens, twelve-year-old Astrid and her best friend, Nicole, are going on a dreaded "cultural appreciation" field trip with Astrid's mom, which they both know will be horrible and boring. They are pleasantly surprised when Astrid's mom takes them to see their first roller derby match. Astrid is immediately smitten by the action and the cool names, like Scrappy Go Lucky and Yoga Nabi Sari (get it?—you gonna be sorry). Nicole, on the other hand, is terrified by the violence and begins a journey of her own—away from her former best friend. The two friends split up for real when Astrid signs up for roller derby summer camp, while Nicole goes to dance camp with a new best friend.

At first, Astrid has a rough time at roller derby camp. As a novice skater, she falls a lot and gets bumped around when she does learn to stay on her feet. To make matters worse, she has lied to her mom about Nicole being at the camp, so she has to skate home every evening, claiming she's getting a ride from Nicole's mom. As the camp draws to a close with a junior bout to be played at the professional bout, Astrid must learn important but painful lessons about friendship and growing up to be her own person.

Figure 4.2. *Roller Girl* by Victoria Jamieson. From ROLLER GIRL by Victoria Jamieson, copyright © 2015 by Victoria Jamieson. Used by permission of Dial Books for Young Readers, an imprint of Penguin Young Readers Group, a division of Penguin Random House LLC.

I love how the author uses the graphic medium in this book. Look at the left spread in figure 4.2. In the first panel, the author dispenses with panel lines to let the pain burst out into the readers' mind—you can actually "feel" the hit. Then in the fourth panel, we see an extreme close-up of Astrid's eyes—a suspense-building technique—before she is blasted into outer space in the final panel, magnified by her skates actually busting out of the panel. The art in this book is beautiful and the storytelling is very effective. Even if you're past middle school, this book will appeal to the part of you that mourns for lost friendships and roots for the underdog. Don't let the simplistic style fool you—this is a vibrant graphic style that will appeal to a wide audience.[7]

Smile

Raina Telgemeier's *Smile* was one of the first really popular graphic novels for middle and high school students. An Eisner Award winner and *New York Times* bestseller, *Smile* is the graphic novel against which all other teen slice-of-life graphic novels are compared. Telgemeier's art style is beautiful and what I would call character forward, meaning she doesn't spend a lot of time on backgrounds, focusing the reader's attention on the characters and their interactions. In that way, it is quite manga-like, although more realistically drawn. This is a powerful style for a book heavily focused on relationships rather than smash-bang action.

Smile could be considered memoir, since it tells Telgemeier's own story through a particular lens: her travails with orthodontics. The first and last panels both feature the author being told to "Smile!" But in between those two frames are four years' worth of dental work, friend troubles and joys, boy problems, face breakouts, ear piercings, and other growing up adventures. In one of the great coming of age scenes in all of teen literature, ninth-grade Raina breaks up with her old friends, who haven't been supportive for a long time.

She tells them, "You guys want a reaction from me? Fine: Karin, I am not a dog. Nicole, I am not a vampire. And I am not going to let the rest of you disrespect me anymore. I'm done. Good-bye." This last line is said as she heads, very dramatically, right into the reader's face, old friends literally and figuratively left behind. That's why this book has such wide appeal—it resonates so deeply on so many levels. The history of this book tells the story of graphic storytelling in the last quarter century: Telgemeier self-published the chapters and sold them at comics conventions until Scholastic approached her about putting them together as a graphic novel. Her other teen graphic novels are excellent as well: *Sisters*, *Drama*, and her adaptions of *The Baby Sitters' Club*, to name a few.[8]

Paste Magazine's Comics for Adolescent Girls

In 2014, *Paste* magazine published an online article discussing the growing number of female comics readers of "all-ages comics." The author, Hillary Brown, quotes comics author Scott McCloud: "Many of the values of the manga generation are merging with homegrown sensibilities and homegrown settings and subjects to ensure a steady flow of new readers—again, mostly female—to help swell American comics' ranks."[e] Its list of ten great comics for adolescent girls may help female readers find something they like. Do you agree with this list or would you add something else?

10. *Spider-Man Loves Mary Jane*, by Sean McKeever, with art by Takeshi Miyazawa and David Hahn (Marvel)
9. *Fray*, by Joss Whedon, with art by Karl Moline (Dark Horse)
8. *One Hundred Demons*, by Lynda Barry (Sasquatch Books) (In my opinion, this may be more suited for older audiences)
7. *Wandering Son*, by Shimura Takako (Fantagraphics)
6. *Primates: The Fearless Science of Jane Goodall, Dian Fossey, and Biruté Galdikas*, by Jim Ottaviani, with art by Maris Wicks (First Second)
5. *Runaways*, by Brian K. Vaughan, with art by Adrian Alphona (Marvel)
4. *Unlovable*, volumes 1–3, by Esther Pearl Watson (Fantagraphics)
3. *This One Summer*, by Mariko Tamaki, with art by Jillian Tamaki (First Second)
2. *Anya's Ghost*, by Vera Brosgol (First Second)
1. *The Secret Science Alliance and the Copycat Crook*, by Eleanor Davis (Bloomsbury USA Children)[f]

Nothing Can Possibly Go Wrong

Faith Erin Hicks is a master graphic storyteller. She took Prudence Shen's prose novel by the same name and turned it into a graphic masterpiece. This is one of my favorite books because it does so many things right. The art is very clean black and white, but shaded in such a way that your eye is fooled into thinking it is seeing colors. The characters are so well conceived and funny that you want them all to succeed, even though they do things that are very unadmirable at times.

Charlie and Nate are neighbors and friends, although they run in very different crowds. Charlie is a star on the basketball team; Nate is a star of the robotics club. Charlie is a peace-loving individual, so when his cheerleader girlfriend Holly breaks up with him (in a text on the first page of the book) he goes along without arguing. But Nate, on behalf of the robotics club, is fuming at Holly because she wants to redirect money earmarked for a national robotics competition to buy new cheerleading uniforms. The principal has decided to let the student council decide who gets the money. Thus is the epic showdown begun: Nate decides to run for student body president against the cheerleaders' candidate . . . who turns out to be Charlie.

Nate and the cheerleaders trade hilariously nasty stunts back and forth until finally the principal has had enough and declares that neither team will get any funding. The two clubs can either quit or work together. They decide to work together by using cheerleader funds to pay for a local robotics competition called the Robot Rumble (figure 4.3), which, if they win, will supply enough money for both groups' needs. Complicate all this with Charlie's screwed-up home life—his divorced mom has decided to visit with her fiancé for Thanksgiving on the day of the robotics competition. Charlie's dad insists he stay home, so he and the group sneak out and commence to let their robot rumble. This is not only a hugely entertaining book, but it is a master class in how to use graphic storytelling techniques.[9]

Awkward

What is your definition of awkward? In *Awkward*, by Svetlana Chmakova, budding artist (and scientist) Penelope Torres (a.k.a. Peppi) defines it a number of ways after she moves to a new middle school. Published by Yen Press in 2015, *Awkward* reads and feels a lot like manga. That seems natural, since Yen puts out a lot of manga series like *Black Butler* and *Soul Eater*. But it also publishes more Western-style graphic novels like *Zoo: The Graphic Novel*. *Awkward* is a fusion comic in the sense that it combines the best techniques of manga with more Western-style art and storytelling.

The opening of *Awkward* starts with a bang as Peppi, new at her middle school, trips over her own feet and falls flat on her face in front of everyone in the hall. When an unpopular student, a member of the science club, helps her pick up her things, she is mocked by some bullies. To save face, she does something cruel to Jamie, the boy who is helping her; this act of bullying haunts her for weeks. When she joins the art club, she finally finds her people, but her unresolved guilt stays

Figure 4.3. *Nothing Can Possibly Go Wrong by Faith Erin Hicks and Prudence Shen. From NOTHING CAN POSSIBLY GO WRONG © 2013 by Prudence Shen. Illustrations © Faith Erin Hicks. Reprinted by permission of First Second, an imprint of Roaring Brook Press, a division of Holtzbrinck Publishing Holdings Limited Partnership. All Rights Reserved.*

Online Innovator Faith Erin Hicks

Faith Erin Hicks was born in British Columbia, Canada, and grew up in Ontario. After studying animation at Sheridan College, Hicks wrote a web comic called *Demonology* that brought her to the attention of comics lovers and publishers. She followed that with *Zombies Calling* in 2007, which was inspired by zombie movies. She continued to write web comics, including the dystopian *Ice*, which ran from 2003 to 2010.

A number of her graphic novels have won enduring audiences, such as *Friends with Boys, Nothing Can Possibly Go Wrong* (with Prudence Shen), and *Bigfoot Boy: Into the Woods* (with J. Torres). Her original series *The Adventures of Superhero Girl*, which was serialized online as well as in a weekly print newspaper, won an Eisner Award in 2014 for Best Publication for Kids.

Hicks frequently serializes her comics online before their print publication. She started this practice with *Friends with Boys*, published in 2012. "There's usually a year in between finishing a book and having it published, which is horrifying," she explains. She posted a page of the book online every weekday, then blogged about it and interacted with readers. By the time the book came out, it already had a loyal fan base. This practice has led her publisher, First Second, to serialize other graphic novels as well, a practice that famous comic writer Jeff Smith (*Bone*) has dubbed "the Faith Erin Hicks model."[9]

The first book in Hicks's new trilogy *The Nameless City*, about the unlikely friendship between a "conquering" teenager and a "conquered" teen in an occupied city, was published in 2016. Her work is truly redefining the perception of graphic stories as "kid's stuff."

with her, especially when Jamie is chosen by the science teacher to tutor her for science class. To make matters worse, there is a war on between the art club and the science club; whoever wins a contest created by the principal will win a coveted table at the school fair. Peppi must face her fears and become a leader or her club will be canceled for good.

When I first read this book, I had not read much manga, so I didn't notice how many manga techniques the author/artist, Svetlana Chmakova, employs here. Now when I read it I see them: distorted faces to display emotion; subjective motion lines; eyes that change shape with mood; quick, loud bursts of emotion; character-focused scenes with no background detail; all of these are common techniques in manga. And yet the number and shape of the panels on the page, the coloring, and the fairly detailed characters (most of the time) reflect Western comics influence. This is not only a very entertaining and heartfelt comic, but a great example of East meets West in style and content.[10]

V for Vendetta

V for Vendetta, written by Alan Moore with art by David Lloyd, is one of the most respected graphic novels ever written. Are you getting the idea that Alan Moore (author of *Watchmen*, *Swamp Thing*, *Batman: The Killing Joke*, and many more) is one of the great craftsmen in this genre? It's true. He has penned the scripts for some of the most talked about comics and graphic novels of the last forty years. *V for Vendetta* is one of his most respected and complex books.

Written in the early 1980s, the story is set in a fictional 1997 in which much of the world has been destroyed in a nuclear war. The country of England has survived but is ruled by a totalitarian government that is eerily believable. After the recent chaos, the people of England are docile and submissive, satisfied to just have food on the table and strong leaders telling them what to do. The leader of the country, simply called Leader by his subordinates, readily admits to being a fascist, believing himself to be the most benevolent solution to a hurting country's needs.

Against this backdrop of totalitarianism comes a costumed figure known only as V. This vigilante, who wears a smiling white mask, destroys the symbols of authority and systematically kills an entire group of people who had worked at a notoriously vicious "resettlement camp" a few years earlier. The leaders of the country eventually find out that V was a prisoner at the camp but the knowledge comes too late; the anarchist has effectively brought down the totalitarian government in a creative and ruthless manner. Although V does not make it out of the story alive, he trains a disciple whom he saved from a rape at the beginning of the story. She takes up the mantle of V to try and rebuild the country she has learned to love.

V for Vendetta is a masterful use of sequential art to tell a complex story. Like *Watchmen*, many stories are interwoven to produce a tapestry of action that the reader can only recognize at the end. One of the techniques *V for Vendetta* uses to great advantage is what Scott McCloud calls a "parallel combination" of words and pictures. He comments that this arrangement can create a "dense, layered texture" and is often used to "transition from one scene to another." In one stunning section in chapter 6, a creepy bishop who is about to molest a child quotes from a religious text: "Thou who art our fate and our final destiny. . . . Help us to clearly perceive thy will. Help us to perceive the wiles of the evil one and stand firm in thee." These words appear in captions over scenes of violence as V takes out the bishop's armed guards and climbs a drain pipe toward the bishop's window. The effect is ominous, with the action outside the mansion giving the hypocrite's words a deeper layer of meaning, in effect acting as a foreshadowing of the retribution about to come.

Caution: *V for Vendetta* is meant for an older audience. Actually it is meant for an adult audience, but older teens will be able to grasp the subtleties and keep track of the story line. Younger teens will probably have a difficult time figuring out what's going on in certain parts; for instance, one entire section is written as a vaudeville song, with the art switching back and forth between V playing the piano and action occurring in the outside world. Some of the themes are for mature readers too, and the violence is a little rough in places. So if you're in middle school or the first few years of high school, my recommendation is that you wait a couple years to tackle *V for Vendetta*.[11]

Bone

The superheroes of the 1980s and 1990s were gritty, rather dark characters whose stories were increasingly meant to appeal to adults. This is understandable, as the mainstream publishers wanted to widen their audiences and the rival independent publishers were putting out mature content that attracted older readers. It's ironic, isn't it? Although comics were originally meant to appeal to young children, the comics of the day were leaving out this demographic.

Enter *Bone*, written, illustrated, and self-published by Jeff Smith starting in 1991. Although *Bone* has been reissued in color, the original comic series was in black and white. The *Bone* series has been compared to *Lord of the Rings* because the characters embark on a quest that involves a company of friends against a supernatural foe intent on taking over the world. The story even contains just enough romance to keep it interesting to readers looking for a relationship drama. In the end, the characters have all developed and matured, the true queen takes her throne, and the evil has been vanquished—although at great cost. The Bones finally find their way back home, albeit much wiser than when they left. This series is truly for all ages. Geared for older elementary or middle school, the story and art are so great that older teenagers and adults regularly pick it up too.

The main characters in this fantasy story are a trio of blobby white cousins who look like a cross between Casper the Friendly Ghost and Pogo, the possum in the old newspaper comic strip. At the outset of the story, Fone Bone has just saved his greedy cousin, Phoney Bone, from an angry mob in their (former) home of Boneville. The people are angry because Phoney has just swindled them out of their money—a running theme throughout the entire series. The two cousins, along with the happy-go-lucky Smiley Bone, become lost and inadvertently enter a world that includes locust hordes, dragons, warrior princesses, and giant rat creatures who try to eat them at every turn.

One of the most interesting characters is Thorn, the princess who doesn't know she's a princess. She works on her Gran'ma Ben's farm, little knowing her royal past or her prophesied future. The moment Fone Bone meets her, he falls in love. At the end he must choose to stay and be with his love or help his cousins find their way back to Boneville. Gran'ma Ben, who is more than she appears to be, leads the ragtag bunch against an impossible host of foes. Gran'ma has to come to terms with her own past if she is to make up for the mistakes she has made in her life. There is a dragon whom nobody but Fone Bone seems to believe in, and the Lord of the Locusts, who is trying to come back physically into the world from which he was banished. The story is gripping, and you fall in love with the characters right away. I'm sure some old-school readers prefer the original black and white, but the colorized version is fantastic, so I recommend trying to get ahold of those.[12]

Brotherman: Revelation

In chapter 1 I told the story of *Brotherman*, a self-published series from the early 1990s that featured an entirely African American cast of characters. The brothers who produced the series let it lie dormant for over a decade before picking up the pencil again, so to speak. After raising some cash through a crowd-funding site in 2015, Dawud Anyabwile (formerly known as David Sims), along with his brother Guy Sims and colorist Brian McGee, created the first of a planned three-part graphic novel series telling the full story of Antonio Valor, also known as Brotherman: Disciple of Discipline. The first book is called *Revelation* (figure 4.4).

In *Revelation*, Valor discovers the inspiring story of his father, Leonard Valor, a community activist and teacher. Much of this is told through a flashback in the Valors' home. When the novel gets back to real time, Antonio and his father leave for a community meeting, while his mother and sister go to a sewing class his mom teaches. A crooked businessman plants a bomb in their house to send a message to the Valors, who have been opposing the building of a soul-crushing housing project in their neighborhood. Both meetings are suddenly canceled, and the family heads back home from two directions. As the clock on the bomb literally ticks, the creators do a great job of building tension for the reader. Will one or both of Antonio's parents get caught in the blast? On the last page of the novel the explosive answer is revealed. The characters, dialogue, action, and setting combine to make this an enjoyable and inspiring comic experience.[13]

Figure 4.4. *Brotherman: Revelation* by Dawud Anyabwile, Guy Sims, and Brian McGee. *From* Brotherman: Revelation *by Dawud Anyabwile, Guy Sims, and Brian McGee © 2015 Big City Entertainment. All rights reserved.*

The Arrival

To call Shaun Tan's graphic novel *The Arrival* a story about the immigrant experience is like calling the New England Patriots a sports team. Yes, it does chronicle an immigrant's experience in a strange, surreal world, but the book is so much more than that. Without any words, Tan manages to communicate perfectly by way of his gorgeous narrative pictures. The absence of words might cause some readers to see *The Arrival* as a children's book, but this book will appeal to people of all ages. Anyone who's ever found themselves in a new and unfamiliar place will be able to relate.

The opening page shows a series of normal, everyday items for a family of three: a tea kettle, a mantle clock, an origami bird. But on the following pages it is clear that someone is leaving. A suitcase is being packed, a bundle of papers is being tied in a string. It turns out the father is leaving due to a large tentacled creature that is threatening the family's town. We follow the father on his journey to a strange new country. The book is a showcase of graphic storytelling; during the father's journey over the ocean on a ship, the passage of time is shown on one spread in the form of sixty small pictures of cloud formations, as if viewed from his cabin window.

The new city that the father arrives in is not only strange to him; Tan has created a fantastical world that is at the same time beautiful and frightening to the reader, too. One of the reasons this book resonates so strongly is that the bizarre city makes us feel like strangers along with the characters. After a series of false starts and lost jobs, various kind strangers put the father on the right track. Soon he has enough money to send away for his family. The reunion that occurs will warm the coldest of hearts.[14]

Marvel 1602

Technically this is a superhero comic. Only it's set in 1602 and written by one of the great literary writers of our generation, Neil Gaiman. So maybe it's a literary graphic novel? Or possibly a historical fiction superhero literary comic? Whatever it is, it's a great read. The characters are well-rounded and consistent—both with their modern Marvel personas and with the Renaissance England time period—and the art is nuanced and beautiful. Oh, and the story is complex and gripping. What's not to like?

In the foreword to this book, comics historian Peter Sanderson explains the brilliance of Gaiman's work in *Marvel 1602*: "In reconceiving these classic Marvel heroes and villains in terms of Renaissance England, Gaiman shows us what remains the same about each character in such different circumstances. In other words, Gaiman demonstrates the timeless essence of Stan Lee and his collaborator's greatest creations." In other words, Nick Fury in 1602 can be recognized as the Nick Fury of modern S.H.I.E.L.D. comics, although he is serving Queen Elizabeth before the publication of Shakespeare's *Hamlet*. He even has an eye patch.

The story opens in the private chambers of Queen Elizabeth as her majesty discusses the odd weather patterns with her chief spy, Sir Nicholas Fury, and her new court physician, Dr. Stephen Strange. The talk turns to a Templar weapon being brought from the Holy Land to England, and the various entities—one of whom is Otto Von Doom—that are seeking to capture it. The next scene is a heart-rending full page illustration of a man with wings chained up in the High Tower of the Palace of the Inquisition. We are quickly introduced to the Renaissance version of the X-Men, called the Witchbreed, who factor heavily in the story. The mutant is saved by two other mutants who take the boy to a school in England run by Carlos Javiar. The story contains numerous twists and turns, including the queen being murdered and replaced by King James of Scotland, who wants to kill all the mutants—a recognizable theme to anyone who's ever read the modern *X-Men* comics. The Templar weapon falls into the hands of Count Otto Von Doom, so Fury enlists the mutants to help him recover it.

In a manner that displays Gaiman's intricate craftsmanship, all the extraordinary people of the Marvel universe somehow end up in the New World by the end of the story, where Captain America makes a surprise appearance. The story is very entertaining, but it also has a serious element to it as the writer reveals the underpinnings in some of our beliefs about the world that we take for granted.[15]

The Dumbest Idea Ever

This book is for anyone who began writing or drawing as a child and dreamed of making it in the comic book industry. Actually, almost anyone will be entertained and inspired by this story, but especially those who've thought about trying their hand at comics. Professional comics creator Jimmy Gownley tells the story of how he got into comics as a teenager, which is why it's a memoir. But the story has all the elements of a good teen story, no matter the genre: romance, humor, friendships (and broken friendships), a basketball championship, arguments with strict instructors who are also nuns, and sickness at the worst possible moment in history.

The story opens with a fifteen-year-old Jimmy being filmed for a television special about publishing his first comic book. When the interviewer asks him where he gets his ideas from, Jimmy launches into his story. The reader learns that the budding artist is a good student and a star basketball player at a Catholic high school in rural Pennsylvania. He also loves comic books and is out to prove to his English teacher that comics can be an integral part of the class. While he convinces her that comics are serious stuff, she continues to ban them in class—demonstrating the still-strained relationship a lot of adults have with comics.

As Jimmy looks for a good subject for a new comic book he wants to write, his friend tries to convince him that, "You should write a comic book . . . about us!" At the time Jimmy retorts, "That's the dumbest idea I've ever heard!" But soon he realizes the truth—that his life is a perfect subject, and that he has important things to say. As he faces a number of challenges—picking up chicken pox days before the championship game, his girlfriend breaking up with him, coming to terms with his own inexperience—he realizes that these are, indeed, the struggles that readers want to read about. His comic book takes off, and the rest is history.[16]

Skim

Skim, with words by Mariko Tamaki and drawings by Jillian Tamaki, is a beautifully told story about a tenth grader named Kim—nicknamed Skim because she is not skinny—who may or may not be goth; who may or may not be studying to be a witch; who may or may not be in love with one of her teachers; who may or may not be battling depression; but who is *definitely* tired of the cheery new club called Girls Celebrate Life! that is formed after the suicide of one of her classmate's boyfriend. The creators are cousins who bring out the humor and anguish of being a sixteen-year-old girl at an all-girl private school in the aftermath of a tragedy that affects everyone at the school.

The main character falls for one of her teachers, who, as the story progresses, disappears from the pages and from Skim's life. The illustrations carry a lot of weight in this book. In figure 4.5, the first few panels show a technique the artist uses to highlight the subject in the foreground while deemphasizing what's in the background. The reader can feel Skim cowering and hiding while the popular girls of the school walk past outside the door. After a conversation with her friend Lisa, informing her that Ms. Archer has left the school for good, Skim runs outside via a panel without any borders and searches for her, only to find an empty parking lot.

The absence of panels makes the reader feel the vulnerability of Skim as her heart begins to break. The cowering on the left spread gives way to surprise, then desperation, then despair as she stands alone in the barren-looking lot. All this emotion and storytelling with only a few words of narration and dialogue. Teen readers will connect with the angst of this character and her quest to find her place in the world.[17]

Figure 4.5. *Skim* by Mariko Tamaki and Jillian Tamaki. *Skim* text copyright © 2008 by Mariko Tamaki and illustrations copyright © 2008 by Jillian Tamaki. Reproduced with permission from Groundwood Books Limited, www.groundwood books.com.

Anya's Ghost

When a book is endorsed by Neil Gaiman saying "A masterpiece!" on the front cover, you sit up and take notice. And for good reason, in this case. *Anya's Ghost*, by Vera Brosgol, is very entertaining, and has a lot to say to a teen audience. What would your life be like if you had a ghost for a friend? Anya Borzakovskaya, a teenage immigrant from Russia, finds out after she falls into a well that houses a century-old ghost. When Anya brings up the ghost by inadvertently putting a bone in her book bag, her life changes in some unusual ways. Usually a ghost character is pretty static, included in the story as a sort of catalyst for change in the main character. In *Anya's Ghost*, Emily, the ghost, is a fully developed three-dimensional character who grows and changes in the story, as does Anya. You can begin to see her change on this spread as Emily manipulates Anya and starts picturing herself in a new way.

One day Anya arrives home to discover that Emily has been reading fashion magazines. The ghost convinces Anya to give herself a makeover to try and impress a boy she likes. Emily makes herself useful in many ways, including helping Anya on tests by looking at other people's answers and getting her invited to parties. All of this seems too good to be true—and it is. Emily has her own agenda and a past much less innocent than the sob story she tells about her family being killed a century ago. The friendship turns to antagonism as the two girls—one alive, one dead—struggle to manipulate each other to get what they want.

Ultimately, both Emily and Anya learn that the person they are—or were—is pretty special, and there is no need to covet the looks or possessions (or boyfriend) of anyone else. This is a very entertaining graphic novel with great art and a moving story line.[18]

This One Summer

There are stories in which the setting is sort of incidental—meaning it could take place in any number of locations. Other stories have been conceived in a particular setting and couldn't take place anywhere else. In those stories, the setting plays such a large role it could almost be said to be a character in the story. *This One Summer*, by cousins Jillian and Mariko Tamaki, fits that description. The story takes place in the little lakeside town of Awago Beach, where Rose's family has been taking summer vacations for as long as she can remember. The beautiful art brings out the sights and sounds and tastes and smells of summer so clearly that it almost feels like summer vacation.

In an effort to get away from her fighting parents after her family arrives at the cabin, Rose seeks out her friend Windy, who is a year and a half younger. Rose, at twelve, is on the cusp of being a teenager, while Windy is still closer to childhood. Rose gets interested in the love lives of the older teens she sees at the town's tiny convenience store, while Windy still says things like "Barf!" when they see a couple kissing. This is a beautiful, wise, entertaining, smart story about growing up. While the characters are twelve and ten, it's not really a story for middle schoolers. Not so much because of the language (which is rough in places) and sexual talk (which is quite raw in places) but more because preteens won't fully comprehend the subtle nuances of the theme of growing up.

The Tamakis do a great job of using graphic tools (remember visual language grammar from chapter 2?) to draw the reader into the story. For instance, they incorporate sound into the story to a greater degree than most graphic novelists. After the girls are caught using the word *sluts* without really knowing what it means, Rose walks back to the cabin with her mom. Her flip-flops squeak as they walk, making a noise that sounds like, "Slut. Slut. Slut." It's barely noticeable, but it reflects her state of mind as she processes being reprimanded for using that word. The creators use the same tool later when Rose is dipping her head under water, thinking about the boy at the store, on whom she has a crush. The sound made by popping under water is "Dunk. Dunk. Dunk." And the boy's name? Dunc, of course. This is one of those books that stays with you a long time.[19]

Nimona

Great fantasy and science fiction authors can build a world that is very different from ours, yet completely consistent within itself. The world of *Nimona*, created by Noelle Stevenson, feels medieval, with dragons and jousting knights, but it also features technology that feels modern: television, laser guns, wireless communicators, and refrigerators. Oh, and there's also some magic thrown in to create mystery. These elements are seamlessly woven together into a tale about the power of friendship, the allure and distraction of love, the mix of good and bad in everyone, and the danger of totalitarian rulers. The art in this book is beautiful, and the hand-drawn letters give the story a nostalgic quality.

Nimona is a shape-shifter who wants to create mayhem and destroy the nefarious Institution, which may or may not have created her in a lab. She invites herself to be the sidekick to the "evil" Ballister Blackheart, who is not nearly as evil as anyone thinks, including himself. Blackheart and his nemesis, the "good" hero Ambrosius Goldenloin (yes, the names vaguely referring to private parts, both physical and metaphorical), have fought for years like the two sides of a coin. But the more you read, the more you realize the Blackheart and Goldenloin use these battles to see each other. They are old friends—or maybe more.

Nimona, turning herself into animals as varied as a cat, a triceratops, and a fire-breathing dragon, helps her boss take down the Institution with a carefully crafted plan. But things get out of hand when the director of the Institution commands Goldenloin to kill Nimona in order to save Blackheart's life. After Nimona goes rogue, burning down a portion of the city, Blackheart must use a magical device that keeps Nimona from changing her shape to save the kingdom from her fiery wrath. After a furious battle, Blackheart and Goldenloin end up in the hospital and Nimona has disappeared. Or has she? Did the same nurse walk in twice and give the same order?

One way to come to an appreciation of the power of a graphic novel is to ask yourself, "Why couldn't this story be told in prose or in film? What would it lose?" In a great graphic novel, the style of artwork, the pacing of the action through the frames, the variation in viewing angle, closeness, and background all contribute to the story. In *Nimona*, the rhythm of the frames is as important as it is in music. Sometimes it speeds up; sometimes it slows down. As much is told through character expression and gesture as through dialogue—more perhaps. In one scene, Blackheart and Nimona are watching a zombie movie; the boss is incredulous that after taking out a whole squadron of soldiers, his sidekick is scared of a poorly done film. After taking the movie apart bit by bit for five panels, there is a panel with no dialogue, followed by Blackheart saying, "Oh come on! That is NOT what intestines look like!" She answers in exasperation, "SHUT UPPPP." This scene is laugh-out-loud funny. But the humor isn't through silly jokes or pratfalls. It's the rhythm of the dialogue interspersed with the silence, the very real patter of two very different people watching the same movie in different ways.[20]

Cardboard

Doug TenNapel, the author/illustrator of *Cardboard*, has produced some of the most popular graphic novels for kids and teens. *Cardboard* is an entertaining story about a father and son trying to survive after the death of their wife/mom. Mike, the dad, is down to his last seventy-eight cents because no one in town is hiring carpenters. He really wants to buy something nice for his son, Cam, on his birthday, but all he can afford is a box of cardboard from a mysterious cheap toy dealer near his home. As he presents his "gift" he is thoroughly mocked by the creepy rich kid down the street.

Cam is a good sport and declares that making something with his dad will be a fine gift. They make a boxer (as in a cardboard man that looks like a boxing champion). But this is no ordinary cardboard. When they wake up in the morning, the cardboard man is alive. As they experiment, they make other creatures that come alive. Cam's dad realizes he can make more cardboard by making a cardboard maker out of the cardboard. Marcus, the rich kid, realizes the cardboard is special and steals the cardboard maker. Meanwhile, Mike, the dad, is struggling with his attraction to his pretty single neighbor, while trying to hold on to his past relationship.

Mike and Cam must come to the rescue when Marcus's evil cardboard creations take over his house and start threatening the neighborhood. Even though Marcus has been a bully, Cam rescues him from being eaten by a giant cardboard version of himself just before the entire house disintegrates in the rain. Although the cardboard is completely destroyed, including Cam's boxer friend, Bill, the boys are saved thanks to Cam's bravery. Marcus's father hires Mike to build him a new house, and Marcus seems to have learned his lesson. In a surprise twist, a man named Bill, who looks remarkably like a human version of the cardboard man, shows up one day asking for a job. The book ends on a romantic note as Mike shows up at his neighbor's door with a bunch of roses. The story is very entertaining and the art in this book is beautiful—well worth the read.[21]

Graphic Novels Adapted from Prose Novels

Some English teachers turn their noses up at prose novels turned into comics. These same teachers eagerly send you out to see the movie adaptation of prose novels, which are many times worse than the graphic version! Film scripts have to be very selective, leaving out a great deal of plot detail and even eliminating major characters. Somewhere in the middle, between the detail of prose and the streamlined skeleton of film, lies the graphic novel adaptation of a prose novel.

When I was growing up, I read comic adaptations of many older novels and plays from a series called Classics Illustrated. I read a lot of adventure stories such as *Treasure Island* by Robert Louis Stevenson, *Ivanhoe* by Sir Walter Scott, and *The Three Musketeers* by Alexandre Dumas. But the series also included adaptations of longer, more mature adult novels such as *Moby Dick*, *Crime and Punishment*, and *Les Misérables*. I enjoyed the stories so much that as I grew older, I read the original books. I'm sure many other people have similar stories of falling in love with the classics through beautiful and well-written comics. In recent years, Classics Illustrated has been revived, with new editions and new printings of old editions. I love that, because titles that have fallen out of circulation are being introduced to readers who might never have come across them otherwise.

It's not just the classic novels written before 1900 that are being adapted to comics. Many great novels of the twentieth and twenty-first centuries are being adapted to the medium. These are longer, more developed, and superior in a literary sense than the old Classics Illustrated versions. So many have been adapted in the last twenty years that I don't have room here to name them all. I will talk about some of the best ones I've come across.

Fahrenheit 451

One good example of a graphic adaptation is Ray Bradbury's *Fahrenheit 451*, adapted by Tim Hamilton. Everyone used to read this novel in middle school, but several middle schoolers have recently told me they've never heard of it so maybe the powers that be—the ones who choose curriculum for school classes—feel that other books are more worthy of study. But *Fahrenheit 451* is a great book with some powerful ideas to wrestle with.

The art in this book is beautiful with lots of muted colors and dark, brooding scenes. Then suddenly, fire will erupt and transform the entire spread into bright chaos and danger. The fire comes from future firemen, who don't protect the public from fires; they seek out book owners and torch the stash of books—often with the owners. The story follows Guy Montag, a fireman who is not quite at ease burning books and their owners with them. He meets and begins talking with his odd neighbor, Clarisse, who stokes his dissatisfaction with his seemingly comfortable life. As he explores what is wrong with himself and his world, he comes to realize that books may hold the answers to his questions. While on a fire call, he steals a book, a copy of the Bible, possibly the last copy left in his region.

Of course, this lands him in trouble and soon it is his house that is burned due to his collection of books. Montag goes on the run with another book lover, and the two join a company of people who have memorized books to keep them alive. The last frames on the final page show scenes of nature, as the narrator quotes Revelation 22:2: "And the leaves of the tree were for the healing of the nations." As dark as the novel is, the last page leaves the door open—even if it's just a crack—that hope still exists and the knowledge and stories of the past will guide humanity in the future. If you have read *Fahrenheit 451*, this is an enjoyable adaptation. If you haven't read it, this comic is worth checking out.[22]

A Wrinkle in Time

Another interesting novel adaption is Madeleine L'Engles's *A Wrinkle in Time*, adapted and illustrated by Hope Larson. Illustrated in blue and black, the art is beautiful and provocative. Since I am not a visual artist, I was stunned by how many effects Larson achieves only using three colors—blue, black, and white. The inclusion of blue gives the tale a cool quality, while at the same time providing a three-dimensionality that black and white comics don't usually achieve.

Most of you have read the story, but the graphic novel shifts the point of view from close third person to first person. As we've discussed in other sections of this book, first person works very well in graphic novels because of the intimacy of the medium. In the bonus materials at the end of the book, the illustrator was asked what challenges she faced in adapting one of the great novels of the twentieth century. Larson's answer explains a lot about the adaptation process:

> I couldn't figure out how to abridge the book—I didn't want to cut anything out, because every part of that book is precious to someone—and we resolved that issue by including every scene and almost every word of dialogue in the graphic novel.[23]

Fans of the original will recognize the brilliant dialogue, along with great illustrations for this classic story.

Gris Grimly's Frankenstein

Gris Grimly is a writer and illustrator known for his gothic horror style. He is well-known for his work illustrating *Gris Grimly's Wicked Nursery Rhymes* and *Edgar Allen Poe's Tales of Death and Dementia*. He had always been fascinated with Mary Shelley's *Frankenstein*. Technically, Grimly's adaption is not so much a graphic novel as an illustrated novel, since a good portion of Mary Shelley's original prose is included outside of the panels on each page. But there are enough illustrations and they appear in frames in such a way that the illustrations collaborate with the prose to tell the story. So maybe it is a graphic novel. Whatever you call it, this *Frankenstein* is darkly stylish, beautiful, frightening, intensely inviting, and in a metaphorical sense puts muscle and skin on the bones of Shelley's original story. You will never think of *Frankenstein* as a movie again.

One section in particular is brilliantly moving. In chapter 3, the creature finds Frankenstein in the mountains as the creator tries to lose himself in obscurity. Using the language of legal procedure, the monster begs that Frankenstein hear his tale before passing judgment. As the creature relates the story of his awakening, the illustrator tells the story in pictures to bring the reader into the very mind of a newborn without language. If you've ever wanted to read the original *Frankenstein* but were intimidated by the old language or the size of the novel, Grimly's illustrated version is an excellent entry point. He dispenses with all the goofy Hollywood fantasies and tells the original story, illuminating its haunting brilliance.[24]

Beowulf

If you take a college lit class, you'll probably read *Beowulf*, the thousand-year-old tale of a Scandinavian champion who vanquishes a monster named Grendel. Before he dies, Beowulf also fights a dragon that threatens his people. This version of the story, adapted by Gareth Hinds, is a beautiful and exciting rendition of those heroic tales. The language is understandable, while feeling old-fashioned at the same time. But it is the art in this volume that stands out. At the end of book 1, as Grendel and Beowulf duke it out, there is a sequence of ten spreads without any words at all.

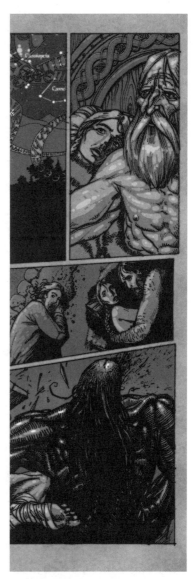

Figure 4.6. *Beowulf* adapted by Gareth Hinds. *BEOWULF. Copyright © 1999, 2000, 2007 by Gareth Hinds. Reproduced by permission of the publisher, Candlewick Press, Somerville, MA.*

In figure 4.6, the reader feels the tension and brutality of the fight without an explanation. It's a masterful combination of art and action that draws you right into the scene. *Beowulf* praises both the bravery and loyalty of a man whose exploits are still told today. Both exciting and beautiful, this is a superhero story without the modern costumes.[25]

The Graveyard Book

The Graveyard Book by Neil Gaiman is a remarkable book in its original prose. But P. Craig Russell's adaption of the book is superb in its storytelling and beau-

Gaming Graphic Novels

Many bookstores have their graphic novel shelves divided into sections: a DC section, a Marvel section, a manga section, and so on. Many also have a Gaming section, where popular video games have been converted into graphic novels, or famous comics have been converted to video games. In these books, the reader is often in the role of a player in that game.

But in one graphic novel, however, the reader is not in the game, but watching a character play a game, along with its real-world ramifications. *In Real Life*, written by Cory Doctorow with art by Jen Wang, tells the story of Anda, a girl with a lot of game. She is recruited to play in an MMO (massively multiplayer online) game where she is part of a team that kills all the gold farmers they can find. These are players who gather precious objects and sell them to players who don't have the patience to earn the stuff themselves.

In the course of playing, Anda discovers that these gold farmers are real people living in China—it's their job. She suggests to one player, whom she has gotten to know through the game, that he organize the workers to demand better wages and benefits. When the Chinese worker is fired for stirring the pot, Anda is devastated. But other workers pick up the cause and they eventually strike for better wages. The book ties games to their economic realities in other countries, which Western gamers don't often think about. Jen Wang's beautiful art makes this book even richer.

tiful in its artfulness. Each chapter is illustrated by a different artist, so although the styles are unique, they meld together to form a coherent whole. The design of each page enhances the storytelling: shapes, colors, arrangement of panels on the page, dialogue and lack of dialogue—all are used to great advantage in this story. You can learn a ton about graphic tools from this book.

The main character in this story—Nobody Owens, known simply as Bod—is being raised in a graveyard. His friends are ghosts and his guardian is a vampire. He dares not leave the confines of the graveyard because of a mortal danger to his life: the killer known as Jack, who has already killed the rest of his family, is looking for him. Bod's adventures are strange and wonderful, as he meets ghouls (hilariously named the Duke of Westminster and the Bishop of Bath and Wells) as well as a pretty girl named Scarlett Amber Perkins. He also meets Liza Hempstock, a witch buried in the Potter's Field, the portion of the cemetery where the suicides and witches are buried.

After Bod gets himself into a pickle by sneaking out of the graveyard and running into some men who want to take advantage of him, it's Liza who helps him out of the jam. To Bod's questioning about why she is out of the boundaries of their home, she replies, "Rules don't count for those as was buried in unhallowed ground. Nobody tells ME what to do, or where to go." This volume ends with a beautiful celebration shared by the living and the dead as they "dance the Macabray," an ancient ritual that the living don't remember and the dead refuse to talk about. This is a wonderful book about being human, about the meaning of death, and the comfort of friendship.[26]

GENRE-BENDING GRAPHIC NOVELS

When people think of comics in the United States, they normally think of superhero stories. And superhero stories do dominate the industry. But there have been plenty of other graphic stories published in the past fifty years. Chapter 4 of this book contains quite a few reviews of graphic novels that are taken seriously as works of literature. Most of those were fiction or adaptions of well-known prose novels, although there were a few other types discussed as well. In this chapter, I want to introduce you to graphic novels that bend the boundaries of traditional graphic novels—genres you might not have thought about before in terms of graphic storytelling. These genres include history, memoir, true crime, journalism, and western stories. These creators do a terrific job of using graphic elements to enhance the telling of these stories.

"Some people will read only one comic and decide that all comics must be bad because the one they read happened to be one of inappropriate content. They start to think all comics must be violent and gruesome. They are wrong. Not all comics are meant for kids but, they are definitely not all meant for adults. In fact most comics now have a rating clearly printed on the front or back cover. So for any parents who don't want their children introduced to violent or sexual scenes there are comics that are rated A (all ages) or T (Teens) may even be appropriate depending on the child's age. For the younger kids who are just getting into comics there are series like Marvel Heroes that are meant for a younger audience. But, just because it's written for younger kids does not mean it's a children's picture book."—Reas S., Cannon Falls, Minnesota[a]

History

Bookshelves around the world groan under the weight of nonfiction books written about historical events. Most of these are written in prose; writers must describe every little detail to draw an accurate picture in the reader's mind. Graphic history books, by contrast, immerse the reader directly into the world of the story without using all that detailed prose that can slow the story down. That's why graphic storytelling techniques are a powerful way to relate history. Following are a few of the most excellent historical comics about a variety of past events.

March: Book One

One historical comic that has won numerous awards, including the National Book Award—the first graphic novel to do so—is *March*, a trilogy of books written by Congressman John Lewis and Andrew Aydin, with art by Nate Powell. Drawn in black and white, *March* tells the story of the civil rights movement through the eyes of one of its most important leaders—John Lewis. The book begins with a bang, literally, as the reader is taken to the famous walk over the Edmund Pettus Bridge in Selma, Alabama, in 1965. Most people know that the Alabama state troopers beat up the protesters on the bridge, but the medium of the graphic novel makes readers feel like they are on the bridge with the marchers as the violence begins.

The story then cuts to the morning of January 20, 2009, as Congressman John Robert Lewis wakes up and prepares to attend the inauguration of President Barack Obama. This sets a precedent in the story for going back and forth in time, a device that works very well to tell the history and show how that history has impacted the present. As Congressman Lewis gets ready in his office, a mother walks in with her two young boys, anxious to show them a part of their history. Lewis enthusiastically tells the boys his story, beginning with taking care of—and preaching to—the chickens on his parents' farm in rural Alabama. He tells the story of his childhood, when all he wanted to do was learn, to his heading off to college. There he studies the ways of nonviolence and joins the students who stage sit-ins in Nashville department stores.

Here again the graphic portions of the novel achieve something prose alone cannot: they immerse readers in the protest in a visceral way. As the protesters are beaten, showered with hot coffee, and verbally insulted, the reality of what they faced is brought home. The black and white art is very expressive, with multiple scene and angle changes to enhance interest. Frequently panels are drawn in innovative ways or without any border at all to give special emphasis to a portion of the scene. This is not only an educational story; this is a very enjoyable comic. Each time the scene switches from 2009 to the past, some visual or spoken cue makes the transition nice and smooth without requiring a caption to tell readers where they are. This masterful work is the first of three volumes that make up the *March* trilogy.[1]

Boxers and Saints

Another masterpiece of graphic history is *Boxers and Saints* by Gene Luen Yang. You may have briefly studied the Boxers Rebellion that took place in China at the end of the nineteenth century. This book duet features the history of the Boxer Rebellion through the eyes of two young characters: one a Christian convert, the other a nationalist fighter. The two characters interact at the beginning and end of the story, but in between their paths take completely opposite directions. The brilliance of the story is that the reader can empathize with both characters; neither is the good guy or the bad guy.

The Christian convert, Vibiana, is a lonely outcast who seeks refuge in the Catholic Church. When we first meet her in *Saints*, she is named Four-Girl, which is a homonym of the word *death* because her grandfather refuses to name her. She runs away from home and becomes a caregiver in an orphanage, where she seeks to find her place in the world. Joan of Arc, who appears to her in spirit, helps her choose a path of action (figure 5.1).

In the *Boxers* portion of the story (figure 5.2), Little Bao, a romantic young boy who loves watching the operas that come to his town, gets pushed into a nationalist fervor by the very church members who have received Vibiana. As teenagers, Vibiana and Bao meet in a village that is under siege by Bao's Society of the Righteous and Harmonious Fist. Bao sends Vibiana to her end, but not before she teaches him a Christian prayer—a prayer that eventually saves his life when the Society goes to war with the foreigners in Peking.

Boxers and Saints is a gripping story that accomplishes something very unique in a historical story: it helps the reader see both sides of a conflict by humanizing the struggle. Since each group is represented by an actual person, the reader comes to see that both sides had legitimate grievances, and both sides committed atrocities. The story has a lot to teach, not only about being empathetic, but about the history of one of China's greatest identity conflicts.[2]

Tales of the Mighty Code Talkers

On November 13, 2013, the Cherokee Nation was awarded a medal recognizing the role of a group of Native Americans who provided a vital service during World War I. *Tales of the Mighty Code Talkers: We Speak in Secret* is a comic by

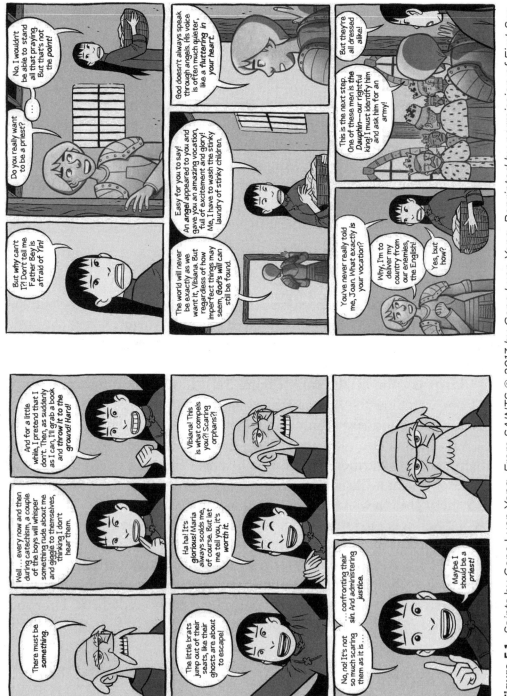

Figure 5.1. Saints by Gene Luen Yang. From SAINTS © 2013 by Gene Luen Yang. Reprinted by permission of First Second, an imprint of Roaring Brook Press, a division of Holtzbrinck Publishing Holdings Limited Partnership. All Rights Reserved.

Figure 5.2. *Boxers* by Gene Luen Yang. From BOXERS © 2013 by Gene Luen Yang. Reprinted by permission of First Second, an imprint of Roaring Brook Press, a division of Holtzbrinck Publishing Holdings Limited Partnership. All Rights Reserved.

Roy Boney that tells the story of Runabout Smoke, a Cherokee soldier in World War I. Runny, as his Cherokee friend calls him, is in a position that keeps getting hit by German artillery. He suspects the Germans are intercepting the Allies' signal—or possibly reading their minds! Out of sheer frustration, the Cherokees devise a plan to speak in their native language, which is not based on any language the Germans have heard. As they suspected, the enemy eavesdroppers are completely confused and the Allies speak freely in their new "code." The visuals in this digital comic are really interesting and the story swings back and forth between heroic and nostalgic.

You can learn quite a bit about the Cherokee soldiers in World War I in this text, including the author's interpretation of why the soldiers had volunteered in the first place—even though they were not at that time legal American citizens. "It's a good question, one full of contradictions—at first," Runabout Smoke says when asked why he joined the fight. "Once you start to examine our history, it all becomes clear. No matter the threat, we have always fought for our family—whether it's here in bloody trenches, or back home in the civil war, brother against brother . . . it's always for family. History might try to take and take from us. Sometimes it may even shed blood, but we never lose ourselves."[3]

The comic is published by Native Realities Press, formerly INC Comics. The company also produced a print comic book named *Tales of the Mighty Code Talkers: Annumpa Luma Code Talker* with story and art by Arigon Starr. This older version of *Code Talkers* is quite different from the digital comic by Roy Boney. Figure 5.3 shows a scene from Starr's version (available only in print on the website, www.nativerealities.com).

This is a compelling version of the story, and nicely illustrated.[4] Both stories can teach readers about Native American history and the contributions Native soldiers made to the war effort. And both are available in a new anthology of *Code Talkers*, published in December 2016.

Yummy

One of the best historical graphic novels I've read is *Yummy* by G. Neri, illustrated by Randy DuBurke (figure 5.4). The book won a Coretta Scott King Award for the author. Although I've called it historical, the book slides between genres. Part crime drama, part history, part psychological thriller, *Yummy* is important for many reasons. The title of the book comes from the nickname of a real teenaged gang member who was killed in Chicago in 1994. Although he is the focus of the book, Yummy is not the main character. The narrator, eleven-year-old Roger, is another boy living on the South Side of Chicago, trying to make sense of Yummy's short life and violent death.

Figure 5.3. *Annumpa Luma Code Talker* by Arigon Starr. *From Tales of the Mighty Code Talkers.* © 2014 Arigon Starr. All Rights Reserved.

As Roger reflects on Yummy's life, he delves into uncomfortable questions about whether Yummy, a gang member who shoots a fourteen-year-old girl in a gang-related crime, is the monster everyone thinks he is. The story flip-flops back and forth between Roger's quest for truth and gripping action sequences on the streets of Chicago. One of the most touching scenes in the story is when Yummy is sent to a juvenile detention facility and is abused by the older boys for carrying around his teddy bear. The symbolism of the teddy bear helps the reader see the truth of Yummy's troubled childhood. When asked to write a paper at school on the incidents surrounding Yummy's death, Roger asks, "I tried to figure out who the real Yummy was. The one who stole my lunch money? Or the one who smiled when I shared my candy with him? I wondered if I grew up like him, would I have turned out the same?"[5]

This graphic novel is regularly used in schools for social studies classes, psychology classes, and general English classes. Because there are fictional storytelling elements, the book can't technically be called nonfiction, but it follows real-life events that have been faithfully researched and retold. The result is a powerful book that uses great art to bring the reader right into the dangerous world of Yummy's South Side Chicago streets in a way that a prose telling could not.

Indeh

The slow takeover of the western United States by white settlers is a complicated story. Early Hollywood movies treated Native Americans as bloodthirsty savages and celebrated their killing as acts of heroism. Later Westerns treated Native Americans as gentle hippie types who, although they committed atrocities out of desperation, enjoyed a mystical connection with nature. Once in a while a work is produced that tells the complicated story with honesty and an understanding of the motives on both sides of the conflict. *Indeh*, written by actor/director Ethan Hawke, with art by Greg Ruth, is such a book.

Indeh tells the story of the Apache Wars in the 1870s in the United States through the lens of the white soldiers and the Apache themselves. The opening section tells the story of Goyahkla, who lost his family in a fight with the Mexicans and became the great warrior Geronimo. After fighting the Mexicans, the tribes discover a new threat to the Apache nation: the "white eyes," or white settlers from the East. In the ensuing series of fights and raids between the Apache tribes and the "blue coats," or United States Army, the story is told from both sides to give the reader perspective. Both sides committed brutal acts of violence, and the creators do a great job in showing that both sides felt justified in what they were doing. They resist the modern tendency to make it look like all the white

Figure 5.4. *Yummy* by G. Neri and Randy DuBurke. *From YUMMY, published by Lee & Low Books, Inc.* © 2010 by G. Neri. Illustrations © 2010 by Randy DuBurke. Reprinted by permission. All Rights Reserved.

characters are straight evil and all the Native characters straight good. There is complexity in all the characters.

This book will keep readers turning the page with realistic characters and gripping battle scenes. The art makes you feel like you are riding a horse through the mountains of New Mexico without using any colors. Artist Ruth achieves a depth of focus and rich detail rarely achieved in comic books. Each frame is a work of art with shading that makes each person and horse and rock look like they can be touched. This is a beautiful book with an important historical message. It is not sugarcoated, but it isn't presented as a hopeless mess of betrayals either. One of the American soldiers tries to explain to a new general why the fight has lasted as long as it has, despite the Apaches lack of nineteenth-century Euro technology and numbers: "An Apache can find water and food to live on for a year in a desert that would kill a white man inside three days," he says. "He can hide on bare ground fifty feet away so well you can't see him. . . . What you're talking about, General, is the tiger of the human species."[6] The title of the book means "the Dead" in the Apache language, a reflection on how life changed for the Apache nation due to the events of the story.

Nat Turner

Slavery is a difficult topic to talk about. The story of Nat Turner, who led a brief but explosive slave rebellion in Virginia in 1831, is especially divisive. To some people, Turner is a hero of an oppressed people, a precursor to the civil rights movement. To others he is a violent butcher who murdered innocent women and children. Almost everyone hears about him in U.S. history class, but few people know any details about his life. Kyle Baker, author and illustrator of this amazing book, aims to change that. Baker is the author of many books, including *Truth: Red, White and Black*, which is the story of the highly regarded Captain America series reviewed in chapter 3.

Baker tells Nat Turner's story in Turner's own words, using his confession as a type of narration. Other than these blocks of narration, the entire story is told in nearly wordless pictures. But how expressive those illustrations are! The faces in this book are as detailed and expressive as any faces I've encountered in any of the graphic novels highlighted in this book. The injustices and atrocities perpetrated on slaves come to life in this heavily researched story. Eight spreads that take place on a slave ship are deeply affecting, as a mother throws her new baby into the mouth of a shark to keep it from being raised in her personal hell. Likewise, life on the plantation is captured in a series of snapshots that will make you thankful that you were not a slave during that period.

Was Nat Turner a freedom fighter? Many will say so. Was he a brutal murderer? Many will say yes to this as well. What comes to light in this story that I have never heard before is Nat Turner's religious zealotry—he truly thought he heard the voice of God telling him to fulfill his destiny and rise up to gain his own freedom. Despite being a terrible soldier and haphazard battle tactician, Turner managed to get farther than anyone believed he could with his untrained, uneducated companions. Viewers of Turner's eventual hanging note how calm and still he was as he was executed, a further sign of his religious devotion. This brings up a warning: this book contains some graphic violence which may bother some younger teens (in truth, I hope it bothers older teens, too).

A note on the jacket cover says the art in this edition is "now colored in duotone from the original digital files." The second color gives it a warmth and richness not possible in black and white. This book is one of the most affecting graphic novels I have read in my journey and I highly recommend it.[7]

True Crime Stories

Crime comics became popular in the 1940s and have never gone away. Murder mystery is still a popular form now that graphic novels have by and large replaced serial comics. Solving crimes is rich soil for graphic storytelling. One true crime story caught the attention of reviewers a few years back because the book was written by the son of the detective who spent years trying to identify and catch a serial killer.

Green River Killer

On the cover of *Green River Killer: A True Detective Story* by Jeff Jensen, illustrated by Jonathon Case, is an endorsement from famous novelist Stephen King: "The novel as a whole makes compelling stay-up-late reading. Great, creepy stuff." The "creepy stuff" is the story of a detective trying to catch one of the most notorious murderers in U.S. history—Seattle's so-called Green River Killer—who was responsible for killing more than forty-eight women and girls in the 1980s. In the book's brief and terrifying opening, the murderer, Gary Ridgeway, appears as a handsome young man who murders a young boy in cold blood. Stephen King calls it "the scariest opening sequence I've read in years."

After the prologue, the focus switches to the detective who worked for twenty years to bring him to justice. The real story begins in 2003 as Tom Jenson, a detective in the King County sheriff's department, is preparing for a strange visitor—Gary Ridgeway—who will be living in the sheriff's office for a month to try and answer some burning questions. Questions such as "Why did you do it?" and "Where are the rest of the bodies?" The story jumps back and forth between 2003 and the 1980s as Jensen and his family try to cope with the stress of the responsibility of trying to catch the killer. The writer, Jeff Jensen, knows all about that stress, as he is the detective's son and lived through the ordeal. The tension mounts as Ridgeway tries—and fails—to lead the police to the bodies he has buried twenty years earlier. In the end, Jensen is only mostly convinced Ridgeway is the real killer.

The author writes in the back matter of the book: "*Green River Killer: A True Detective Story* is . . . not intended as history or memoir." That's because he has created dialogue that had not been recorded, and he reimagined some of the characters for the sake of a streamlined story. Jensen goes on to say, "The Green River Killer's victims were prostitutes, but to their families they were daughters, sisters, and mothers. They stand for a larger group of women and children victimized through sex and labor exploitation, brought into prostitution by force, fraud, and coercion."[8] Readers who enjoy detective stories will like this book, as well as history buffs who want to get inside the mind of the detective and the killer himself.

Memoirs

According to author Matilda Butler, in a post on *Creative Writing Ideas Blog*, a memoir differs from an autobiography in the sense that an autobiography includes lots of different events in a person's life crammed together chronologically. A memoir, by contrast, is "a slice of your life. It could be just one time period, and it could be just one aspect of your life. For instance if you have diabetes, it might go across multiple years, and you might look at the diagnosis and how you manage. You might decide, I am not talking about the other things that happened to me. I am not talking about my relationships. I am not talking about my education. I am talking about living with diabetes."[9] The story is focused around one aspect of a person's life. The following books are great examples of memoirs told in graphic art.

Tomboy

A great example of this life story told with a focus, and a great graphic novel, is *Tomboy* by Liz Prince (figure 5.5). *Tomboy* is the story of Prince's life as she struggles with understanding society's gender expectations for a woman, then learning to disregard them. Prince reveals in the opening spread that, even as a little girl, she threw temper tantrums when forced to wear a dress. Her boyish

Figure 5.5. *Tomboy* by Liz Prince. *From Tomboy, published by Zest Books. © 2014 by Liz Prince. All rights reserved.*

outfits and behavior led to bullying and misunderstanding growing up, but she eventually learned to be comfortable in her own skin. Throughout the book she is labeled a she/he, a lesbian, and many other things as her peers attempt to put her in a box. As she grows, she crushes on boys who like her, and boys she thinks of as friends reveal crushes on her. Through all the drama, she continues to wonder, "What kind of girl am I? Should I have been born a boy? Why do I feel like I do?"

> "Since the 1930s, comics have been witty and thought provoking when it comes to issues like racial tension and gay rights. People discover themselves within them, just like I found myself in the Runaways."—Emma S., Plymouth, Minnesota[b]

Eventually she meets tomboys like her and embraces her idiosyncrasies. At the end of the story, grownup Liz says, "What a revelation I'd had . . . I subscribed to the idea that there was only one form of femininity and that it was inferior to being a man. I don't want to be a girl on society's terms . . . I want to be a girl on my terms."[10] The art in *Tomboy* is very clean and enjoyable. The conflicts and struggles throughout the book make it an interesting read, and the conclusion has something to teach all ages and genders.

Persepolis

Another of the masters of the graphic memoir for teens is Marjane Satrapi. Her book *Persepolis* tells the story of growing up in Iran immediately before and after the Islamic Revolution of 1978. Although some of the main movers and shakers of the revolution possessed a socialist or communist bent, a group of fundamentalist Muslims took power in the country. For educated, secular families like the Satrapis, this meant women were required to wear the veil, pretending to be religious, or even fleeing the country. As family and friends either left the country, experienced death in the subsequent war with Iraq, or had family members thrown in prison, the teenage Marji grows up quickly.

Satrapi is a master of pacing and visual storytelling. In one spread, she uses a seething crowd of deliriously happy people, all wearing vibrant designs, to bring home the ecstasy of the celebration when the Shah was overthrown. On the very next page, she uses a symbolic frame—made up of a snake—to show that evil is never far away, and is in fact closing in on the family even as they celebrate. The impact is magnified by the contrast between the monster about to strangle them and her parents' flippant conversation. Her dad proclaims, "Let's enjoy our new

Students Talk *Persepolis*

Students from a high school English class that had studied *Persepolis* were asked what they liked and didn't like about the graphic novel. Here is what they said:

- "I liked how you can connect to the characters through the emotions displayed on the page, compared to just reading about it" (Timothy, 17).
- "I liked how they went over life in Iran from a teen/preteen's point of view" (Lucas, 18).
- "I liked that it was on a topic I didn't know much about that showed view points from a child to an adult" (Olivia, 18).
- "I liked the story and then it helped me picture some of the stuff that I am not used to seeing better" (Justin, 18).
- "It told a good story from a point of view that I could relate to. Liked the cliffhanger ending" (Amelia, 18).
- "It helped visualize the story and reach the reader. Didn't like bland character and story" (Dane, 18).
- "It was good to change up the style of books we read in English but it got a little boring at parts" (Chris, 18).
- "Liked learning about the culture" (Damon, 18).
- "It taught some great lessons and showed us how there isn't that much global awareness between different countries" (Crispin, 18).
- "I enjoyed the simplicity of the art style, for it served as juxtaposition for the intensity and maturity of the storytelling" (Ashlyn, 18).
- "It was easy to read and I like how I was able to understand it. But I didn't like how the narrator or main person was so easily influenced" (Destiny, 18).
- "It was a fun and easy read. It had a lot of fun and interesting events that happened within the book and gave great insight on the actual events that had occurred in Iran. This book though could sometimes get slow at points but overall great book" (Austyn, 17).
- "I like the use of visuals to illustrate the events occurring in Iran" (Connor, 17).

- "[Liked] the realness of the book, they didn't sugarcoat the events. I didn't really like the length, I felt the book could have been longer" (Anthony, 18).
- "I like how the book engaged the audience with the comics. I didn't like the lack of words" (Natalie, 18).
- "It conveyed a powerful message about a powerful topic while still keeping a witty sense of humor" (Alex, 18).
- "It gave a whole new perspective of how a normal girl went through a dramatic change in her country rather than hearing news on the TV" (Alina, 18).
- "I liked how it was easier to read and how you can make it more of a movie in your head. What I didn't like is how it was hard to follow sometimes because there wasn't any description to explain to you what was going on" (Makayla, 18).
- "I liked the content and how much I learned. I didn't like all of the pictures because not all of them made sense" (Bailey, 18).[c]

freedom!" and is answered by her mother, "Now that the devil has left!" All the while, a serpent or dragon is encircling them and staring at them out of the corner of its beady eyes. The impact of the entire spread is very powerful.

Persepolis is being used in classrooms for many reasons: as a history education tool; as a literary masterpiece; and as an example of accomplished visual story-telling. The art style is bold and straightforward, without a lot of environmental detail, which has the effect of highlighting the characters and the action in the story. This is important because concentrating on the Iranian backdrop might cause some readers to make judgments before they get to know the characters in the story. Students come to like the story because it's fast paced and written in the perspective of a teenager like themselves. Caution: younger readers should be aware that some parts of the story contain explicit violence, such as a torture scene. The scene is important for the background of the story, but it may be intense for some readers.[11]

Comics Journalism

Closely related to memoir graphic novels are journalistic graphic novels, or comics journalism. You haven't heard of any of those? That's because there aren't

"The comic book creators were like the journalists and reporters of the Vietnam War, who felt it was their duty to enlighten the people to the true nature of the war. The Vietnam War was a tumultuous time in American history; it represented America finally growing up. As the country grew up, we lost the childlike innocence and plunged into a nostalgic and cynical view of the world. All of American society was affected, especially the comic book writers. In their stories the Superheroes reflected the pain and problems that America was experiencing. No longer did superheroes fight for the American way, they began to question their own role on the earth; just as America did. The Vietnam War changed America and its superheroes."—Olivia R., La Jolla, California[d]

many out there. Taking a medium that many people don't take very seriously to begin with and trying to use it to relate an "accurate" account of historical events is a stretch for many readers. Nevertheless the use of comics to tell nonfiction events, especially recent events, is growing. There are now several print journals and online sites dedicated to comics journalism. Check out the website the Nib (medium.com/the-nib) if you want to see some entertaining and educational comics journalism.

Palestine Series

Joe Sacco is one of the pioneers of comics journalism. In late 1991 and early 1992, Sacco spent two months with Palestinian people in the Occupied Territories in the Middle East. When he returned to the United States, he began to write about the conversations and events he had witnessed. He used graphic storytelling to appeal to the widest possible group of readers. The classification of this book is difficult, as with all nonfiction books. Can every word be authenticated? That is not possible, although the events he records are easily corroborated in other sources. He mentions that he takes notes during conversations but he is relying on his memory to make the conversations accurate. In the end, I don't think it's important to quibble over whether *Palestine* is truly nonfiction. The truth of the series is apparent and reading the accounts of the suffering Palestinians will help shed light on one angle of the situation that rarely receives any attention. Sacco's nine-issue comics series won a 1996 American Book Award.

Reading *Palestine* takes time. Most of the pages are crammed with either narration in captions or dense conversations in dialogue bubbles. Not a lot happens per se, although Sacco records many trips and visits to people in Jerusalem and in the Occupied Territories. He has many confrontations with Israeli soldiers and Palestinian extremists, which give the account an air of danger and intrigue. Many of the events you learn about secondhand, from people suffering in a hospital or strangers the author meets on the street or with whom he shares a cup of tea. The account ends in a very disconcerting way, with his bus driver lost and asking directions from locals.

The last page ends with high tension. As the bus wanders into a Palestinian town, the situation grows dangerous: "You could see the kids in the distance taking cover on each side of the road. . . . If we continued that way, we were going to get stoned. . . . The driver backed the bus up and turned it around. . . . He stopped at a small army post an asked for more directions."[12] This ending is significant because Sacco doesn't treat the conflict between the Israelis and the Palestinians as if one side is completely at fault. Although the Palestinians have been sorely mistreated, the story ends with Palestinian youths about to stone his bus. This is a true-to-life story that tries to shed light on oppression but refuses to bring easy solutions where there are none.

A.D.: New Orleans after the Deluge

What was life like in New Orleans after Hurricane Katrina in 2005? You may have heard news reports about it or met a classmate who had family in New Orleans at that time. But hearing news reports is not as impactful as actually following the stories of victims of the disaster. Cartoonist Josh Neufeld has created a hard-hitting comic book that tells the stories of five people (and their families) who experienced the hurricane and its aftermath. As if to answer any doubters that this is true journalism, Neufeld explains in the afterword how he met all the people in the book and what they are doing now.

The opening of the book takes us from a serene view of earth from space, with a smattering of clouds over all the continents in view. As we move in closer to the southeastern United States we begin to see a swirl of clouds beginning to form over Florida and the Caribbean. We move closer still to view the city of New Orleans, then a particular neighborhood with a canal running between two walls. In a dramatic panel we notice a breach with a surge of water beginning to bust out. Then we see the neighborhood underwater. This is the story in a nutshell and we haven't even met any characters.

After this ominous introduction we meet the characters: Leo and Michelle, twenty-somethings who decide to leave before the storm hits and head to Houston; the middle-aged doctor, who rides out the storm in his home with his friends; Kwame, a high school senior who can't leave town until his father, a pastor, finishes his Sunday morning service; Abbas, a convenience store owner who waits out the storm with a pistol to discourage looters; and Denise, who must take care of her mother, her niece, and her niece's baby in the midst of the flood. We see them all before the storm, during the storm, and after the storm. Some of the scenes are truly heartbreaking, for instance, when Denise and her family arrive at the convention center, only to find it bursting at the seams with people who have nowhere to go. They had been picturing a place of respite, only to find an overcrowded shelter with no plumbing or water for the mass of refugees. You will never think of the Hurricane Katrina disaster in the same way after reading *A.D.: New Orleans after the Deluge*.[13]

Faction

In recent years, literary critics have been discussing a new genre—if it is really a genre at all—called faction. The word is a combination of *fact* and *fiction*. It either puts real characters in a fictional setting or treats real historical characters as if they were fictional characters. I don't know what genre the recent graphic novel *Trashed* would be, but as I understand the definition of faction, it seems to fit.

Trashed

The author and illustrator of *Trashed*, Derf Backderf, can talk trash with the best of them. He worked as a garbage collector in 1979–1980. After writing some shorter pieces based on his experience, he decided to write a long-form graphic novel about the business of garbage. But instead of making it autobiographical, he decided to create a work of fiction loosely based on events he experienced as a trash collector. So why am I not calling it fiction? Because of the educational piece, which appears on almost every page. By the time you're done with *Trashed*, you will know more than you ever thought possible about Americans' "throw away" culture. But few people would read a simple informational pamphlet on garbage, so Backderf sets the information in a humorous, engaging story about a young man who becomes a garbage man.

The main character in this story is J.B., a twenty-one-year-old college dropout who is looking for a way to make some money so he can move out of his parents' house. He and his buddy, Mike, get jobs at the village municipal department picking up trash. As the friends learn the job, they are confronted by one hilarious incident after another and get to know the very quirky civil servants who perform the jobs no one in town ever notices—until they screw up. Readers get to see the real life of garbage men in our country, from loading an entire piano into the truck and then hearing it "sing" as it gets crushed to being deliberately scraped off the truck onto a mailbox by the driver.

Along the way, the author lectures about our garbage habits and where they're taking us. As J.B. and the crew struggle through Heavy Trash Day, the author makes his point:

> Built-in obsolescence keeps the economy humming. Many economists argue it's a vital component of the system. We never stop replacing stuff, stores never stop selling stuff, and factories never stop making stuff. The downside, of course, is we also never stop throwing stuff away.[14]

Far from making the book boring, readers will never quite see their trash habits the same way. An entertaining story keeps us reading, great art helps us enjoy the story, and important information will hopefully help us change our habits. Caution: some strong language and sexual innuendo make this more appropriate for older teens.

Horror

Let's face it—most people love the spine-tingling feeling of watching a horror movie or reading a scary book. Horror comics combine the visuals of movies with the dialogue and pacing of a prose novel, making it the perfect medium for scary stories. Indeed, the horror genre has been well developed since the late 1940s and 1950s, when superhero comics fell out of popular favor after World War II. Titles such as *Tales from the Crypt*, *The Vault of Horror*, and *Weird Science* scintillated audiences with their dark portrayals of evil and the dark side of science. In fact, many readers of the day felt that the comics companies had gone overboard with gratuitous violence and gore.

This outrage was one of the contributing factors to the advent of the Comics Code Authority, or CCA. This symbol became the publishers' way of demonstrating to the public that they were restraining certain kinds of material in their books and magazines. Nevertheless, comics publishers never quit writing and illustrating horror stories, because the reading public can't get enough. The following are a few of the best horror comics I've come across. Please note that some horror comics are more appropriate for older teen audiences.

Saga of the Swamp Thing

There really is something out there . . . *Saga of the Swamp Thing*, published in 1983, is written by Alan Moore, with art by Stephen Bissette and John Totleben (figure 5.6). The comic is equal parts horror, superhero, and romance. The presence of monsters, demons, and mad scientists gives the book a spine-shivering vibe that only comes with a horror or monster comic. Yet it's got villains trying

Figure 5.6. *Saga of the Swamp Thing* by Alan Moore, Stephen Bissette, and John Totleben. *All DC comic artwork, its characters and related elements are ™ & © DC Comics.*

to take over the world and the presence of the Justice League to lead readers into thinking it's a superhero romp. And a growing relationship with a damsel in distress provides just enough spark to *almost* make it a romance. *Saga of the Swamp Thing* is a restart of the original DC comic from the 1970s by Len Wein and Bernie Wrightson.

The story of the so-called Swamp Thing, formerly known as Alec Holland, is about a monster who has just recently discovered that he is, in fact, not human. He is a walking, thinking, loving, and incredibly strong plant-being-thingy. This absence of humanness allows him the freedom to be totally plant, but also leaves a lonely hole where he once had human relationships.

After a prologue that wraps up an old story line, the book opens with a monologue by Dr. Jason Woodrue (a.k.a. the Floronic Man), who is responsible for reviving the Swamp Thing and setting him loose in the world. As a plant-man hybrid, Woodrue seeks to use the Swamp Thing's connection to the plant world in order to control its power. Or is he being controlled by the green, as he claims? Either way, he wants to take over the world, like all memorable supervillains. The Swamp Thing must decide whether he wants to defeat Woodrue and save humanity, even though he has recently discovered that he is no longer a part of the human race.

As Woodrue wreaks havoc on the planet by raising oxygen levels, the Justice League is called in. Although superpowered, they have no idea how to deal with a villain who is being controlled by the world's plant life. Fortunately, the Swamp Thing decides to intervene, partly due to his fondness for Abby Cable, an old friend who is stuck in an abusive and unhappy marriage. Other villains join in the fun, including the antihero demon Etrigan and a monster who embodies and feeds on the fear of humans. By various means, the Swamp Thing manages to subdue them all. These stories are beautifully written and illustrated, making it a book that is on many lists of "essential graphic novels."[15]

Bad Island

While we're on the subject of there being "something out there," imagine you were out on a sailboat with your family and a raging storm suddenly appeared and drove you onto an uninhabited island. And what if that island turned out to be . . . alive! *Bad Island* is part (light) horror comic, part adventure, part family drama, and all entertainment.

Reese is playing football with his friends when his dad announces the family is going on a boat trip so that he, his mom and dad, and his little sis can spend some "together" time. Reese figures he's old enough to stay by himself, so argues vociferously that he should be allowed to stay home. Mom is not thrilled about the trip either, as her rare orchids might be in danger. Little sis Janie just wants someone to help her find her pet snake Pickles. All the members of this dysfunctional family have their own problems, but they must put them aside when their boat is driven onto a mysterious island at sea. They encounter one monster after another on the island as they try and figure out where they are and what they are supposed to do with a mysterious artifact they find in a dead guy's traveling bag. They will have to learn to work together or be destroyed by the alien life trying desperately to keep them from discovering the treasure they have found.

Author/illustrator Doug TenNapel has created several comics for kids and teens. His art is really attractive and his stories move along an entertaining clip. The dialogue is true to character and filled with humor. After running away from a rock monster, the likes of which they've (of course) never seen before, Reese's mom tells him to stay away from rocks. Reese answers, "Well, if I find the dangerous kind again, it will be a good chance for me to practice my karate moves on it." Mom answers, "I didn't think it was possible to make me even more worried! Thanks, Reese." He replies, "No problem, Mom. It's a gift."[16] Nice moments like that between family members show their developing relationships, even as the action crashes around them. If this is horror, it's what I would call heartwarming horror.

Through the Woods

You've heard ghost stories—those frighteningly real stories that people tell in the darkness of the woods at night, or in the gloom of a basement at a sleepover. Well, Emily Carroll is a master of the ghost story. But this is not just hearing the story, when you read *Through the Woods*, you see it in all its spine-tingling splendor. Using moody illustrations and vivid, although minimal, colors, Carroll creates the perfect mood for her tales. Warning: if you choose to read these stories by yourself in a lonely house at night, you may end up sleeping with a nightlight!

This is a book of five separate stories, plus an introduction and an epilogue. The first is called "Our Neighbor's House" and features three sisters who are left alone when their father goes away. They are told to visit their neighbor's house if Father does not return in three days. Well, wonder of wonders, he does not return. One by one the girls dream of a man knocking on the door at night, and one by one the girls disappear until only the oldest is left. She ventures to the neighbor's house to see if she can find her sisters. The second story, "A Lady's Hands Are Cold," features a newly married woman who hears a macabre song in the night about a woman who was killed by her husband. The new bride, going

"Comics are more than that; they have very good, detailed, and well thought out stories and characters. They could easily be turned into full length novels if wanted and some have been. Whereas a picture book only has one or two sentences a page and could never be a full length novel. 'Comics are just as complex as any other literature' [quote from researcher Carol Tilley]."—Reas S., Cannon Falls, Minnesota[e]

mad, finally takes the house apart and finds a pair of cold hands in the wall, arms in the attic, and other body parts in different places. She ties these body parts together and discovers a chilling secret. The other stories are equally frightening and beautifully drawn. These tales are one part romance, two parts horror, all totally engaging—if you don't mind sleeping with the light on.[17]

Locke and Key, *Volume 1:* Welcome to Lovecraft

One of the most well-plotted and dialogued horror stories I have come across is the *Locke and Key* series written by Joe Hill, with art by Gabriel Rodriguez. It is truly scary with its blend of murder, ghosts, mysteries, and a house with doorways that lead to unexpected places. The writing is superb, as themes keep popping up when you least expect them. The art is terrific and terrifying—definitely not for the faint of heart! Caution: this series is geared toward older teens with graphic violence, rough language, and sexual content.

Two teens show up to the door of a house in the very first panel on the top left side of the opening spread. I mention this because comics is unique in its layout—you can see the entire spread as you turn the page and must choose which panel to read first. This is used to unique advantage in this story, especially on this spread. Even as you look to the top left side of the spread at the faces of the boys, you can't help seeing the same scene at the bottom right of the spread, shown in a long-angle shot from behind the teens' pickup truck in the driveway. In the bed of the truck are two gruesomely murdered bodies covered haphazardly with a tarp. So you are looking forward and backward in time all at once—this is an example of the brilliance of this well-designed graphic story.

The story is told through multiple points of view, but mainly through that of the youngest member of the story, a boy named Bode. He is the youngest of three siblings (with the last name Locke) who suffer the loss of their father due to his murder by the two teens mentioned in the last paragraph. One of the murderers gets put in a juvenile psychiatric ward, from which he naturally escapes. By hitchhiking and performing sexual favors (this, along with the graphic depiction of violence, leads to my older recommendation for the book), the murderer finds the family on the East Coast in a mysterious mansion with magic doors that cause unexpected consequences when a character walks through them. One mysterious character, a woman living in a well whom only Bode can see, is freed by a mysterious key and returns at the end of this volume as a boy who befriends the kids. The muted colors in this book and the beautiful art—most panels look like detailed woodcuts—make it a pleasure to read, although the tale is truly spine-tingling.[18]

Pinocchio, Vampire Slayer

Yes, you read that correctly. Van Jensen and Dusty Higgins have taken the original Pinocchio story, before Disney and others got ahold of it, and turned it into a vampire hunting story. In a uniquely rough black-and-white style, the creators have made an entertaining tale for readers who like monsters and monster hunters. The use of a dot-shading technique to create a grayscale gives the book a sort of retro feel that hearkens back to the old superhero stories that used to be shaded using a similar technique.

After a quick introduction to the original legend, the "real" wooden boy and his ward, Master Cherry, arm themselves to hunt down the monsters who have killed his maker, Geppetto. Cherry's impressive-looking weapon is humorously named the Monsterminator, and it does what it is advertised to do. Until Cherry is killed by a vampire, of course. Ironically, the vampire who kills Cherry reveals himself to be Geppetto, who has been turned into a monster. Pinocchio mercifully kills him to free him of his curse, and with the Blue Fairy (in an older version than some of the more recent retellings), continues in his quest to destroy the creatures threatening the town. Although the violence in this book is not much different than other stories, the depiction of people being hung might upset some readers, so be advised.[19]

Science Fiction/Fantasy

A lot of superhero comics could be labeled as science fiction and fantasy. But there are also a lot of science fiction and fantasy comics that don't contain any superheroes. Science fiction tries to see into the future and what it will look like. Fantasy can take place anywhere, but must follow the author's internal rules. The following are a few excellent examples.

Zita the Space Girl

If you found a remote-control thingy (with a giant red button on it) inside a hole made by an asteroid (or something), would you push it? Zita does! Despite the frightened protests of her friend Joseph, Zita presses the button, whereupon Joseph disappears through a space/time warp to an entirely different planet. Zita must follow after him and bring him home, which is easier said than done. Along the way, she meets a band of companions to help her in her quest: Piper, a flute-playing man who abandons her when things get tough; a flying war orb named simply One; a giant mouse who prefers to be called Mouse rather than his real name, Pizzicato; and a rusty old robot named Randy who lacks confidence but secretly contains the weapon necessary to save their planet from an approaching asteroid.

Zita the Space Girl, which is written and illustrated by Ben Hatke, is a beautiful and exciting story. With themes of friendship and self-sacrifice, this book is a heartwarming read as well as a fun one. The book has a powerful ending, as Zita gives up her ride home, so to speak, sending Joseph home with the last power of the time-traveling crystal from the remote control. Luckily, Piper has had a change of heart—and he has a ship so that the friends can continue their adventures.[20]

Castle Waiting

Fairy tales and legends are the source of many artistic endeavors: movies, books, plays, paintings, you name it. Many comic books, too, have used fables and fairy tales as their source material. *Castle Waiting*, by Linda Medley, makes use of the Snow White legend to start the story off. But this is the town of Putney, which for a while enjoyed good fortune and great leadership from a wise king and queen. But alas, the royal couple could not bear a child. So the king seeks out a school of witches to obtain a charm. The humor in this volume is apparent as the wide-eyed king asks the old lady if the liquid she's holding in her hand is a magic potion. Her answer: "Generally, it's not a good idea to ask a witch what she's cooking . . . however, I'm just making toffee for the little ones."

Unfortunately for the king and the kingdom, a rival witch becomes jealous of the "business" brought by the king (hey, witches have to make a living, too) and curses the daughter who is eventually born. The curse gets softened from death to eternal sleep to be broken only by the kiss of a prince. The real story occurs after these events, as a wandering pregnant woman finds the reawakened castle (minus the princess who has long since left with the prince who woke her). The cast of characters at the castle is loveable and mysterious: a steward who is a stork-man; a nun with a beard; a cook with her simpleton son; a doctor who wears a mask and collects peoples' hair to make magic potions; and a horse-man who is a warrior champion. Yes, there is a lot of drama and humor in *Castle Waiting*!

A good portion of this volume is occupied with telling the stories of characters at Castle Waiting. In particular, the nun with a beard, Sister Peace, tells the story of her happy years at an abbey of other bearded women. Most of these women had been outcasts but found a place with the Solicitine Sisters, who make it a point to follow the intent of their patron saint by giving people what they need, not necessarily what they want. *Castle Waiting* is a delightful tale about redemption and the beauty of tolerance, drawn in beautiful, detailed black-and-white art. A word on form here: normally it is not recommended to tell a flashback within a flashback because the reader can get lost; when a particular story comes to a conclusion and the reader goes "back" to the present, he might get confused when the present is still embedded within a story being told by a character in the actual present. But Linda Medley pulls it off in a very entertaining fashion.[21]

Foiled

Most people only think about the sport of fencing—sword fighting—when the Summer Olympics comes on TV every four years. But the main character of *Foiled*, written by veteran children's author Jane Yolen, with art by Mike Cavallaro, features a high school student who is an accomplished fencer. She is not so accomplished in dating, however, which leads to some epic adventures as the story progresses. A foil is a type of weapon that is thinner and lighter than other types of swords. The double entendre in the title is interesting, referring both to the type of weapon Aliera competes with and to the complications to her plans to get a date with Avery, a cute boy in her school.

This graphic novel is a good example of a first-person point of view. Not only does Aliera (who is colorblind) tell her own story, but she actually breaks the "fourth wall" by looking straight at the reader (or the camera, depending on how you want to look at it) and delivering lines right to the audience. This helps the reader feel the frustration Aliera experiences when Avery, now her lab partner, flirts with her and she just stutters in response. Aliera's life runs a predictable and boring course until the day Avery asks her out on a date. They meet at Grand Central Station in New York, but Aliera's world is thrown into chaos when she dons her fencing helmet in the station and sees colors for the first time . . . as well as fairies and goblins and other mythical creatures! The creators use color for the first time in this otherwise monochrome comic, and the experience is shocking to the senses, as it is to Aliera. We have literally seen the world through her eyes— merely shades of gray—until she puts on the helmet and sees color.

There are many reasons to read *Foiled*, not the least of which is because it is entertaining and beautifully drawn. But you can also study how comics creators use foreshadowing, suspense building, changing color palettes, panel variation, and many other tools to make a good graphic story. Jane Yolen has achieved greatness in many other genres, and now she shows her prowess in comics. At the end of the story, the beautiful red queen promises Aliera that Avery, who turns out to be a troll (literally), must come to her aid in her future adventures. Maybe it isn't the date she was looking for, but this defender gets marching orders for future adventures.[22]

Amulet, *Book 1:* The Stonekeeper

Author/illustrator Kazu Kibuishi has had a huge impact on the graphic storytelling industry. Not only with his graphic novels but as editor and promotor of short graphic story volumes such as *Flight* and *Explorer* (see the reviews later in this chapter). But Kibuishi is best known for his *New York Times* best-selling series *Amulet*. At first glance, readers may think the story is for younger children because the characters in the story are kids, but readers of all ages enjoy it. Indeed, several high school libraries I've visited contain copies of *Amulet* and are enjoyed by older teens on a regular basis.

Kibuishi has a special gift for beautiful art. Every panel could be framed and sold as fine art. Especially beautiful are his splash pages and full spread illustrations. Such a spread occurs on the last page of the book. I don't want to ruin it for you, but suffice it to say you will never see another spread that looks anything like this one. The author includes these larger illustrations sparingly, but when you turn the page and see them, they are breathtaking.

Emily and Navin have just lost their father in a tragic car accident. When they move into a creepy old house "out in the middle of nowhere" with their mom, the wheels of the story begin to turn. Emily finds a strange amulet, which she puts around her neck. When her mom gets kidnapped by a strange creature in the middle of the night, the children descend an old staircase and find themselves in a strange new world. The amulet has special powers and gives them instructions to save their mom. They aren't sure whether to trust it or not, which is a foreshadowing of the struggle in future volumes. A hooded figure saves them from trouble and leads them to a house full of strange but loveable characters to help them on their quest. Emily is dismayed to discover that she is the subject of an ancient prophecy that she is "The One" who will free the land of Alledia from tyranny. Navin, who turns out to be quite a pilot—also a foreshadowing of future adventures—flies the team through a dangerous tunnel where they attempt to save their mother. But their adventures are only just beginning as the story ends—and the entire house stands up and begins to walk! (Sorry, I said I wasn't going to ruin it, and then I did. Read the book, you'll understand why it's a best seller!)[23]

Godzilla: History's Greatest Monster

This volume collects the first thirteen issues of IDW's popular series *Godzilla*, which came out in 2014. The writing, by Duane Swierczynski, is unique in that it tries to set up this monster story with real, three-dimensional characters. The story opens in Mexico City, where a giant spider ruins the wedding of Urv, a former soldier. Like all the other characters in this book, Urv loses a loved one to monster mayhem—in this case, it is his husband who is killed. The next character we meet is Boxer, who is a bodyguard for a rich family. He, too, has lost a loved one—his daughter—which gives him a strong motivation to form a monster hunting squad that turns out to be pretty effective. The group has developed a sort of ray gun with a "headache beam" that renders the monster inoperative until they can move in heavier equipment.

While the story is engaging, it's the art (by Simon Gane) that really stands out in this series, especially at the end. Joshua, an eighteen-year-old student writing in the magazine *VOYA*, complained that the opening chapters didn't have enough monster action: "Godzilla, Volume 1 is rather disappointing. For starters, the title is a lie, at least for this volume, because you hardly get to see him. He's in a few panels, but that's just about it."[24] I can understand Joshua's complaint but this volume collects more stories, and the art at the end of the monsters fighting is both beautiful and epic. While it has a gritty reality to it, the colors are vibrant and the detail is amazing. The last section, in which the world is coming to an end until Godzilla and a few of his pals show up to destroy the monsters trying to destroy the planet, is breathtaking. Boxer, after helping save the world, goes after Godzilla by jumping into his mouth with a giant gun. In the last panel, the monster is seen swimming away. Has Boxer destroyed Godzilla, or has the man been destroyed by the monster? It seems there are more adventures to come.[25]

Think Tank

The front cover of *Think Tank*, by Matt Hawkins, with art by Rahsan Ekedal, claims, "Reading this book will make you smarter." I don't know if I'm any smarter, but my imagination is definitely expanded! The author says in the back matter that he wants "people to like science." He describes touring government research facilities, and even the declassified gadgets make you feel "like you're stepping into the future." His adventure/science fiction series will teach you a lot about science but will also thoroughly entertain you!

The protagonist of the story, Dr. David Loren, is a genius in his midtwenties who has been working in a secure research and development lab since he graduated early from Cal Tech. He seems more of a prisoner than a scientist, however. Dr. Loren builds weapons for the U.S. military to use in its operations overseas. He has seen firsthand what those weapons can do and he's had enough. He wants out, only he's too valuable to be let go. And the truth is, he enjoys creating things—even destructive things. His supervising officer, Colonel Harrison, nails this as he brings the young doctor home from an unsupervised night on the town (figure 5.7): "I know your type," the colonel says through gritted teeth, "The thought of your inventions killing people makes you want to pretend that you don't live for this. . . . You may not like it, but don't fool yourself . . . you love it."[26]

Nevertheless, Dr. Loren plans a brilliant and entertaining escape that rivals any spy thriller in prose or on screen. Using inventions that his superiors think are total failures, Loren escapes and takes his girlfriend—who is being questioned by interrogators—with him. The suspense in this section is incredible, as the two lovers run from one impossible situation to another, outwitting the military at every turn. Or do they? I will not ruin the twist at the end, but suffice it to say, David Loren may not be as much in control of his own fate as he thinks he is!

Hybrid Graphic/Prose Novels

In recent years, prose authors who have recognized the power of comics have begun incorporating sequential art sequences into their books. There is no rule about how much of the book has to be graphic to be recognized as a hybrid graphic/prose novel. But the rule of thumb is that there needs to be a narrative reason to include the graphic sections, such as a dream sequence or a part of the story that can't be told by a character for some reason (like he's a squirrel and can't talk).

The Invention of Hugo Cabret

Possibly the most famous hybrid of recent decades is *The Invention of Hugo Cabret* by Brian Selznick. The book, which states on the title page that it is "a novel in words and pictures," won a host of awards after it was published in 2007, including the prestigious Caldecott Medal for illustration in children's books. Rather than opening the book with prose to explain the world of the characters, the author-illustrator chose to start with pictures. And although the pictures all encompass an entire page instead of using smaller panels, the sequential art is still considered comics, according to Scott McCloud's definition (explained in chapter 1).

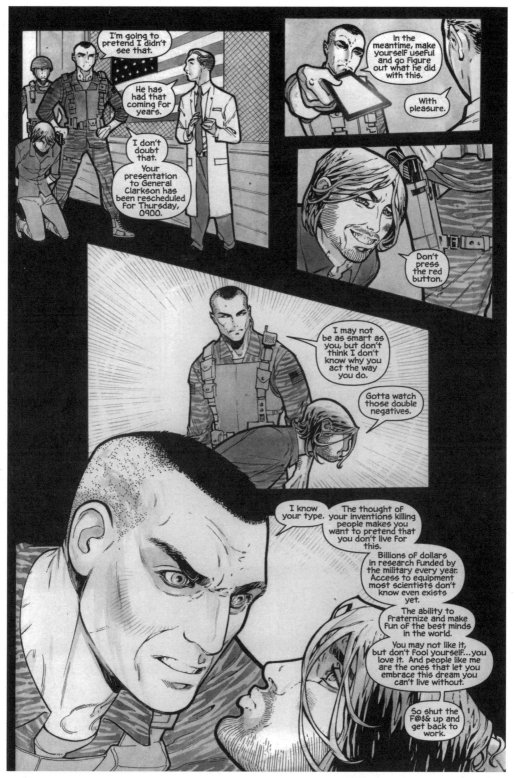

Figure 5.7. *Think Tank* by Matt Hawkins and Rahsan Ekedal. *From* Think Tank *by Matt Hawkins and Rahsan Ekedal © 2013 Image Comics. All rights reserved.*

The opening sequence begins with a close-up of the moon, a symbol that will be important later in the story. The pictures then focus on a twelve-year-old boy in a crowded train station in Paris and follow him into the walls where he lives, unseen by the people who frequent the station. The sequence ends with a close-up of the eye of filmmaker Georges Melies, who will become a father figure to the protagonist, Hugo. The beautiful artwork is drawn in a unique, old-fashioned way, in a style that is explained on the very last page of the book.

One of the most striking sequences in the book is near the end when Hugo escapes from the custody of the stationmaster and accidentally falls onto the tracks, right in the path of an approaching train. With each page turn, the engine gets closer and closer, and the detail on the nose of the engine becomes clearer and clearer. Another hybrid author, Swati Avasthi, whose interview appears later in this chapter, notes that the "visceral, physical response to that is so different than a scene with a train bearing down on you in prose." Indeed, as the train gets so close you can see the number and count the rivets on the front, you can't help but feel a little claustrophobic. Which is why the last picture in the sequence is so beautiful and tension releasing (I won't ruin it for you).

As with all the works for younger readers that I've included in this book, *Hugo Cabret* is not just for kids—it is a book for all ages. Everyone can relate to the feelings of loneliness Hugo feels, and the joy of becoming part of a family in the end. The film version is wonderful too, but the book is a graphic/prose hybrid masterpiece.[27]

Chasing Shadows

One expertly written hybrid novel is *Chasing Shadows* by Swati Avasthi, with art by Craig Phillips. This is the story of three teens who are freerunners. They use their Chicago landscape to perform aerial feats and move around on the edge of excitement and danger. The main character, Savitri, always figured the most dangerous thing she and her two best friends—twins Corey and Holly—did was freerunning at night in the urban jungle. The event that shatters their lives does not come vaulting from rooftop to rooftop but in the form of a random shooter who targets the twins as they stop at a red light. How to deal with the pain of a loved one's death and the onset of mental illness, how to care for yourself when you're caring for a grieving friend, all these themes come together in a mystery as the two survivors seek to find the shooter in the streets of the Windy City.

One of the questions always asked of a hybrid novel like this is, "Why?" In other words, is the author just trying to do something cool and cutting edge, or was a hybrid style the best form of communication for this story? In this case, almost all of the graphic episodes are story elements that occur inside the head of

An Interview with Swati Avasthi

Swati Avasthi is the author of *Chasing Shadows*, a popular hybrid prose/graphic novel that came out in 2015. She is also the author of the prose young adult novel *Split*, as well as a mom and a university creative writing professor. She was gracious enough to answer some questions about the hybrid graphic novel process.

Randall Bonser (RB): For *Chasing Shadows*, did you develop your story first, then decide, "Wow, a hybrid form would be better to tell my story?" Or did you say, "I'm going to write a hybrid novel, let me think of a story that allows some graphic elements?"

Swati Avasthi (SA): It's the former of the two. I had a story about a girl who faced the loss of someone she loves through violence. There are moments when we all experience this change from feeling invulnerable to vulnerable. And in that moment when you can see that world shift, that loss of innocence, it's like the whole has gone a-kilter and it will never come back. I was trying to talk about that moment, and the intensity of that moment. I was also thinking on an intellectual level about how graphics can do things differently in storytelling than prose. And so I said, "Why don't I have this incredible break be in graphics?"

RB: Is the story based on something that happened in your own life?

SA: In the summer between high school and college, a friend I knew from middle school, Kaitlynn Arquette, was killed in a drive-by shooting, in a case that has still not been solved today. In middle school, we'd done sleepovers and birthday parties and she had the most infectious laugh. I wanted to be an author, even then, and she was the daughter of a well-known YA novelist, Lois Duncan. Lois was the first author I'd ever met and I wanted my life to look like hers—husband, kids, novelist. That family left an important impression in my life. But Kait and I had lost touch when she went to another high school.

Hearing about Kait's shooting on the news was one of those moments for me when I went from invulnerable eighteen-year-old to vulnerable. For a moment,

I had absolutely no access to language. I couldn't think, I couldn't talk words, I couldn't do anything, it was such a shock. I'm a wordy person, I love words, writing is my profession, it's what I have wanted to do my whole life. So it was absolutely something I was thrown by, this lack of access to language. So that's what I was looking to explore. I said, "Let's use graphics to show how this changes the consciousness." So that was really where the idea for a graphic section came from.

RB: What does graphic storytelling allow you to do that prose doesn't?

SA: Have you read *The Invention of Hugo Cabret* [by Brian Selznick]? There's a passage in that book where a train is bearing down on Hugo. As you turn the page, the train gets closer and closer and closer. And the visceral, physical response to that is so different than a scene with a train bearing down on you in prose.

RB: I'm thinking of the scene in *Chasing Shadows* where the gun is pointed at the reader at the beginning of the book. What did you want to accomplish there? It seems different than the mental illness scenes where Holly is in the Shadow world?

SA: Right, it is different. During the shooting, I wanted the reader to have a visceral, physical experience along with Holly, to let the reader experience the wordlessness of fear.

RB: So words are failing her at that moment and she's just feeling something emotionally, or as you say viscerally, and you're trying to pass that on to the reader?

SA: Exactly. And then for the remainder of the text, when we're in the Shadow world, I'm thinking about sort of levels of consciousness. That which is explicable, it's still about words, and language, and logic. But as you're slipping away from reality. . . . My experience with people close to me that have struggled with mental illness is that they get submerged into a world that is pretty inexplicable to the rest of us. So the graphic became a way of showing her consciousness and the world that she was enveloped in. I think graphics do a better job of submerging a reader into a world, or a faster job, a cleaner job, of submerging a reader into a world that is unknown to them.

RB: Are there any rules in creating a hybrid form like this?

SA: No. One of the greatest things about creating a hybrid form right now is that there are absolutely no rules. You can do whatever you want because it's so new. I think people are still figuring out what the rules are. I do think it's better if you set rules within the narrative for when you're in graphics and when you're in prose. For instance, my rule for *Chasing Shadows* was that whenever Holly was losing touch with reality in any way, she was in graphics. So the moment, even when she was being shot at, just felt unreal to her. So all of that to me was about a sort of psychotic break. Incorporating a graphic section has to make emotional or logical sense within the story you've created. Each book has to establish its own rules for how it's supposed to be read. I think it's easier for a reader to understand those shifts if there's an emotional logic to it.

RB: Did you choose Craig Phillips to be the artist, or did the publisher choose him?

SA: The publisher chose the artist. My editor showed me his work and I was very excited by it. I thought the communication process was going to be a mess but I was very impressed with the way it worked. I thought it was going to be like a game of operator, and those never turn out well, right? What I mean is, I would talk to my editor, who would talk to his art editor, who would talk to him. And back and forth and back and forth. But I couldn't believe the results. I think that he did an amazing job.[f]

Holly, who is struggling with mental illness. For that reason, the graphic elements are very powerful. They allow us to see scenes that the character herself cannot, or will not, articulate.

In one sequence, the graphic scenes are used as a flashback, implying an abortion that is never mentioned in the story. In the first panel, Holly and her then boyfriend, Josh, are talking about her positive pregnancy test. She says, "Josh, are you sure?" He, obviously distraught, answers, "I don't know. Maybe it's not mine." The following three panels show two other girls whispering to each other. In the first, a girl says, "[W]onder how many other guys she's slept with." It's followed by another in which she says to someone else, "The dad is an old-fashioned Catholic." The trilogy of panels ends with a close-up of the gossiper's lips as she says, "But Holly isn't. Obviously."

In many of the comic sections, the main character is a half-man, half-snake named Kortha, whom Holly imagines as a sort of god of death as he leads away the character who was shot. It turns out that Kortha is a kind of perversion of Yama, an actual Hindu god. This becomes an important subtheme in the story due to Savitri's Indian heritage.

The final graphic sequence in the story takes place in the shadow lands of the teen struggling with mental illness. She has been traveling back and forth between the real world and this one in an effort to bring her brother back. In the final panel, her brother steps through a door with one last look at her. It is at once heartbreaking and encouraging, as we get the sense that Holly is finally letting go of her brother. The rope that has been around her neck, symbolizing her desire to die, is finally thrown on the ground, allowing her to come back to the real world once and for all. This use of graphic art to symbolize an internal world that only she can see is extremely powerful.[28]

Flora and Ulysses

Flora and Ulysses, by Kate DiCamillo, illustrated by K. G. Campbell, is technically a middle grade novel, but people of every age group read it because the story is beautiful and the graphic parts are superbly conceived and illustrated (figure 5.8). This is the story of Flora, a ten-year-old girl who is looking for love and adventure and says things like "This malfeasance must be stopped!" which she gets from her favorite comic book, *The Illuminated Adventures of the Amazing Incandesto!* She finds all of this, and more, when her next-door neighbor accidentally kills a squirrel by vacuuming him up in a giant indoor/outdoor vacuum cleaner. The squirrel, Ulysses, comes back to life with superhuman—or supersquirrel—powers: he can lift large objects, understand human speech, fly, and write poetry. When Ulysses's archnemesis—Flora's mother—kidnaps him and takes him out to the woods in the middle of the night with a shovel, he must use his super powers to escape.

Flora and her new friend William, who is experiencing "temporary blindness induced by trauma," discover the crime and set out to find Ulysses. With the help of her father, who lives in a nearby apartment building terrorized by a savage cat, Flora is reunited with Ulysses and experiences the truly superhuman power of

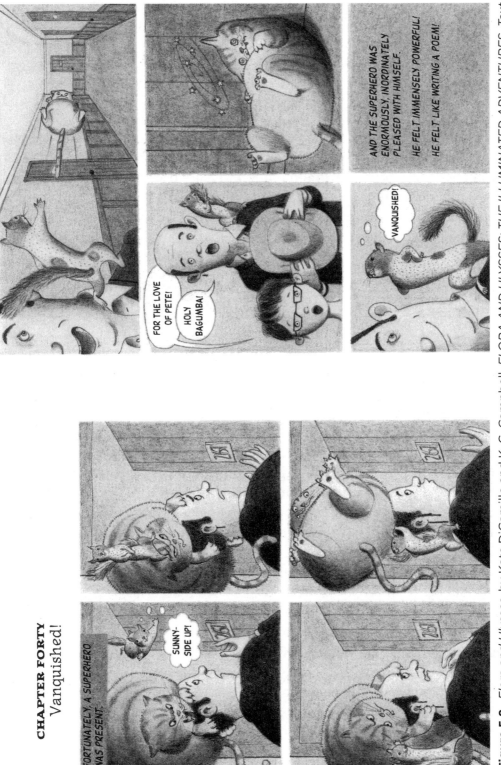

Figure 5.8. *Flora and Ulysses*, by Kate DiCamillo and K. G. Campbell. *FLORA AND ULYSSES: THE ILLUMINATED ADVENTURES. Text copyright © 2013 by Kate DiCamillo. Illustrations copyright © 2013 by Keith Campbell. Reproduced by permission of the publisher, Candlewick Press, Somerville, MA.*

love. Kate DiCamillo is one of the great writers of our time; her characters are complex and loveable, and the action is humorously engaging. The graphic parts of the story show the feats of Ulysses, who obviously can't talk. This is a brilliant hybrid work by a master storyteller.[29]

Plays as Graphic Novels

We've talked about a number of genres represented as comics in this chapter. Some of them work more naturally as graphic stories than others. I had my doubts about a play done as a graphic novel. That's because much of theater is visually static, depending on dialogue to produce conflict. But graphic plays do exist, and so with an open mind I explored the idea of expressing a Shakespeare play as a comic book. I looked at *Hamlet*, since that's one of the Bard's most well-known plays.

Hamlet

The best adaption of *Hamlet* as a graphic novel is, in my humble opinion, the *No Fear Shakespeare Graphic Novels* version, adapted and illustrated by Neil Babra. The text is a hybrid of Shakespeare's original language (think "To be, or not to be—that is the question . . .") and the modernized language of the *No Fear Shakespeare* series. If you're a purist and insist on 100 percent Shake-spearean words, this adaption is not for you. If you don't care about the original language and just want a quick interpretation, there are other, shorter versions of the play, including a manga version that is quite simplified. But Babra's adap-tion contains enough original language to give you a good flavor for the Bard, with the right amount of modernization so that readers will understand what's happening.

This *No Fear* adaption is especially strong in its transmutation of Hamlet's famous soliloquy from act III, scene 1, which I referenced in the preceding para-graph. This is a famous speech quite apart from the play in which it appears, and entire productions are judged on this single two-minute stretch of time. In the same way, any graphic version of *Hamlet* must be faithful to the meaning of this speech, while utilizing the unique qualities of the comic medium to help the reader understand what's going on. I saw several versions that shorten the speech too drastically, or convey it faithfully but are visually boring. Babra's rendering of the speech is visually stunning, faithful to the text, and helpful for getting in-side the Prince of Denmark's addled head. One panel is especially powerful. As Hamlet says "or not to be, that's the question," he kneels beside a pond in which he can see his reflection—but the face staring back at him is that of a skull, symbolizing his fantasy of what it would like to be dead.[30]

Kill Shakespeare, Backstage Edition

A few years ago I was browsing around at a college bookstore in Atlanta when I came across a large, beautifully bound graphic novel called *Kill Shakespeare, Backstage Edition*, by Conor McCreery and Anthony Del Col, with art by Andy Belanger and color by Ian Herring. I had never heard of it or seen anything like it so I picked it up. And fell in love with it. I will caution that it contains some graphic violence in the story (such as a man's eyes being gouged out and a head getting chopped off in a battle), but honestly, you can witness these atrocities in an actual Shakespearean play such as *King Lear* or *Titus Andronicus* (although without the trail of blood dripping off the dagger, or course). For this reason, and because the language can sometimes be a bit . . . Shakespearean, this book would probably be for older teens.

The authors have taken Shakespeare's characters and set them in a world in which all of the Bard's plays are actual events. The story is set one month after Hamlet's father, the king of Denmark, was murdered, and one week after his tormented son has mistakenly murdered Polonius. The young man Hamlet leaves on a ship for England, where he meets Richard III. A villain in the play by the same name, the reader cannot tell whether Richard is good or bad as he enlists Hamlet in an effort to rid the land of the mysterious god/prophet/saint called William Shakespeare. If Hamlet can just kill Shakespeare and retrieve his magic quill (as in an old-fashioned pen) and hand it over to Richard, all will be well . . . maybe.

No one's ever actually seen the mysterious Shakespeare, but followers such as Juliet Capulet, Falstaff, and Othello the soldier are rallying support amongst the commoners to fight Richard III in the name of their hero. Hamlet must decide which side he's on, since both groups consider him the Shadow King of an ancient prophecy that guides them all. This is very entertaining stuff, especially if you are familiar with the real Bard's material, because characters are tossing off lines and ideas from various plays in the course of the action. In the end, William Shakespeare makes an appearance, but it is not what anyone had imagined.[31]

Religious Graphic Novels

Religious leaders have been using visual teaching aids for thousands of years. If you've ever been to Europe and seen the storytelling stained glass windows, you will know what I mean. But it's not just the Christian religion, other religions are using graphic art to explain their holy books or tell the story of their famous figures. I've listed just a couple here, but there are many more.

The 14th Dalai Lama: A Manga Biography

This manga biography of the life of the Dalai Lama is important for a number of reasons. First, it brings the reality of this very complicated political situation to a level where students can understand it. Second, it is a strong advocate of nonviolent solutions, as it reflects the personal beliefs of the Dalai Lama. Third, it is a great introduction to the teachings of Buddhism. The story doesn't pull any punches—it's a very sad and difficult story—but by focusing on the life and emotions of the Dalai Lama, the Tibetan struggle comes to life in a personal way. Tetsu Saiwai, the creator, has taken books and movies about the Tibetan spiritual leader and included the most significant and powerful events.

The first scene in the story shows the people of Tibet mourning the passing of the thirteenth Dalai Lama. Following a vision, a group of leaders travel to the house of a peasant family and proclaim two-year-old Tenzin Gyatso the reincarnated Dalai Lama. He is taken to the country's capital, where he engages in religious and political studies. When communist China sends tanks and troops into Tibet to "liberate the country from foreign imperialists," the Dalai Lama— only a teenager at the time—must decide how to resist. When the Chinese army attacks his palace and city, the young leader leaves the country in a daring night-time escape to take up residence in India. You've probably heard about things the Dalai Lama has said and done to promote the independence of Tibet or to teach Westerners about Buddhism. This story, which is very well told with wonderful artwork, has continuing ramifications today.[32]

The Bible

Some people are going to think the Bible as a comic book is sacrilegious, especially since one of the laws in the Old Testament is "You shall make no graven images." Well, the definition of what is a graven image is probably debatable. But lots of people have bought Kingstone Comics' versions of Bible stories. They retell the drama in a way that lets the reader see what the world might have been like at that time. The company has produced books on many of the Bible's main characters: Adam (and the creation), Sampson, Elijah, David, Jesus, and many others.

The graphic adaption of the biblical book of Esther is interesting. A Hebrew working-class girl is taken to the palace as part of a contest to find out who will be the next queen for Emperor Xerxes of Persia. It's almost like the first reality TV show, only five thousand years before TV was invented! After a year of preparation, Esther is chosen to be the king's new wife. She uses her position of influence to counteract the work of Haman, one of the king's officials who is trying to wipe out the Hebrew people. The famous line "For who knows whether or not you have been in your position for such a time as this" is from the book of Esther. It's interesting to see the garb the people of the day wore and learn about their customs through the graphic medium.[33]

Historical Fiction

The power of a comic or graphic novel is that the illustrations transport the reader into the landscape of the world. That's why the medium is powerful for science fiction and fantasy. In a prose book, the world is described, but it's up to the reader to visualize it. The author of a comic can take the reader right into her world without the long descriptions. That's why historical fiction, like science fiction, is a natural genre for comics. The following books are good examples of this genre.

War Brothers: The Graphic Novel

War Brothers, written by Sharon E. McKay and illustrated by Daniel Lafrance, is based on the novel by the same name published in Canada in 2008. This adaption, which was published in 2013, is a powerful retelling of this fiction story based on real experiences by the boy soldiers in Uganda. The author spent time in Uganda hearing the tales of boys who had been abducted and trained as soldiers for the Lord's Resistance Army (LRA), a brutal revolutionary militia. Lush colors and vivid illustration make this already gripping story come alive.

In the past twenty years, many stories have surfaced about the boy soldiers being abducted and trained in war-torn countries. In this story, fourteen-year-old Jacob has just traveled to a boarding school run by the Catholic Church when soldiers from the LRA overpower the school's guards and kidnap all the male students. The boys are made to carry the soldiers' equipment through the jungles; if they kill people and become soldiers, they can eat. If they refuse to become soldiers, they are either killed themselves or made into slaves of the LRA. Late one night, after several of his friends are beaten, Jacob decides to escape with his friends from school. Their harrowing escape through the jungle, over the Nile with its nocturnal wildlife, and then trying to convince government soldiers that they are not a threat, will keep you glued to the book. Interestingly, after Jacob escapes, his troubles are not over: his family and neighbors don't trust that he is back to normal—they think he may go off and kill someone at any moment. This story will help provide a window on a tragic situation still very much ongoing to this day.[34]

Law of the Desert Born

For all the Western comic books written in the 1940s and 1950s, there are relatively few graphic novel Westerns—yet. In my view, it's just a matter of time. *Law of the Desert Born* by Louis L'Amour—adaptation by Charles Santino, script by Beau L'Amour and Katherine Nolan, and art by Thomas Yeates—is an adaptation of a short story written by one of the most prolific writers of American Westerns in the twentieth century. Millions of Louis L'Amour's westerns have been printed and read. I have read a lot of them myself. So when I saw that one of his stories had been adapted to a graphic novel, I was interested.

This is not one of L'Amour's most famous stories, because the distinction between bad guy and good guy is more subtle in this story than most of his novels, in which you easily side with one of the characters. This moral ambivalence is a hallmark of recent western movies, which is why I think *Law of the Desert Born* is well done. Thomas Yeates's art is clear and expressive, although it is in black and white. The structure is fairly traditional, but the artist allows characters to break the boundaries of their panels, which adds to the theme of characters not being pigeon-holed as good or bad.

You can see in figure 5.9 that the artist has done some really innovative things with his paneling. On the left spread, the fight begins in a fairly standard square panel. A few fists are thrown, then the two men get tangled up as the scuffle gets more violent. The artist demonstrates this by removing the panel borders to allow the reader to "feel" the impact of the men hitting the ground—the energy practically shoots off the page. As the fight dies down on the next page, the artist returns to rectangular panels, although he still allows a fist or a hat to slip out of the frame, as a visual clue that the anger and passion are still there. Yeates uses a wash technique that provides a compelling sense of distance (Beau L'Amour explains a little bit about this on page 196). There is a fair amount of fist fighting and shooting in this story, which you expect from a western, but none of the stereotypically staged gun battles of old movies. If you like westerns, this book will appeal to you.[35]

Short Story Collections

There are a lot of anthologies of short stories in the world. There are even anthologies of short graphic stories. These are collections that feature the best illustra-

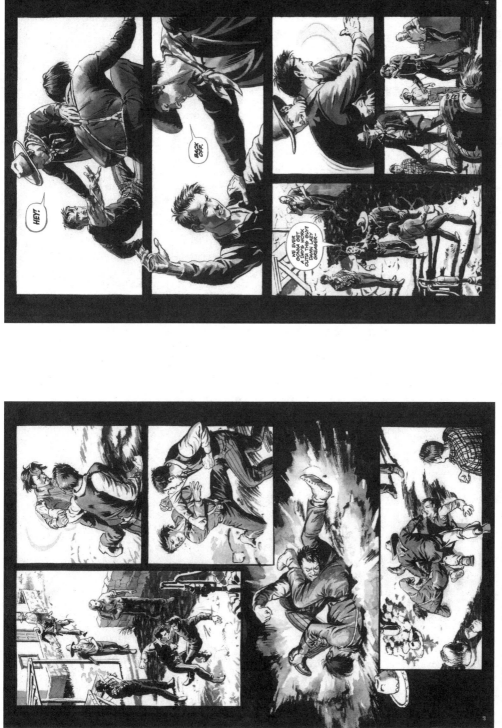

Figure 5.9. *Law of the Desert Born (Louis L'Amour)*, by Charles Santino, Beau L'Amour, Katherine Nolan, and Thomas Yeates. Excerpt(s) from *LAW OF THE DESERT BORN (GRAPHIC NOVEL): A GRAPHIC NOVEL* by Louis L'Amour, adapted by Charles Santino, script by Beau L'Amour and Katherine Nolan, illustrated by Thomas Yeates. Text copyright © 2013 by Beau L'Amour; illustrations copyright © 2013 by Louis L'Amour Enterprises, Inc. Used by permission of Bantam Books, an imprint of Random House, a division of Penguin Random House LLC. All rights reserved.

Adapting Prose to Comics

Beau L'Amour is the son of Western novelist Louis L'Amour and the driving force behind the adaption of *Law of the Desert Born* into a graphic novel. I asked Beau about some of the challenges of adapting a prose story into a graphic story. He was kind enough to send this answer:

Dealing with a novel or short story, every reader has their own imagination of what a narrative is about, what it looks like, and how the characters interact. That's the magic of prose. In doing an adaptation you have to accept that the story may change. The most important thing is to make it your own, get inside and respond to it without worrying about the original material. That said, as you work on it, you have to listen to what the *story* tells you it wants to become. You serve the adaptation, not the original. Also, keep what you do in the planning stages simple; if you are really sensitive to your characters and aware of their situations then complexity will arise and you'll need room to deal with it. Simple is best because things won't stay that way.

Visually, the main challenge in *Law of the Desert Born* was to find an artist who could really sell the feeling of distance—not just width, but depth. When we first spoke with Thomas Yeates, he suggested the wash technique, where the lighter tones of what is essentially a watercolor give you the sense you can see atmospheric distortion, dust, and haze. It gave us exactly what we were looking for.[9]

tors and writers out there at a certain time. Most of these collections are put together for adults, so read them advisedly. But there are some anthologies that are great for teens, too. The first great one is *Flight*, volume 1, originally published by Image Comics in 2004. Comics legend Scott McCloud wrote a tongue-in-cheek afterward for the book entitled, "The Year Comics Took Flight," supposedly written by his brain in the year 2054. In 2007, the anthology was republished by Villard with *Amulet* creator Kazu Kibuishi as editor. That was the first of eight

The Elements of Style

I have deliberately not included illustrated or picture books in this volume because they are not technically graphic stories—in most cases, the art doesn't move the story forward; it just illuminates the prose. I do want to include one illustrated book, however, because it is so unique. You've probably heard from your English teacher about *The Elements of Style* by Strunk and White. It's a great book with the power to improve the writing style of anyone who studies it.

Until now, the book was difficult to sit down and read unless a person was forced to do so for a class. But Penguin released a version of the book in 2007 with whimsical paintings by artist Maira Kalman. The illustrations are paired with sentences from the text that provide great humor and insight. For instance, one painting shows a group of people lounging placidly in a well-appointed living room, with a person lying in a pool of blood in the middle of the room. The caption reads, "He noticed a large stain right in the center of the rug." The original sentence is meant to illustrate keeping important words together, but in the context of the art, it takes on a wry, darkly comical meaning. If you want to improve your writing, or giggle at the surreal combinations of art and prose, this engaging book is a great read.[h]

volumes of *Flight*, each one gaining a broader audience for the beautiful art and poetic storytelling. Many of modern comics' great illustrators got their start or are featured in that series.

Kibuishi also edits and headlines the graphic story compilations called *Explorer*. This series features famous author/illustrators creating beautiful stories centered on a certain exploration theme. Volumes include *The Hidden Doors*, *The Mystery Boxes*, and *The Lost Islands*. Remember as you read them that these are short stories. Serial comics already have us exposed to short stories, but as you finish a serial comic, you know the story will continue in the next episode. With these books, the story ends with a mystery or other type of open-ended conclusion and some readers feel dissatisfied, like they want more. But short stories are like that, whether prose or film or graphic.

Science Comics

More and more educators are using comics to engage students in learning a subject. Take, for instance, *Primates* by Jim Ottaviani and Maris Wicks. This is the story of three women who are responsible for much of what we know about monkeys, chimps, and gorillas: Jane Goodall, Dian Fossey, and Birute Galdikas. Because some of the dialogue is made up, it can't be technically considered nonfiction, but readers can sure learn a lot about the lives of these scientists!

Many of the pages in this graphic novel are straightforward, with symmetrical panels in three tiers. But the creators occasionally break the pattern to produce a powerful effect on the reader. For instance, as Dian is learning to follow gorillas, she takes the trail the wrong way—toward where the animals have been. After being corrected by a photojournalist, she starts up the mountain in a frameless panel that serves as a background to most of the page. The effect is one of a steep grade and tired feet—it's almost exhausting to read it![i]

This is the type of science that students really enjoy reading. And researchers have found that people retain more information than just reading prose, too. (See chapter 7 for a discussion on these studies.)

JAPANESE COMICS/ MANGA

Walk into any bookstore to look for graphic novels or comics, and you will find another, probably larger section right next to it: Manga! Interestingly, the word *manga* is hardly used in Japan itself anymore, but we in the West use it to describe Japanese comics of all kinds. Most people in Japan use the ubiquitous word *comic*, which covers a broad range of Japanese comics and graphic novels.[1] It is not uncommon in Japan to see people of all ages and life situations on the street or riding public transportation, all the while reading thick manga books and bright manga-filled magazines.

People aren't just reading action-adventure or romance stories, either. Popular books on economics, cooking, and technical manuals are written as comics. Many schools are utilizing manga-style textbooks to interest students in past events. One series about the history of Western art features da Vinci, Picasso, and other great artists inviting children to explore their artworks. Manga in Japan is fairly inexpensive and is sold at newsstands and magazine stores, reminiscent of the way comics used to be sold in the United States in the mid-twentieth century. One writer estimates that manga comprises nearly one-third of all written material in Japan.[2] This will undoubtedly change in the coming years as more consumers read their favorite stories on mobile devices.

> "I honestly like manga a lot better than comics because reading manga is completely different than reading comics . . . manga seems to be a lot more fun to read than comics. Manga has much more romance and comedy and action in one book than comics do, and sometimes they tend to be slightly over exaggerative and sometimes over exaggerative can make it much more fun to read. So in a battle between manga and comics I think manga wins completely."—Micah E., Wilmington, Delaware[a]

Manga—along with its requisite art style—is on the rise in the West, having found its way into libraries and bookstores, as well as onto the Internet. Popular series have been made into television shows and movies. The stories are often action packed, full of humor, and brimming with relational hijinks. If you haven't been introduced to manga, go ask your school librarian or check out the huge selection at your local or online bookstore. You can find descriptions of some popular series at the end of this chapter.

History

Modern Japanese manga is an amalgamation of Eastern art culture with Western comic forms. But many scholars think the Japanese people were, in a way, predisposed to excelling in comics because of Japanese history and culture.

The first cartoon-like drawings in Japan were carved in ceiling beams by workmen around 700 AD.[3] In the twelfth century, a Buddhist priest named Toba Sojo created picture stories on scrolls that featured anthropomorphized animals such as frogs and rats (see figure 6.1 for other animals pictured on scrolls). These

Figure 6.1. Teen artist rendering of animals on Japanese scroll. *Illustration courtesy of Chris Burns*

scrolls told stories, often humorous or satirical. For instance, monks (represented by animals) are seen bathing in preparation for a ceremony, while in another a monkey thief is running from some frogs.[4] Although not technically manga as we know it today, the pictures were important because they told stories visually without words. The tale unfolded as the viewer looked from right to left. From the seventeenth to the nineteenth century, single-panel woodblock prints known as *ukio-e*, which captured moments of pleasure or humor, were printed and sold.

The first use of the word *manga* is from 1798 in the work of poet-artist Santo Kyoden. Then in 1814 Aikawa Minwa published a book called *Manga Hyakujo* (*100 Girl Cartoons*). The Chinese characters making up the word *manga* were *man*—meaning "involuntary" or "in spite of oneself"—and *ga* for "pictures." Hokusai was describing the fantastical nature of his prints, which is how manga came to represent "whimsical pictures."[5]

In 1861, after Japan opened its borders to the world for the first time in several hundred years, a British journalist and artist named Charles Wirgman arrived in Japan. He started a satirical magazine called *Japan Punch* that included politically and socially relevant cartoons. Western-style comic strips, with their multipanel arrangement, also made their debut at this time. This Western style of cartoon art caught on in several other magazines started by Japanese citizens. These new political cartoons, which had been forbidden for hundreds of years, paved the way for Japanese readers who ate up the humorous combination of words and

---

! **New York Times Manga Best Sellers October 2016**

Every week the *New York Times* publishes the list of the bestselling manga books during that week. It gives a snapshot of what's popular at a certain time. The October 9, 2016, list at NYTimes.com looks like this:

1. *One-Punch Man*, volume 1 (Murata)
2. *Tokyo Ghoul*, volume 1 (Ishida)
3. *Goodnight Punpun*, volume 3 (Asano)
4. *One-Punch Man*, volume 8 (Murata)
5. *Haikyu!!* volume 3 (Furudate)
6. *Mysterious Girlfriend X*, volume 3 (Ueshiba)
7. *Attack on Titan*, volume 1 (Isayama)
8. *Tokyo Ghoul*, volume 8 (Ishida)
9. *Monster Musume*, volume 9 (Okayado)
10. *Tokyo Ghoul*, volume 2 (Ishida)

pictures. Several magazines for children published around the turn of the century also helped pave the way for modern style manga.[6]

In 1902, the Sunday edition of *Jiji Shinpo* featured an insert called *Jiji Manga*, a humorous comic strip about a couple of country bumpkins in the big city. The strip serial was the debut manga of political cartoonist Rakuten Kitazawa, widely thought of in Japan as the father of modern manga.[7] *Jiji Manga* is considered to be the first modern use of the word *manga*, although it didn't look much like the manga that would be seen after World War II, the era in which the style we know today was created.

In 1931, a famous character made his debut—a talking animal whose exploits would pave the way for many characters through the succeeding decades. That was the year the mangy orphan dog Norakuro appeared in the pages of children's magazine *Shonen Club*. Lovable Norakuro is accident-prone but heroic as he fights with his dog regiment. Compiled into hardcover books, Norakuro's adventures sold over a million copies before World War II.[8] His creator, Suiho Tagawa, was one of the twentieth century's most successful manga artists.

Disney's animal characters were very popular in Japan in the 1930s, and this influence can be seen in Norakuro's design. Mickey Mouse even helps Norakuro round up some naughty monkeys in one of his adventures. This was possible because there weren't very many enforceable international copyright laws at the time.[9] Norakuro was popular for a decade until World War II forced magazines to shut down due to paper shortages. But the brave canine has been featured in several TV series and movies, and his merchandise remains popular to this day.

Another enormously popular manga character of the 1930s was Tank Tankuro, created by cartoonist Gajo Sakamoto. Tankuro was the first of many manga robot characters and had a strong influence on Osamu Tezuka's Astro Boy, among others. With a round iron shell, Tankuro could produce all kinds of gadgets and weapons for every occasion. He could sprout wings or become a ship as well.[10] Tankuro's nemesis, Kuro-Kabuto, was equally resourceful. His iron mask, with only two holes for eyes, gave him an eerie appearance and foreshadowed other masked villains.

In 1946, budding artist Osamu Tezuka published his first comic in a children's newspaper called *Mainichi Shokokumin Shinbun*. He was seventeen at the time and had been drawing comics since he was a little boy. Tezuka's first book-length project, *Shintakarajima* (*New Treasure Island*), appeared in 1947, when Tezuka was nineteen. The surprising success of this book—which sold more than four hundred thousand copies—launched Tezuka's meteoric career in comics. Although comics had been seen in Japan for a half century, Tezuka brought film techniques to the page—zooming in or panning across a scene like a film camera. He didn't draw his scenes full form, from one viewpoint, as if the audience were watching a play; instead the scenes were drawn from many different angles, which changed from panel to panel.[11]

Tezuka has been called the "God of Manga." That's because his influence on Japanese comics and animated movies (called anime) is so profound. One Japanese newspaper wrote, "One explanation for the popularity of comics in Japan . . . is that Japan had Osamu Tezuka. . . . Without Dr. Tezuka, the post-war explosion in comics in Japan would have been inconceivable."[12] He has been called the Japanese equivalent of Walt Disney. His forty-plus-year career, from 1946 to 1989, is synonymous with the period that saw Japanese comics transformed from children's entertainment to serious stories targeted to all age groups.

Throughout his life Tezuka wrote and drew 150,000 pages for six hundred manga titles and sixty animated works.[13] He was driven by his horrific experiences during World War II to promote peace and respect for life through the medium of comics. His nuanced stories explored the deepest human emotions of identity, loss, love, and injustice. Tezuka "helped revolutionize manga and launch the artistic explosion that became anime."[14] His stories were not just action packed; they also explored social issues such as racism, terrorism, and ecology. Tezuka's emphasis on a compelling story, as well as his art style, was passed down through the many famous author/artists he trained, and his innovations continue to inform manga creation today.

Robots and Robot Boys

In 1951, Tezuka's *Astro Boy* flew into the minds and hearts of readers in Japan. The original Japanese title, *Tetsuwan Atom*, emphasized his atomic-powered capabilities. This is ironic, considering how the mechanical boy tries to achieve peace in the wake of the atom bombs that had been dropped on his homeland less than a decade before. Astro Boy has special powers. He can fly, speak sixty languages, and detect whether a human being is good or bad. He fights to protect the world from people and robots who would harm others. In addition to another of Tezuka's characters—Kimba the White Lion—Astro Boy became an animated television character in the 1960s, finding fame in the United States as well.

In 1956 a second popular robot appeared to challenge the popularity of Astro Boy. That's when Mitsuteru Yokoyama, a protégé of Osamu Tezuka, created *Tetsujin 28-Go*, popularly known as *Gigantor* in English. This giant mechanical leftover from World War II was controlled by the ten-year-old son of the robot's inventor. Lots of giant mech robots showed up in manga during the middle decades of the twentieth century, but like Gigantor, they played mostly a defensive role against criminals and aliens.

Similarly to how comics were marketed in the United States, many Japanese comics during this era were targeted at boys. In 1959, two weekly manga magazines began publishing on the same day: *Weekly Shonen Magazine* and *Weekly Shonen Sunday*. These contained multiple manga serials written for the boys' market. They joined several other weekly magazines devoted solely to manga for other segments of the population. Today, there are more than a dozen weeklies aimed at all segments of Japan's manga reading public.[15] Here in the States, we can find serial comic strips in daily newspapers or online, but we don't really have any print equivalent to the weekly manga magazines in Japan.

More robot manga appeared in the 1970s, when Go Nagai's *Mazinger Z* became the first story about a giant robot controlled by a pilot inside the robot. The television anime version followed soon thereafter, cementing its popularity in Japan. Nagai struck gold again in 1974 when *Getter Robo* was published, introducing the concept of combining robots to make bigger, more dangerous machines.

Women Take the Stage

Before World War II, girls in manga had been drawn by male writers and artists. Most of the story lines encouraged girls to aspire only to "refinement, romance, marriage and motherhood."[16] After the war, Machiko Hasegawa, dubbed the "manga princess,"[17] began writing a strip called *Sazae-San*. This rather ordinary Japanese woman and her domestic struggles became one of Japan's most beloved manga and anime characters. For several decades, this humorous yet unglamorized portrayal of a Japanese Everywoman resonated in the hearts of Japanese readers. In fact, *Sazae-San* is the longest-running anime series in the world.[18]

Wanting to create a strong female character, Osamu Tezuka wrote *Princess Knight*, featuring Sapphire, a girl who is born with both a girl's and a boy's soul. *Princess Knight*, which began to appear in serial form in 1953, is widely regarded as the first adventure manga series for girls. Other female characters had appeared in various stories through the years, but Sapphire was the first hero to headline her own series.[19] In order to take her eventual place on the throne, Sapphire disguises herself in public as a prince. Although in the end her male soul is removed and she marries her prince, Sapphire kicks butt when she needs to. According to Helen McCarthy, "She inspired generations of manga artists, animators, and game designers to create fighting female heroes."[20]

One example of this type of fierce female character is *Rose of Versailles*, a story set during the French Revolution by Riyoko Ikeda, published in 1972. In order to fulfill her father's ambitions, the main character, Oscar, must (like Sapphire) pretend to be a boy in public. Oscar eventually rises to become captain of the guard, but in the end renounces her life of privilege to join her nonaristocratic lover,

CLAMP

Most manga books you will pick up have the author/illustrator's name on the cover. However, there are several series—*X, Tsubasa RESERVoir CHRoNiCLE*, and *Legal Drug*, among others—where the name CLAMP appears as the author. Who in the world is CLAMP, you ask?

CLAMP is a group of four female writers who work together and share all the duties associated with creating manga. Their pen names are Igarashi Satsuki, Mokona, Nekoi Tsubaki, and Ohkawa Nanase. Although their process is somewhat mysterious, they are known to write and illustrate as a group without drawing attention to any one member's work. Although they are best known for their magical girl stories, they have produced a wide variety of stories, including the apocalyptic *X*, which takes place at the (possibly) world's end in 1999. Their website claims they have sold nearly one hundred million copies of their works worldwide.

CLAMP's first published work was the serial *RG Veda* in 1989. Since then they have produced hit after hit, many of which have been turned into anime. Some of their best-known works are *xxxHolic*, *Drug and Drop*, *Clamp School Detectives*, and *Angelic Layer*. Characters from one series sometimes appear in other series, giving rise to what some call the CLAMP universe.

Although each artist came to the group with a different and original style, the group works to achieve a unified artistic style, employing a different look for each type of work. Their styles range from cutesy and lighthearted to brooding, detailed, and realistic.[b] Most artists employ assistants to do the more menial work, but CLAMP employs no assistants, doing all the penciling and color work themselves. Their appeal is not in their originality, says one writer; rather the group "excels at creating manga stories that perfectly mesh the conventional attributes of *shonen* and *shoujo* manga. . . . [The stories] are able to appeal equally to both male and female readers, and feel like substantial, involving narratives."[c]

"Created by CLAMP, an all-female Japanese manga artist group, *xxxHolic* starts out as a fairly simple paranormal-investigator series. It takes readers through the colorful world of Japanese mythology, introducing monsters and spirits in a beautiful ukiyo-e style. But anybody familiar with CLAMP's work knows that nothing that starts simple ever stays that way. Unlike many of their other works, *xxxHolic* is strongly character-driven. Although offering no truly intense moments, there's more than enough to tug at your heartstrings. Despite a slow beginning, *xxxHolic* is certainly worth the read."—Alyse A., West Lafayette, Indiana[d]

Andre. Manga historian Paul Gravett explains why Rose is so popular to this day: "To growing girls dealing with the demands of femininity, Ikeda showed Oscar as a girl who had been denied the outward trappings of her sex, but who finds the courage to be her own woman and relate to her man as a true equal."[21]

In the 1960s, before female writers became common, two male writers wrote stories for girls that helped define the "magical girl" genre. Fujio Akatsuka's *Secret Akko-chan* is about a normal girl who receives magical powers from an object—in this case a mirror. Another version of a magical girl came in the form of *Sally the Witch*, written by Mitsuteru Yokoyama (of *Gigantor* fame). Sally comes from another world and is believed to have been inspired by the American television show *Bewitched*.[22] These magical girls paved the way for many more girls with magical powers, including the super popular *Sailor Moon* series.[23]

In the late 1960s and early 1970s, women began to write and illustrate manga, forever changing the way women were portrayed. A group of female creators became known as the Magnificent 24s, after the year *Showa* 24, or 1949, when most of them were born. They created more interesting, active, and convincing female characters than the traditional demure stereotypes created by male authors. These writers also took storytelling to a new level by letting go of the linearity of straight boxes in favor of irregular panels—or getting rid of panels—in order to better tell the emotion of a story. Women have continued to make strong contributions to manga to the present day.

The Darker Side of Manga

By the late 1950s, the children who had started reading manga in the 1940s had become older teens and adults. They still enjoyed reading comics, but the material and art seemed too childish for them. For this changing audience, a group of writers led by Yoshihiro Tatsumi began to develop a darker style of manga called *gekiga*. In 1959, together with Takao Saito and several others, Tatsumi formed the Gekiga Workshop to develop a new style of graphic art.

Exploring darker and more violent themes, these artists strove to represent realism in a fashion similar to the experimental and noir films of the 1960s. Their mystery, action, and horror comics contained little humor and influenced a new generation of artists.[24] A good example of this style of manga is the series *Golgo 13*, the story of a professional assassin who both hunts and is hunted by the world's most dangerous people. *Golgo 13* is still being published in Japan after more than forty-five years. The term *gekiga* lost its meaning in the mid-1960s, as pretty much any action was labeled as such. But the shift to a more cutting-edge art style and subject matter changed the industry forever.

Stories of the American West, although popular in the United States and Europe, never really caught on in Japan. By contrast, Samurai and ninja stories have always been popular subjects for manga. The new freedom to tell tales with more violent and emotionally intense content gave rise to many popular series during the 1960s and 1970s. One such series was *Lone Wolf and Cub* (*Kozure Okami*) by Kazuo Koike and artist Goseki Kojima, which ran in weekly segments from 1970 to 1976.

During this time of great change in the industry, writers in Japan began to create honest, graphic stories about the bombing of Japanese cities by the United States during World War II. One manga creator in particular is remembered for his accounts of the bombing on Hiroshima. In 1966, Keiji Nakazawa's mother died. This traumatic event brought back memories of the harrowing events of 1945. Nakazawa began to chronicle those events, first in a fiction series called *Struck by Black Rain* about war survivors involved in the black market, followed by the autobiographical story *I Saw It*. In 1973, the boys' magazine *Weekly Shonen Jump* began to publish his most famous work, *Barefoot Gen*. The serial, which ran from 1973 to 1985, is a fictional story about a boy named Gen Nakaoka that nevertheless reflects the author's own experience of living through the Hiroshima bombing. *Barefoot Gen* has been adapted numerous times for television, anime, and live-action movies.

Many manga titles could be—and should be—mentioned for their role in diversifying Japanese comics between the 1960s and 1980s. We don't have room to mention them all. But one apocalyptic series many teens to this day find interesting began publication in 1982. *Akira*, by Katsuhiro Otomo, is set in Neo-Tokyo in the year 2019, nearly three decades after a nuclear explosion has destroyed the original city of Tokyo. *Akira*, which you can find now compiled into ten volumes, contains something for everyone: motorcycle gangs battling for territory, the authorities looking for people with special powers, and a gang of misfits trying to find their place in this crazy world. The movie version of *Akira* was instrumental in the breakthrough of anime into English-speaking culture.[25]

Many manga titles popular today made their debut in the 1990s. It was a time of great creativity and productivity by manga creators (often called *mangaka*) in Japan. Two series that gained huge followings in the 1990s were detective stories. *Young Kindaichi's Case Files* (*Kindaichi Shonen no Jikenbo*) was first published in weekly segments in 1992. The story features a teenage detective who investigates murders performed by killers who are presented not as heartless psychopaths, but in an almost sympathetic way.[26] The second series, *Case Closed* (*Meitantei Conan*) by Gosho Aoyama, features a teenage genius who is transformed into a child by a mysterious poison. While awaiting a cure for his condition, the child detective solves murders and lets others take the credit in an effort to keep his identity hidden. As of this writing, *Case Closed* is still going strong after all these years! Both of these series have inspired numerous anime and live-action films in Japan and elsewhere.

Over the years, Japanese publishers worked to diversify their subjects, marketing their stories to specific segments of the population. Although there is a lot of crossover within these categories, manga is generally divided into six categories: *kodemo*, *shonen*, *seinen*, *shojo*, boys' love or *shonen-ai*, and *josei*. As you seek out manga titles, knowing these categories may help you find stories suitable to your age and subject interests.

Kodomo

Kodomo manga are written and published for younger children, elementary aged or younger. In the United States, this category is limited, although it is growing as manga becomes more and more popular. *Pokémon* is among the most popular titles in this category. Other titles include *BakéGyamon* by Mitsuhisa Tamura, *Dinosaur Hour!* by Hitoshi Shioya, *Ninja Baseball Kyuma* by Shunshin Maeda, and *Leave It to PET!* by Kenji Sonishi. To give younger children an appreciation for manga, publishers are also creating chapter books of some of their older lines, such as *Naruto*.[27]

Shonen

During the 1950s, uplifting stories about sports, from baseball to boxing, became popular in manga magazines for boys. These stories were not only exciting; they also influenced a generation of Japanese children to take up sports. There is a famous story about the 2002 Japanese World Cup men's soccer team. Although soccer was not popular in Japan in the 1970s, writer Yoichi Takahashi, who had been present at the 1978 World Cup in Argentina, set about popularizing the sport through his series *Captain Tsubasa*. A number of the 2002 World Cup players from Japan credited that series with igniting their interest to play soccer.[28]

These ideals of friendship, effort, and victory are often seen in *shonen* manga, which are written for and marketed to boys, ages ten to twenty.[29] The stories are

Dragon Ball's Creator, Akira Toriyama

One of the most popular *shonen* series of all time is *Dragon Ball*, by Akira To-riyama. The artist was born in Nagoya, Aichi, Japan, in 1955. His first popular series, *Dr. Slump*, was an irreverent comic serial published between 1980 and 1984 in *Weekly Shonen Jump*. The series has spawned several anime series and sold over thirty-five million copies in Japan.[e] He followed that up with *Dragon Ball*, which was serialized from 1984 to 1995.

Dragon Ball became an instant hit, leading to anime adaptions, movies, and video games. At the beginning, the series was more comedic, but as time passed and readers responded to what they liked, the story became more of a pure fighting tale. Eschewing the Western "big equals powerful" character motif, the heroes of this series were rather small, a trend that has continued in Japanese manga. *Dragon Ball* traveled quickly across the world, becoming spectacularly popular in Europe and the United States, selling more than 240 million copies worldwide.[f] The publisher, Shueisha, claims the manga is its second-best seller of all time, after its megahit *One Piece*.[g]

Although *Dragon Ball* is far and away his best-known title, Toriyama has been involved in many other projects. He worked on the design of characters in several video games, including *Dragon Quest*, *Chrono Trigger*, and *Tobal 1* and *Tobal 2*. Most of his work is done by himself without a staff of assistants, a relative rar-ity among in-demand mangaka. Most of the manga Toriyama has produced since *Dragon Ball* have been shorter, including *Cowa! Kajika*, and *Sand Land*—all of which were serialized in *Weekly Shonen Jump* as fourteen chapters or less.

Many manga artists claim Toriyama as an inspiration to them, for both story and art style. In an interview about his legacy, the artist stated that, "I just wanted to make boys happy. . . . The role of my manga is to be a work of en-tertainment through and through. I dare say, I don't care even if [my works] have left nothing behind, as long as they have entertained their readers."[h]

not all about sports: mystery, comedy, horror, and many other genres are represented. Nevertheless, the winning formula of following the underdog through his rigorous training to see him compete on the big stage is a major theme in many of the books. A series that has appealed to boys for over thirty years is *Dragon Ball*, which debuted in *Weekly Shonen Jump* in 1984. The spinoff *Dragon Ball Z* has also been phenomenally successful. In 2012, the publisher, Shueisha, proclaimed *Dragon Ball* its second most successful manga series ever, trailing only its series *One Piece*.[30]

Shonen comics are the most popular form of Japanese comics in Japan, and many titles have become available in the West as well. Because they emphasize action and spend relatively less time focusing on characters' emotions, *shonen* comics are a quick read and translate well to other languages and locations. Many of these characters have their own movies and TV shows, which allow them to become popular in several mediums. Some popular titles include *Naruto* by Masashi Kishimoto, *Ranma 1/2* by Rumiko Takahasi, *One Piece* by Eiichiro Oda, and *Bleach* by Tite Kubo.

Shojo

Although a lot of female readers cross over and read *shonen* comics, there is a category aimed specifically at girls aged ten to twenty: *shojo* (sometimes spelled *shoujo*) manga. These stories generally emphasize the characters' emotions and relationships, even when they contain a good amount of action. The first *shojo* title was *Princess Knight (Ribon no Kishi)* by Osamu Tezuka in 1953. After the 1960s, female writers began to create many of the stories. A group of women famously called the Magnificent 24s changed the industry by writing stories in which the women were less bound by tradition.

These new storytellers began playing with the layout of their tales as well. They utilized innovative panel sequences and shapes, and used the entire page to tell the story, rather than sticking to the traditional frame-by-frame structure.[31] While relationships are at the crux of *shojo* manga, the stories are represented by different genres: historical fiction, fantasy, mystery, romance, and many others.

One of the most popular *shojo* manga series of all time is *Boys over Flowers (Hana Yori Dango)* by Yoko Kamio, the story of an ordinary girl sent to an elite school for the purpose of snaring a rich young man. Some other popular *shojo* titles include *Fruits Basket* by Natsuki Talaya, *Vampire Knight* by Matsuri Hino, *Ouran High School Host Club* by Bisco Hatori, *Say I Love You* by Kanae Hazuki, and *Black Butler* by Yana Toboso (although this is a good example of a crossover title that appeals to both boys and girls).

Boys' Love (*Shonen-ai*)

Boys' love manga, also sometimes known as *yaoi*, is homosexual in nature, although it is written for, and mostly produced by, women. Some titles are explicitly sexual, while others are less graphic. Why do women enjoy these stories of homosexual boys and men? The reasons are varied, according to those who write about manga. One writer quotes a reader who says that women in Japan "are disillusioned (and bored) with male-female relationships where the sexual roles are still very fixed. They are seeking a new romance in which neither partner has to pretend to be weaker than the other." Or maybe "these boys provide an unthreatening way for Japanese girls to fantasize about the opposite sex without competing with another female presence."[32] Another writer theorizes that "while the characters are males, they are the embodiment of female ideals."[33] Whatever the reasons, these dramas about characters who live outside of traditional sexual expectations have a dedicated fan base. Some popular boys' love titles include *Boy Princess* by Seyoung Kim, *Only the Ring Finger Knows* by Satoru Kannagi, and *Little Butterfly* by Hinako Takanaga.

Seinen and *Josei*

Seinen manga is written for older teen boys and adult men. Stories encompass a variety of genres: crime dramas, sex comedies, mystery, historical fiction, and others. These books often include intense action or violence and mature sexual content. *Josei* manga is written for older teen girls and adult women. The majority of *josei* creators are also women. Generally, these stories deal with relationships, and many feature single women.

Visual Storytelling—Japanese Style

So what makes Japanese manga different from Western comics? What are the similarities? Neil Cohn, a researcher who studies how graphic stories are structured and understood, explains: "Most people can identify Japanese Visual Language (JVL) by the most salient feature of its graphic structure: the stereotypical way that people are drawn with big eyes, big hair, small mouths, and pointed chins."[34] Although Japanese artists exhibit a great deal of diversity in their work, this "stereotypical" style of drawing figures sets manga apart from comics created in the Western Hemisphere. Indeed, this art style can be seen outside of comic books in Japan, as Cohn explains: "JVL extends beyond manga into nearly all aspects of visual culture, such as animation and advertising."[35]

"Manga and comics may have the same bubbles with words in it but that's the one thing they have in common. Think about it when you touch a manga book for the very first time you notice that the manga book starts in the back of the book and comics start on the front. Well in case you don't realize manga is actually made in Japan."—Micah E., Wilmington, Delaware[i]

Figure 6.2. Manga-style art. *Illustration courtesy of Chris Burns*

Other aspects of JVL are less "representative" of real-life objects. For instance, *shojo* manga often make use of abstract signs or symbols in the backgrounds of their panels, using cascading flowers or sparkling lights to set a mood or hint at underlying meaning.[36] Because manga panels often utilize spare backgrounds, these symbols can set a mood or heighten the emotional impact of a scene. Sometimes characters are depicted with animal characteristics to portray strong feelings, such as fangs and claws to denote rage or dog paws and ears to suggest begging (as in figure 6.2). Most readers are familiar with the vocabulary of these transformations—they understand that the character is not turning suddenly into an animal!

Japanese artists visualize motion quite differently than their American counterparts. At least they did until the 1990s, when Western artists began to copy manga styles. The classic superhero motion lines made famous in the 1960s—

Figure 6.3. American-style motion lines. *Illustration courtesy of Chris Burns*

and still popular today—show the path an object has already traveled by placing sweeping motion lines *behind* the object (figure 6.3).

Japanese artists, on the other hand, often blur the entire background while keeping the moving object static. This results in motion lines behind and *in front of*, the subject (figure 6.4).

This gives the illusion that the viewer is moving at the same speed as the object itself. These types of panels support artist and author Scott McCloud's theory that Japanese manga is more subjective than American comics. This basically means that Japanese artists put the reader in the shoes of the character, rather than as an objective viewer of the scene.

These types of motion lines, as well as many other manga techniques, give the reader the feeling of actually participating in the drama unfolding on the pages. Whereas many Western comics keep the reader on the sidelines as an observer, manga tries to bring the reader right into the frame to experience the emotion or

Figure 6.4. Japanese-style motion lines. *Illustration courtesy of Chris Burns*

the action as a participant. That is why so many manga artists distort their characters when they are feeling strong emotion (figure 6.5). Suddenly the character will look almost deformed, with only the screaming mouth emphasized. This is meant to involve the reader in whatever the character is feeling.

Frequent close-ups of people's heads and faces is another technique illustrators use to bring the reader into the minds of the characters. Sometimes these close-ups are not accompanied by words, just iconic expressions. Mangaka will use scene changes and still-life drawings to create resonance in readers as well. Western artists who grew up reading manga in the 1990s and 2000s are now incorporating many of these techniques into their art, bridging the gap between Western and Eastern comics.

Finally, remember that manga is read in a different direction than Western comics. You start from what we would think of as the end, then work right to left. Figure 6.6 is an illustration of the direction a sample manga would be read.

Figure 6.5. Faces are often distorted for effect in manga. *Illustration courtesy of Chris Burns*

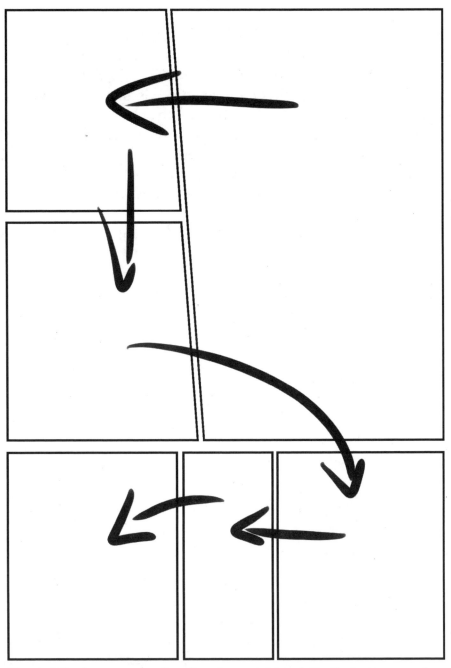

Figure 6.6. Japanese reading flow from right to left. *Illustration courtesy of Chris Burns*

Manga You May Encounter

If we took a look at every popular manga series, this book would be very long! And not all manga series are appropriate for preteens and teens. So I will highlight a few of the most popular series with teens.

Black Butler, *Volume 1*

Black Butler, by Yana Toboso, is very popular with middle school and high school teens. The story features Sebastian Michaelis, a fashionable butler who seems to be able to do everything well: he cooks, landscapes the garden, cleans the mansion, fights masters of many different martial arts—he even teaches dance lessons!

His charge is the diminutive teen, Ciel Phantomhive, head of the wealthy Phantomhive family and owner of the Funtom Corporation, one of the leading toy makers in the country. When Ciel is taken from his bed one afternoon, the butler must seek out the kidnappers and bring his charge home—all before dinner gets cold! How could a butler be so good at so many things and be so utterly charming and debonair? A villain named Vanel in book 1 asks this question after being rebuffed from trying to bribe the butler away from his master. Sebastian answers,

> My apologies, Mister Vanel . . . but I have no interest in man-made rubbish, coin or other-wise. For you see . . . I am a devil . . . of a butler. So long as the young master possesses the "mark of the covenant." . . . I am his faithful dog. And a "covenant" binds me to my master. Until I claim his soul.[37]

This series is very entertaining and the characters are well developed. The cook, Chef Baldroy, the groundskeeper, Gardner Finnian, and the maid, Housemaid Mey-Rin, are all bumbling, lazy characters whose jobs are mostly done by the butler (see figure 6.7). They do more standing around and complaining than they do actually working, meaning that the butler has to do all their tasks in record time before guests come or some other shenanigans ensue.

Vampire Knight, *Volume 1*

Who doesn't love a good vampire story? The blockbuster series *Vampire Knight* by Matsuri Hino, is set at Cross Academy, which houses a day class and a night class. Guess who make up the night class? Not just any old vampires, but extremely beautiful vampires. Two human students, Yuki Cross and Zero Kiryu, make up the "disciplinary committee," protecting the day students from the night students. They are also charged with keeping the vampires' secret identities. Yuki and Zero are run ragged as they take classes, patrol the grounds at night, and keep the human students from getting too close to the attractive vampires.

Everything goes smoothly thanks to the handsome leader of the vampire class, Kaname Kuran, who protects the protectors, as it were. The background

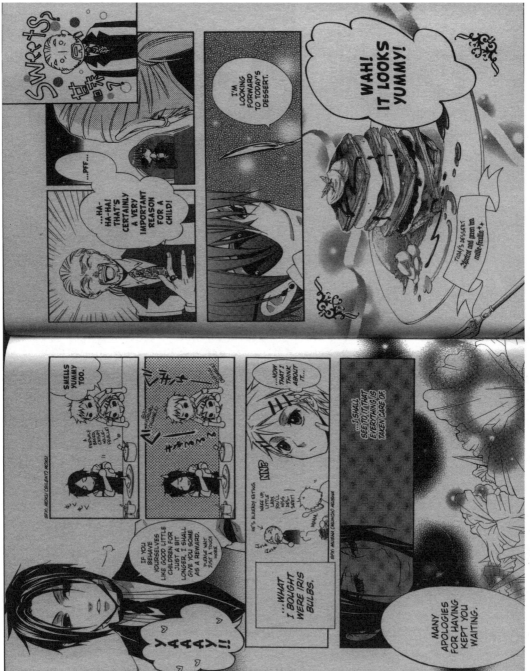

Figure 6.7. *Black Butler* by Yana Toboso. © *Yana Toboso / SQUARE ENIX*

of the story is that Kaname saved Yuki when her family was slaughtered by vampires when she was five years old. Of course, she now harbors a secret crush for Kaname, which can only lead to trouble! Zero, like Yuki, was orphaned when his family was killed by vampires. But unlike his fellow protector, Zero was bitten by a pure blood vampire at the time.

As the story opens, Zero is still hiding the truth from Yuki and everyone else. But when he begins to show signs of becoming a vampire himself, Yuki and Kaname discover the truth. Should Zero join the vampires in their Moon Dormitory, or should he stay with the human students, thereby endangering their very lives? The mix of romance, tragedy, action, and humor in this story has made it one of the most popular manga series in the world. The author-illustrator regularly comments in the margins, which has led to an almost cult following of her fans, who feel like they know her personally.[38]

Fruits Basket

Fruits Basket, or *Furuba*, by Natsuki Takaya, is an entertaining story that combines fantasy, romance, and action. Published in English by Tokyopop in 2004, *Fruits Basket* was a fan favorite in Japan before it crossed the ocean to the West. Like other popular manga series, it has been turned into an anime series that has gained many followers. I have wondered why the publisher left the goofy translation of the title, but it refers to a game the main character played as a child that involved a fruit basket (or fruits basket). She did not fit in with her classmates at the time, and she has been trying to find her identity ever since.

The story begins with the heroine, Tohru Honda, waking up and going to school. But this is no ordinary home—Tohru lives in a tent. As an orphan, she is subject to every whim of fate, and the latest whim is that her grandfather, with whom she is living, has asked her to stay with someone else while he remodels his home. Having no place else to go, Tohru puts up a tent in what she thinks is an uninhabited area. Unbeknownst to her, she is staying illegally on land owned by the Sohma family, near the house of three amazingly attractive Sohma family boys. In the course of the story, Tohru learns that the Sohma family has a secret— they are possessed by the vengeful spirits of the Chinese zodiac. So whenever a family member is hugged by a person of the opposite gender, they immediately turn into the animals of the zodiac: a dog, a rat, a boar, and so on.

Once Tohru has learned their secret, they threaten to erase her memory. Their kinder natures (and a healthy dose of self-interest) prevail as they decide to let her stay with them in exchange for some cooking and cleaning duties. As more members of the Sohma family show up, the situation becomes complicated—and more fun. When Tohru is called back to her grandfather's house, it looks like all the fun is over . . . or is it? Can the new friends (and possible love interests) scheme Tohru back into their lives? This is a lively, humorous, and romantic comedy that has become a fan favorite of boys, girls, and adults alike.[39]

Bleach, *Volumes 1–3*

Bleach, by Tite Kubo, has become a media franchise, with an animated series, feature-length animated movies, video games, even a series of rock musicals based on the books. The story opens with Ichigo "Strawberry" Kurosaki, an orange-haired teenager who can see ghosts, fighting to protect a ghost who has been disrespected. Ichigo soon meets Rukia Kuchiki, who is a soul reaper—one who escorts the souls of the dead to the Soul Society, or afterlife. Another role of a soul reaper is to destroy evil spirits—called hollows—who are out to destroy both humans and ghosts.

When Rukia sacrifices herself to protect Ichigo from a hollow, she must transfer her power to him. Ichigo, a prickly personality on his best day, is at first unwilling to put his life on the line for souls he doesn't know, but he soon decides to pursue his new calling. An interesting twist occurs in volume 2 when Ichigo and Rukia encounter a powerful "modified" soul created by the Soul Society in an attempt to create a superpowerful warrior to help them fight hollows. The experiment is deemed a failure, and the Soul Society destroys all the mod souls—or they think they have.

When this mod soul briefly inhabits Ichigo's body, he pleads with the two soul reapers not to destroy him in words that eerily echo the creature's words in Mary Shelley's *Frankenstein*: "I was created, then the Society ordered the destruction of all mods. The day after I was born, the date of my death was set! So I sweated in that pill, just waiting to die. I had a lot of time to think about things. I decided no one has the right to take a life. I exist! I should have the right to live and die freely! Like humans, or even bugs. Even a mod should have that right." Needless to say, the mod soul is saved and becomes a character in the story as the soul reapers try to save those around them from evil spirits.[40]

Ranma 1/2, *Volumes 1–2*

Ranma 1/2 by Rumiko Takahashi is another of those series that breaks gender barriers. In this case, this is literally true as the main character, Ranma, is a teen boy who frequently turns into a girl. This immediately causes drama as Ranma and his father visit some old friends—with three teenage daughters. The female Ranma and the youngest daughter Akane go to bathe, but Akane and a strange boy emerge after the bath. It turns out that when Ranma encounters cold water, he transforms into a girl, turning back into a boy only when he is doused with hot water. This is a result of falling into a cursed spring while on a martial arts training trip to China with his father (who is cursed by turning into a panda in the same way). Fights and duels abound in this story, with both boys and girls taking part in the action. When an old rival of Ranma's named Ryoga appears, the story moves into high gear as Ranma learns that Ryoga, too, has fallen into a cursed spring and transforms into . . . a tiny pig.

Is the story an action/martial arts story? Yes. Is it a romance? Yes, very much so. Is it funny with quirky characters? Indeed. Should you find a copy and read it? Of course![41]

Kitchen Princess *1*

Najika Kazami is an orphan growing up in the Japanese city of Hokkaido in this story by Natsumi Ando and Miyuki Kobayashi. The innocent but resilient teen is known for her cooking skills but is unaware of how talented she is in the kitchen. Najika dreams of meeting her "Flan Prince," a boy who saved her life as a young child and gave her a parting gift of the sweet treat. Discovering that the spoon the boy left behind bears the insignia of an elite Toyko boarding school, Najika earns her way into the school and leaves the orphanage.

The school is not at all what she thought it would be; it's full of snobby students who consider themselves better than everyone else, and Najika is teased and rejected by the other girls. Fortunately she meets two cute boys who are kind to her. The boys happen to be brothers who are not on good terms with each other. Najika brings the boys together with her near-magical cooking skills, and earns herself a measure of fame in the school. As she watches the brothers eat a meal she cooked to bring them together, Najika says, "There's magic in making food taste good. The key is . . . to eat with someone important." She cooks because she wants "to see the smile of the person who eats it."

Kitchen Princess is an entertaining romance series that also dispenses helpful cooking techniques and recipes. Through preparing good food and serving others, Najika wins over the hearts of many of her classmates. Not all though—when the cute boys begin to direct their affection toward her, Najika unintentionally makes some influential enemies. Can she continue to excel despite the jealousies of the other girls?[42]

Tsubasa Reservoir Chronicle

What price would you pay to get something you could only obtain by magic? In *Tsubasa Reservoir Chronicle*, volume 1, Syaoran discovers that Yuko, a mysterious witch, will grant him what he wants, but he will have to give up what is most precious to him. This series by CLAMP, which boasts many volumes translated into English, is one of the most popular manga series of all time. Part romance, part science fantasy, all action, *Tsubasa* crosses over with another of CLAMP's popular series, *xxxHolic*. Characters from other CLAMP series make appearances, too, as part of what some people call the CLAMP Universe.

As the story opens, Syaoran is visited by his childhood friend—and possible love interest—Sakura. The only problem? Sakura is the princess of Clow, and her brother the king doesn't want his sister to fall in love with a commoner. Unbeknownst to any of the characters, Sakura is gifted with great powers that are destined to change the world, powers that are taken away from her in a mysterious event in the ruins that Syaoran, an archeologist, is excavating. To save her memories—and her life—Syaoran is sent to another dimension to see Yuko, the time-space witch. There he meets two other travelers seeking favors from Yuko. The three are thrown together to travel to different dimensions where they will collect Sakura's memories—if they survive. The price for Syaoran to save the princess is the one thing that he truly values . . . his relationship with her. If he succeeds, she will not remember their relationship at all. Is it worth it? Would you pay that price?[43]

Maximum Ride: The Manga, *Volume 1*

In 2007, famous adult crime writer James Patterson wrote a science fiction series for teens (in regular prose) called *Maximum Ride*. The book is about a group of kids whose DNA has been combined with that of birds. The result is that the kids, who are pretty normal in many ways, grow wings and have certain behavior in common with our feathered friends. The series was a huge hit. In 2009, the first book was turned into manga by Korean artist NaRae Lee. The series has become a huge favorite among manga-loving teens, many of whom have never read the prose novels.

The story, which is mostly in black and white, begins with a splash section in color. Max, the oldest of the kids, who sees it as her job to take care of the rest of her "flock," has a nightmare that includes human-wolf hybrids named Erasers. Thankfully she wakes up and she's safe at their secluded house in the woods. But soon disaster strikes in the form of—you guessed it—Erasers. But these aren't just any monsters; these are Erasers that Max knew in a former life at the "school" where the children were illegally created and detained before they escaped. When the Erasers take Angel, the youngest of the bird kids, Max and the others decide to follow the kidnappers and do what their enemies least expect—that the flock will take the fight right to their doorstep.

Artist Lee has created a very compelling adaption of the story, with lively characters and lots of action. There are also many beautifully drawn pictures of the kids' various types of wings, which is a very nice addition. As beautifully as the bird kids are drawn, the Erasers are just as detailed—and scary. This is an exciting science fiction series that you will not be able to put down. Not to spoil the story, but down the road the romance heats up, too.[44]

Rurouni Kenshin: Restoration

If you like a lot of fighting and swordplay in your manga, along with a touch of romance, this book is for you. *Rurouni Kenshin*, by Nobuhiro Watsuki, reads at a lightning pace and rarely lets up from the first page to the last. This series is a follow-up to his immensely popular series by the same name that ran in Japan during the 1990s and was published here in the United States between 2003 and 2006. After a more than ten-year hiatus, the mangaka decided to begin a new series because of the publicity surrounding the release of the first *Rurouni Kenshin* live-action film in 2012. The series has also spawned numerous anime series and games as well.

Restoration begins with some background for those, like me, who had never read the original series. It recaps the vicious war between the Tokugawa Shogunate forces and the Ishin Shishi pro-imperialist patriots during the Bakumatsu era. The result of the bloodbath was the victory of the Ishin Shishi and the beginning of the Meiji Restoration. One warrior named Hitokiri Battosai in particular gained a name for himself for his fierceness and unrivaled technique. After helping the pro-imperialist forces win the war, Battosai disappeared. Caution: these first chapters contain intense and fairly grisly fighting scenes, so this book may be more appropriate for older teens.

The real story begins during the eleventh year of the Meiji period, when a clueless young man appears on a Tokyo street one day wearing a samurai sword, unaware that carrying swords is banned in public. He is mistaken for a paid swordfighter and finds himself paired against a beautiful swordswoman named Kamiya Kaoru, who is fighting to save her dojo from a crooked businessman. The young man loses the fight but gains a friend. As various killers are sent to the dojo to dispatch him, he handles each one with superior skill and a frightening transformation into the ancient warrior whenever he draws his sword. Fortunately for his opponents, he has taken a vow not to kill and is aided by a reverse-blade sword that does not do lethal damage. The young man, who turns out to be the returned Hitokiri Battosai, has now sworn to protect the innocent and save lives rather than take them. The final story in this series takes place as the young man protects a foreign doctor sworn to heal those who cannot pay for his services. When a native doctor gets angry and sends assassins to stop the doctor's work, Battosai saves the day and reveals that the Western doctor is actually a woman. This is a very entertaining manga, with both exciting fighting and a message about justice for the oppressed.[45]

Parasite

The entire human race becomes threatened when a bunch of alien organisms rain down on the earth in Hitoshi Iwaaki's hit series *Parasite*. This is a great example of a science fiction manga set in modern times. The art in this book is clearly manga, but the style is more realistic and Western than some older manga. The story gets revved up when the worm-like aliens take over organisms and eat their brains. They can take any form they choose, but most have chosen to look like normal humans—until the host's face peels apart to reveal long, slimy tentacles that overwhelm and consume another human!

The only person who knows what the aliens are up to is a high school boy named Shinichi. Instead of letting the alien into his brain, Shin has trapped an alien in his hand. Henceforth the human and the alien must work together to find and destroy the other aliens. You may ask why an alien would aid in the destruction of his own species? Shin asks the same question, to which the alien living in his hand (which he has named Migi) replies, "Only your own life is precious. I've never valued any life besides my own." Migi goes on to warn Shin that if he tries to tell the authorities about the alien, it will not go well. "Shinichi, if you attempt anything that will cause me harm, I will do everything I can to stop you."[46] The boy is forced to comply. This book is filled with great fight scenes as well as romance and humor. The book also contains some rather gross scenes where humans have been mutilated by aliens, as well as strong language and some sexual innuendo. But *Parasite* also raises larger issues about the contradictions inherent in various human beliefs.

GRAPHIC NOVEL AS SERIOUS LIT: ARGUMENTS FOR YOUR ENGLISH TEACHER

We've talked about a lot of graphic novels, comics, and manga throughout the course of this book. Some are fantasy stories about superheroes, while others are history stories about real-life heroes. Some tell the stories of atrocities in other countries or in our own. We've looked at graphic novels that tell heartbreaking love stories and comics that show graphically the story of a teen growing up into adulthood.

I assume if you've read this far that you take graphic novels seriously. The stories told in these books are as deep and challenging as stories told in prose that you read in high school literature classes. In many cases, these books deal with difficult subjects in a way that makes them more affecting and life changing than the same stories would be if told in prose. Why, then, are graphic novels still looked down upon by some in the literary community? Why do librarians and English teachers continue to exclude graphic novels and comics from the classroom and school libraries?

Some teachers are still hanging on to the old notion that comics are for kids. Others say that graphic novels, although more serious than they used to be, are still too easy to read. I even found some who believed that, because teens like them, they couldn't be that serious! In my opinion, that's a terrible answer; wouldn't people read more if they liked what they read? It seems obvious.

"Last year in eighth grade I was sitting in reading class without a book. So I pulled out a comic from my back-pack and began reading. Before long the teacher came and told me to put it away and get a book. She didn't think comics were appropriate reading material. But was she right? Are comics not good to be reading? There is evidence to prove they are suitable reading material. Many reject them without even looking at them because they believe the content is bad. But comics are more educational and complex than anyone thinks.

"Comics are often dismissed before ever being picked up. They have been stereotyped as 'bad' and 'uneducational.' Professor Carol Tilley, from the Department of Library and Information Science, says, 'Any book can be good and any book can be bad, to some extent. It's up to the reader's personality and intellect.' She then continues to say, 'As a whole comics are just another medium, another genre.'"—Reas S., Cannon Falls, Minnesota[a]

Comics as Serious Literature

Let's take a look at the question of whether comics, graphic novels, and manga are serious literature. How does one decide what books are sufficiently excellent and challenging to warrant being studied in a classroom? The definition of serious literature is subjective, of course, which is why "experts" have such wide-ranging opinions as to what is a "great work of literature." Rick Gekoski, at one time a professor of English Lit at Warwick University in Coventry, England, as well as an author and a judge for the prestigious Man Booker prize for literature, was asked what makes a great work of literature. His answer encapsulates a lot of what we believe about the great works:

> What you find in the greatest works of literature often involves some or all of the following: the high quality of the language, complexity of theme and detail, universality, depth and quality of feeling, memorableness, readability. . . . When you read works of this quality you often feel, and continue to feel, that your internal planes have shifted, and that things will never, quite, be the same again.[1]

I love this definition. If I can paraphrase, great works of literature have

- Great writing with great detail
- An emotionally complex and challenging theme
- A universal quality that resonates with many different types of people
- A high-interest factor, so you don't want to put it down
- The ability to not only stick with you but also change you, even after you put it down

Think back to some of the comic books and graphic novels you've read. Some don't meet these criteria, just like a lot of prose books don't. (I'm thinking here of many of the spy thrillers I've read through the years; they were great fun to read, but I can't remember any of the plots or characters, and they certainly didn't change the way I think about the world.) Some comic books have been churned out quickly because a deadline was approaching and not a lot of thought was put into the story or the art. Those comics are fun to read, but nobody would call them great literature.

But then there are some graphic novels that are very challenging to read, require a great deal of thought, have an amazing amount of detail (both verbally and visually), and are so deeply affecting that they change your perspective permanently. I would say those fall into the literature category. Even some superhero comics are deeply and thoughtfully written, asking questions about what we believe and why, with deeply thoughtful writing and great art. Again, I would argue that these books can be considered great literature.

And I'm not alone. More and more teachers are incorporating graphic novels and comics into class reading lists. Kristi Romo, a high school English teacher and reading specialist in Minneapolis, Minnesota, said in an interview that she has used graphic novels at every high school level for a variety of reasons:

- "The comics format forces readers to slow down. One of the most common bad habits I see is students are reading to 'get it done' rather than to make meaning or understand what the words are communicating. When reading a graphic novel, the reader needs to take in both the images and the words together to create the meaning which forces the reader to slow down; the text supports the image and the image supports the text.
- "Graphic novels are also useful because students are more likely to experience a complex story from beginning to end. Because a graphic novel typically has fewer words, it increases the chances a reluctant reader will read it in its entirety. This success is significant for these students, often pivotal.
- "Graphic novels can provide additional support to special education students and English language learners who are in mainstream classes by pro-

viding a visual interpretation of the text. I used www.stickfigurehamlet. com regularly in my English class when teaching *Hamlet*, and having the illustrations increased students' ability to comprehend the many characters and their interactions.

- "Graphic novels are not just effective for remedial reading classes; they are a great way to experience excellent literature with complex ideas. In my English 12 courses, students analyze and discuss *Persepolis* by Marjane Satrapi and *American Born Chinese* by Gene Luen Yang. The ideas they develop are just as intelligent and in-depth as the work they do for the assigned novels.

- "Graphic novels have very limited filters—sometimes no filter. Unlike prose novels, which require a strong narrator, graphic novels are experienced more directly. This, combined with the illustrations, makes the reading experience more visceral than a prose novel."[2]

Serious literature requires more work for our brains and our souls. The following are some more characteristics of serious literature:

- Employs more complex sentences and advanced vocabulary
- Relies less on action and more on internal struggles
- Contains fuller three-dimensional characters
- Generally deals with more complex and darker subject matters
- Uses imagery and symbolism to resonate on a deeper level
- Improves empathy for people different from you in culture, race, gender, sexuality, or socioeconomic background
- Does not shy away from showing uncomfortable parts of life such as abuse, bullying, prejudice, death, suffering, betrayal, heartbreak, broken relationships, moral failure, and other hurtful experiences
- Generally tries to redeem those hurtful experiences, meaning that they are shown in light of some quality or experience gained

"Comic books are awesome. I could go on and on about how they combine art with literature seamlessly or how graphic novels like the *Watchmen* have stood up to novels like *To Kill a Mockingbird* on *Time*'s 100 Best Novels. But that's not why they're special to me, or thousands of other readers. They're special because they represent generations, the reason why characters span across decades."—Emma S., Plymouth, Minnesota[b]

- Makes the reader more human somehow; doesn't treat disaster and violence as entertainment, but blights on the world that need to be redeemed

This is an incomplete list, of course. Your English teacher or professor will have more reasons that some books are taken more seriously than others. Literature is not something that can be tested and proven in a laboratory—literature is an art form that shapes the mind and the soul, so it will by nature be subjective and personal. The case study on the book *Blankets* will tackle some of these issues and provide a sort of test to see if the book should be included in a literature class.

Students on Graphic Novels as Lit

A number of high school Honors English students were asked if they think more graphic novels should be used in lit class. A vast majority said they think more graphic stories should be utilized, but some disagreed. Here is what they said.

Yes, graphic novels should be used in the literature classroom, because . . .

- "It could spark someone's interest other than reading normal books" (Joey, 18).
- "Sometimes when I'm given a book to read in class it may not be in my interest so by having the graphics to go along helps me follow" (Olivia, 18).
- "Some students really benefit from seeing what's happening rather than just imagining it" (Brooke, 18).
- "At least one through a school career. I think this is so that students can get to see all types of literature" (Justin, 18).
- "It helps get out a message to an audience that wouldn't need a reading level on par with the subject of the novel, i.e., a child would be able to learn about war without reading a textbook" (Amelia, 18).
- "It's a nice change from reading regular texts. Gives some variety to the lessons" (Taylor, 17).
- "Graphic novels are easier to read, and understand because of the pictures" (Madelyn, 18).

- "It shows a different way of thinking. It made us have to think about the images as well, which we don't normally have to do" (Kayla, 18).
- "They're less work than normal novels, and [you can] connect what you're reading by seeing it" (Emily, 18).
- "It's a different way to learn. It adds veriety and veriety is the spice of life (excuse my bad spelling!)" (Sophia, 17).
- "It is short enough for people to finish but long enough to teach students lessons" (Crispin, 18).
- "They make reading funner but also having images make it more real" (Michael, 18).
- "Absolutely! They demonstrate many of the themes and elements we research in our studies. Also, it's important to encourage reading, and comics are perfect for those who otherwise hate books" (Ashlyn, 18).
- "Something new to introduce instead of always a chapter book. I feel like teachers may think it's too easy, but it can be hard to understand sometimes" (Destiny, 18).
- "They are easier and more understandable reads and can be just as educational that gives you a picture to make things seem more realistic and relatable" (Austyn, 17).
- "Visual learners are more engaged and greatly benefit" (Connor, 17).
- "They are a good way for more people to read. A lot of people can read them easier and comprehend them better" (Melanie, 17).
- "They are easier to follow and keeps students engaged by using pictures" (Stephanie, 18).
- "Comics and graphic novels are great ways to keep the 'not so readers' in the loop. Everyone is involved and can feel the emotions while seeing them" (Natalie, 18).
- "It helps students learn a different kind of reading. If it wasn't for us reading in class I never would have read a comic. And now I wish I would have read more" (Jillian, 18).
- "An image in a book becomes more powerful when a real image is shown instead of shown in only words" (Alex, 18).

- "Teens [don't] really read books often, and having a graphic novel for us to read in the classroom is amazing because it help us really visualize what's really going in the story to help us to get a better understanding" (Alina, 18).
- "They are for the readers enjoyment and when they enjoy it, maybe they will read more often" (Devin, 17).
- "I think it would help lower level reading ability students because the visual aspect helps to keep them engaged. It also makes the pages seem far less intimidating because less words are used per page. Also if they have a harder time imagining what's going on the pictures help kick start that movie in your head making a book far more enjoyable" (Alex, 18).
- "I think they could be more widely used, especially with kids who are struggling with reading" (Timothy, 17).
- "Educational, sometimes. Pretty. Entertaining. Expand horizons" (Tyler, 14).

No, graphic novels should *not* be used in the literature classroom because . . .

- "Hell no, I read real books" (Josh, 18).
- "[The books] used would not be the stories of interest to students. It would cause students to permanently resent the genre" (Dane, 18).
- "I don't think there are many important literature elements found as commonly in comics and graphic novels. I feel it's more entertainment than learning" (Chris, 18).
- "I think students should be forced to use our imaginations instead of just be given pictures. I feel like my generation is already struggling enough with imagination given the large role technology play in our lives" (Brittany, 18).
- "I do not think it's needed. I really feel like the education system has really fallen behind, books like *1984*, *Fahrenheit 451* are classics that are not taught in our schools that could really teach valuable lessons that are becoming relevant with current issues about personal freedoms" (Anthony, 18).

- "I believe we should read actual books instead of having 18 year-olds read a book with primary pictures" (Walker, 18)

And one person even answered both yes and no:

- "Yes and no. Yes because it's an easier way to learn things and no because it gets too distracting and seems to shy away from the meaning of the text sometimes" (Bailey, 18).[c]

Good for Learning

Besides being great literature, graphic storytelling should be included in classes for another reason: it improves educational outcomes. "Educators agree that graphic novels are useful for teaching new vocabulary, visual literacy, and reading skills," writes Brigid Alverson in an article on the *School Library Journal* website. She mentions a teacher in New York City who regularly uses *Gettysburg: The Graphic Novel* by C. M. Butzer in conjunction with other historical sources to teach about the Civil War. "Publishers often provide lesson plans, information on curricula, and tie-ins to the Common Core State Standards."[3] Students may be interested to know that there is even a Zombie-Based Learning Program where they can learn geography by tracking the undead after a zombie apocalypse!

Graphic novels offer many advantages in the classroom. First of all, because we are at heart visual people, the graphic images help comprehension and retention rates. In Alverson's article, she tells the story of a high school English teacher in Illinois who did an experiment with his class. He made some students read the play *Hamlet* by William Shakespeare. He gave another group the graphic novel adaption of the play. When both groups of students took a test of their understanding and retention of the play's events, the group that read the graphic novels actually scored higher than the prose-only group. The teachers in the article were quick to state that they wouldn't give *only* a graphic novel version of a great play or historical event, but in connection with more traditional sources, the graphic versions raised retention rates.

This higher retention rate bears out other studies done with comic-style textbooks. A University of Oklahoma professor named Jeremy Short conducted an experiment in which he had two groups of business students read a text about management concepts in the business world. One group read a portion from a graphic novel; the other read about the same business concepts in a traditional

The Story of All of Us

What's the best way to get an overview of the history of humankind? The History Channel produced a series called *Mankind: The Story of All of Us*. At the same time, the broadcaster came out with a companion series of graphic novels for elementary and middle school students. The chapters in volume 1 of the series cover specific time periods: early man, the pyramid builders, the Romans and the spread of Christianity, and so on.

Many of the writers for the graphic stories in volume 1 are well-known comics writers, such as Marv Wolfman, who wrote many famous DC superhero comics. Other writers are Nathan Edmondson, Shawn Brock, Neo Edmund, Devin Grayson, and Joe Brusha. The illustrations in this book are top notch, giving readers amazing insight into what life was like thousands of years ago. The illustrators for volume 1 are Tom Derenick, Dennis Calero, Giovanni Timpano, Lara Baron, Javier Aranda, Matt Triano, Mike De Carlo, and Wes Huffor.

The opening story is about a family who must hunt far and wide for food in humankind's early days of hunting and gathering. The main point of the story is that humans differed from the animals in that they learned and passed down their knowledge. With each generation, people learned more, such as how to stay in one place and grow crops instead of following the animal herds. The book then moves to the pyramids and the secrets of storing food in ancient Egypt; discusses Roman roads and the impact that Jesus of Nazareth had on the Roman Empire; and ends up all the way through the crusades, when European knights attempted to take back the Holy Land from the Muslims. This is history in an interesting, beautiful format that you will not easily forget.[d]

textbook. The results surprised some people. "While both groups were able to apply the concepts, the results indicated that participants who read the graphic novel excerpts were better able to recognize direct quotes than participants exposed to the traditional textbook."[4] Retention had been considerably improved just by adding in a visual story element.

Gene Luen Yang, whose name has appeared in a number of other places in this book, is a former high school teacher as well as a writer-illustrator. When he got a job writing *Superman* for DC in 2015 he had to take a break from teaching, although for years he taught and wrote simultaneously. Yang authored a paper entitled "Comics in Education" in which he makes the case that the five strengths of comics can be harnessed in almost any subject or grade to improve educational outcomes.[5] According to Yang, comics aid in education because they are

1. Motivating. Students enjoy comic books, even when they teach a lesson. A researcher in 1973 concluded that teachers would do well to harness the "fantastic motivating power of comic books."[6]
2. Visual. Many studies have shown that people remember visual stimuli better than words by themselves. There is also the issue of different learning styles to contend with—visual learners need visual stimuli to learn abstract material.
3. Permanent. Lectures and films are "fleeting" while words and pictures on a page are "permanent," which allows students to travel at their own pace; the difference is that only comics provides both a permanent and a visual component.
4. Intermediary. Comics can serve as an intermediate step to difficult concepts or disciplines; the medium is especially good at drawing in reluctant readers or students who don't traditionally enjoy the discipline of reading.
5. Popular. Comics can bridge the gap many students feel between their lives in and out of school. As comics researcher Katherine Polak MacDonald says in *Teaching Comics and Graphic Narratives*, "Popular culture is always a good bet for keeping students interested in the writing process, and graphic narratives offer a platform for this."[7]

Yang's recent series *Secret Coders* puts these principles into action as he writes a suspenseful story that also teaches students about computer coding.

Working Out the Brain

I can imagine some people still objecting: "Okay, comics may be considered literature, and they may help with understanding and retention, but aren't they sort of a cop-out because they're simpler and easier to read than straight prose?" A linguistic researcher named Neil Cohn (you may remember his name from earlier chapters on the elements of visual language) has done extensive research on comics and how our brain functions when we read the medium.

Secret Coders

Would you like to sit through a long, boring class on how to program a computer . . . or read a suspense-filled graphic novel that teaches you to do it? Yeah, me too! *Secret Coders* is a graphic novel series by Gene Luen Yang and Mike Holmes geared toward middle schoolers (although high schoolers can learn a lot as well). The main character, Hopper, is a new student at a creepy-looking school filled with robotic birds and odd teachers—including her mom! Hopper starts off on the wrong foot as she picks a fight with a popular basketball player named Eni. The two quickly become friends as they are thrown together to solve a mystery involving a turtle robot, birds with four eyes, and a series of path portals that become more and more mysterious. And does her missing father have something to do with the school's mysteries? The cranky janitor says it's true and sends Hopper and her friends on a mission using their new knowledge about coding to guide them.[e]

Cohn and his colleagues devised an experiment using *Peanuts* cartoon panels (the old comic strip written and illustrated by Charles Schulz). They tested how the brain processed comic strips under a variety of circumstances. Some of the strips were related in content, but there was no clear narrative; other strips had a narrative arc but the panels came from different stories so they were unrelated; the last group consisted of random panels with no narrative structure or thematic similarities. In a nutshell, he found that the experiments "point to a system of comprehension guiding sequential images that is broadly analogous to what is involved in processing verbal language: both sentences and sequential images require the combination of meaning (semantic relatedness) and structure (narrative structure/syntax) to build context across a sequence."[8] In an article in *Discover* magazine, Cohn further explains these findings: "Sequential images have a grammar like sequential words do . . . the brain is processing these different kinds of grammars in a common way."[9] In other words, reading comic books is utilizing the brain in the same way as reading words on a page—it's not an inferior process; it's the same process.

This research goes hand in hand with a conclusion many researchers are coming to; namely, that using comics and graphic novels in the classroom helps

"Until I turned seven years old, I despised reading. In fact I would often find a book, read the first page, then throw it aside and stare at the wall, because at that time, I would rather be bored, than be reading. As I grew older I learned to enjoy reading through comics. I was seven the first time I read a comic, and at that time I wasn't allowed to read most comics, because of my age, so I went with an easy choice that my parents would be okay with, The Simpsons. Since then, I have evolved into an avid reader."—Michael B., Plymouth, Minnesota[f]

improve various types of literacy. The authors/historians who wrote *The Power of Comics* state, "Research over the past seven decades has demonstrated that comics have the capability to motivate readers, to enhance reading skills, and to aid those engaged in learning a second language." This is partly due to the fact that students actually enjoy what they're reading and reach for something else. "Those who reported more comic book reading also reported more pleasure reading in general, greater reading enjoyment, and tended to do more book reading."[10]

This finding—that students enjoy reading comics, and therefore seek out more—is supported anecdotally by every librarian I talked to in writing this book. In fact, the two librarian/authors of the book *Library Collections for Teens: Manga and Graphic Novels* introduce an interesting phenomenon called the expansion effect. The *expansion effect* means that graphic novels "lend themselves to 'literary exploration'—discovering connections among books, authors, illustrators, and other creators." The authors find that this often leads to more reading, even of books that are not graphic stories. They tell the story of Bill (not his real name), a seventeen-year-old library patron in Glendale, Arizona. At a librarian's recommendation, Bill read Neil Gaiman's graphic novel *The Sandman: Preludes and Nocturnes*. He liked that book so much he read the other nine books in the series, as well as the companion books *The Sandman: The Dream Hunters* and *The Sandman: Endless Nights*.

After finishing the *Sandman* series, Bill did some research and discovered that Gaiman had written several spinoff books, which he read, followed by all of Gaiman's unrelated graphic works. Then he read Gaiman's prose novels *Neverwhere*, *American Gods*, and others. Bill went back and read several other Sandman offshoots that were written by other authors. One of these was Bill Willingham, author of the *Fables* series, which he found and read. After that, Bill looked up the original artists on the *Sandman* series, including Craig Russell and Jill Thompson, and procured and read all of their books. The librarians conclude, "Eight years later, Bill has since read more than forty graphic novels, novels, and short story collections on the strength of one recommendation."[11]

Multimodal Literacy

Today's students live in what researchers call "multimodal culture." This means that teens experience the world and communicate using more than one type of medium or communication resource (including written text, spoken language, pictures, and visual/aural messaging like video). For example, most social media formats and websites operate textually, visually, and aurally to communicate messages. This is the world that students operate in, leading some educators to advocate for using forms of literacy that go beyond just text-based literacy. One of these forms is comics.

Researcher Katherine Polak MacDonald says that because comics are multimodal, they teach students to think critically about the complex, layered messages that they encounter all the time. "Multimodality as it is deployed in comics develops the way in which students recognize milieu, and gestures to the way in which they encounter the world in terms of multiple literacies which must be simultaneously read for subtextual elements, as well as for their interrelations." Comics helps students become more discerning by means of

> the examination of the layout of panels on the page, the analysis of what is depicted versus what is relegated to the gutter, how space is used within the panels as well as on the page and the purpose therein and the style(s) of artwork. Drawing attention to the kinds of choices the producers of comics are making helps students better grasp issues of composition and arrangement in texts that are predominantly textual, but more importantly, in texts that combine numerous modalities.[12]

That is a fancy way of saying that readers of comics must figure out how the words and art are working together and infer meaning from what is *not* being said on each page.

A great example of this multimodality occurs in this spread from *Roller Girl*, by Victoria Jamieson (figure 7.1). Astrid, the main character, is trying to explain how conflicted her emotions are. She references a chart with simple faces that her kindergarten teacher used to explore emotions. She doesn't have to explain it; she draws it right on the page. Astrid ends up saying that she's "shad," which is happy + sad. Readers can relate to this combination of feelings immediately, without the need for long paragraphs of explanation.

Figure 7.1. *Roller Girl* by Victoria Jamieson. From ROLLER GIRL by Victoria Jamieson, copyright © 2015 by Victoria Jamieson. Used by permission of Dial Books for Young Readers, an imprint of Penguin Young Readers Group, a division of Penguin Random House LLC.

An article on the website of the National Council of the Teachers of English supports the kind of thinking required when students read graphic novels. One high school English teacher from Alberta, Canada, says in the article, "Every part of each frame plays a role in the interpretation of the text, and hence, graphic novels actually demand sophisticated readers."[13] Another high school teacher, from Rhode Island, explains that she teaches comics for the sake of learning literary terms. "Many of today's comics rely heavily on allusion, satire, irony, and parody to make a point. Students discover they might actually need to know such terms for reasons other than analyzing a Dickinson poem. Making this connection has strengthened their understanding of terms."[14]

Graphic Nonfiction in the Literature Classroom

Adrielle Anna Mitchell, a researcher and university professor agrees that graphic literature is important to include in the classroom. But she takes the argument a step further and makes a case for graphic nonfiction in place of graphic fiction in the literature classroom. One reason is that graphic nonfiction might be more instantly respected than graphic fiction: "For many students (and many of our colleagues as well) in the United States, speaking of comics brings to mind superheroes, garish primary colors, triviality, popular culture, and other jejune pursuits."[15] Bringing in historical and philosophical works can dispel this idea that graphic storytelling is for children. Another reason she advocates nonfiction is that it widens the audience considerably. In the past, comics have been associated with young, white, heterosexual American males; nonfiction graphic novels draw readers from any number of communities, many of whom are nonwhite and nonheterosexual.

Mitchell recommends many of the nonfiction books mentioned and reviewed in this book, including *Palestine* by Joe Sacco; *A.D.: New Orleans after the Deluge* by Josh Neufeld; *Persepolis* by Marjane Satrapi; and *Maus* by Art Spiegelman. And why graphic nonfiction as opposed to prose nonfiction? Because of the sophisticated skills mentioned earlier in this chapter: "Graphic narratives offer the reader a chance to apply cutting-edge critical apparati to a challenging dual-track medium which richly rewards such work." Looking to the work of a French comics theorist, Mitchell points out another way in which graphic literature helps in many other areas of study: reading nonlinearly.

> A strictly linear reading (first page to last) does not do justice to the special nature of a visually-dominant comic text. . . . Students can learn to move around a comic text fluidly, detecting the . . . strong ties between distal panels. This is a lesson I believe students of literature should learn to ap-

ply to all texts, graphic and traditional. . . . Instead of reading the book once straight through and relying on this vectorized reading to support all subsequent critical insights, the student can become more facile at jumping around the text, looking for connections, repetitions, contradictions, etc.[16]

Graphic memoirs, in particular, are useful for teaching critical thinking, according to Mitchell. "Because autobiographical comic artists walk a slippery line between realism and subjectivity, their works offer fertile ground for the active reader to create meaning and co-generate the text while simultaneously inferring the writer-artist's stake in the content, structure, and point of view of his/her text. Graphic memoirs demand a high degree of reader involvement in the form of identification, truth-testing and contextualization."[17]

Case Study 1: *Blankets*

There are a number of graphic novels that should be included in high school and college literature courses—and I don't mean as a transition to reading for reluctant readers. That is a worthy use of graphic novels, but I'm talking about something more advanced. I propose that graphic novels and comics that deal with "serious" subjects in a "serious" way be included with the best American books in lit classes. One of the best is *Blankets* by Craig Thompson.

Look back at the list of attributes we are looking for: well written with vibrant details, a serious subject matter, life changing, focus on characters rather than breathtaking action, and many more. In my opinion, and the opinion of numerous English teachers, *Blankets* fits the bill. On the surface a love story, the book is, down deep, about a boy growing up and deciding to give up his faith. The details of the story are not just given in words, but in the illustrations as well. The world-building is strong—the story could not take place anywhere else; the snow, in fact, becomes a very important symbol in the story. The story is ultimately heartbreaking, as the boy loses both his faith and his first love. And yet there is redemption and growth as the main character learns to follow his heart.

Throughout the narrative, frames with no words require the reader to interpret symbols and judge the passage of time without narration. On one page, for example, the artist shows the teenage boy lying on his girlfriend's bed reading a story from the Bible. He actually becomes part of the biblical story, foreshadowing the struggle he will endure trying to reconcile the teachings of his faith with his very real sexual desires. In the final frame, the boy notices a painting of Jesus, the same painting that hangs in his own room. Does the Jesus of the painting look with disgust at the struggles of the boy, or with forgiveness, or some sort of understanding? It is a mystery at this point in the story.

In another scene, near the end of the story, the main character is a few years older. He is walking through the fields with his younger brother, trying to explain why he gave up his faith. The story of a cave that slowly disappeared one spring is used as a type of metaphor for how the boy's faith seemed to shrink until it finally disappeared from his life. In the second frame on the page, the main character's past experiences get all tangled up in his mind, like the collage of images that appear around him. Just as quickly his brother brings him back to reality, and the scenery disappears. In fact, his brother's words literally become the only scenery in the frame. The reader is left to wonder why the scenery has disappeared, why the artist chose to feature just words and reactions. It's part of the language, the diction, the vocabulary of sequential art—your mind has to work on many levels to understand it.

The final two spreads contain no words, just a hand with a paint roller gradually painting over the image of the boy and girl sitting in a tree, until the final page contains nothing but nothing. Readers are left to reflect on scenes that they have painted over themselves, people they have lost, beliefs that have changed; it is very powerful.[18]

"When compared to other literature comics are at the bottom of the list. They're not considered good. But, what if you were to put a comic to novel form. Anyone who read this would get the exact same story and learn the same things as they would if they were to read a comic. One difference though, is it would take longer and probably be less interesting (depending on personality) than to have read a comic. I believe it is actually more educational reading a comic. In a chapter book it tells you what is happening and you visualize it but with comics it's the exact opposite. They show you what happens and you put it to words in your mind. So why are they so often rejected?

"Those of you who reject comics as literature should open up your minds and try something new. Read a few comics and maybe you'll realize comics are just as good as other books if not better. When you think of it comics really are just another genre."—Reas S., Cannon Falls, Minnesota[g]

Case Study 2: *One Hundred Demons*

Lynda Barry is one of the smartest writers of this generation. Her books make you think, while entertaining you; they make you laugh and, of course, cause you to cry. *One Hundred Demons* is arguably her most well-known work. The story of Barry's growing up through her teen years is not always "exemplary," meaning teens should not necessarily try all the things she tried at that age. But everyone can relate to her struggles. Her commentary resonates on so many levels: "This ability to exist in pieces is what some adults call resilience. And I suppose in some way it is a kind of resilience, a horrible resilience that makes adults believe children forget trauma."[19] In the same panel, the main character is lying on a bed thinking, "Wish I was dead Wish I was dead Wish I was . . ." The narration and the thoughts of the character are working against each other because the narrator is the adult Lynda, while the girl in the bed is her as a teen. This requires some elevated thinking to process why these contradictory elements exist in one panel.

This book shows the life of a teen as it really is with unflinching truthfulness. At the same time, her positive attitude gives us hope that things will get better. The art is wonderful, even though there are more words here than in most graphic novels. This book will cause you to change your mind about successful ways of growing up, honest relationships, the dangers of substance abuse, and many other topics teens are interested in.

And that, after all, is what we ask of literature.

HOW TO CREATE YOUR OWN COMIC BOOKS

Some of you have been reading this book thinking, "I could do that. I could create my own comic." The truth is, *yes you can*! Even if you can't draw, you can write a script for someone else to draw. Or maybe you can draw but don't have an idea for a story. Let someone who's good at stories write the script and you illustrate it. There are many ways to create a comic, so don't think there is a right or wrong method.

There are also many ways to distribute a comic. Some people are fine with just drawing it and letting their friends read their one original copy. Others will want to distribute it to the people in their school. Some may even want to try and distribute their comics to a wider audience, either in print or online. These are all possible scenarios, depending on what your ambition is, and how hard you are willing to work. Of course, the wider the distribution you want the more effort it will entail.

I'm going to talk about both of these aspects of original comics: creation and distribution. Remember, the subject of your comic doesn't have to be superheroes, although that has been a very popular subject in the comics world. As you've seen throughout this book, comics are written about all aspects of life and represent many different genres. So don't be afraid to write a story about any type of subject—even yourself, as the author of *The Dumbest Idea Ever* (see the review in chapter 4) discovered. You will be sure to find someone who is interested in whatever subject you choose! In one chapter we won't be able to cover every aspect of the process, so I will suggest a few more books and websites devoted solely to the creation process for more information. Here are subjects covered in this chapter:

- Coming up with a story
- Panel principles
- Building suspense using visual tools
- Formatting a comics script
- Finding an illustrator

- Different jobs in creating artwork
- Making copies of your work
- Getting your comic to readers
- Print versus online distribution
- Being picked up by a publisher

An Interview with Gene Luen Yang

Gene Luen Yang is one of the most prolific comic creators of our time. He is both author and illustrator for *American Born Chinese*, *Boxers and Saints*, *The Eternal Smile*, and *Animal Crackers*. He is the writer for *The Shadow Hero*, *Level Up*, *Secret Coders*, *Avatar: The Last Airbender*, DC's *Superman* and *The New Super-Man*, and many others. The U.S. Library of Congress named him National Ambassador for Young People's Literature in 2016. He is also the father of four children, a university professor, and the recipient of a MacArthur genius grant in 2016. Yang was gracious enough to take time out from his writing and speaking engagements to answer some questions.

Randall Bonser (RB): How was the reception to the first *New Super-Man*?

Gene Luen Yang (GLY): I think the reception for the entire rebirth/relaunch of the DC comic universe has been pretty successful, so this book has been carried along with that wave, which is really nice.

RB: Have you enjoyed the new comic? And how did you enjoy doing the old Superman that you killed off?

GLY: (Laughs) I did not write those issues where he died, by the way. Anyway, it's a really different experience because Superman Superman—like Clark Kent Superman—is one of DC comics' marquee characters, one of the Big Three: Batman, Superman, and Wonder Woman. So I think there's a lot more pressure involved, and there are also a lot more people involved. Superman is in four books, so there are four different writers and we all have to coordinate. He was also in that big movie last summer so it was a lot more coordination. Because New Super-Man is a new character, I definitely get a lot more elbow room. But I felt like I learned a lot in both experiences.

RB: Would you like to do more of the big, old-school superhero books?

GLY: I don't know. I enjoy the monthly series. I think the pace is really different. I have a really hard deadline every month, I can't blow it off. I have to turn something in, even if I don't think it's ready yet. And I think I have learned a lot because of that pace. It gives you more practice, because you're dealing with plot structure and characterization and all that stuff on a monthly basis. And you're trying to churn this stuff out. So I think just by sheer repetition I've learned a lot.

RB: Were you working closely with your illustrators? Or they just took your scripts and knocked them out?

GLY: Because the timeline is so compressed I definitely had fewer interactions with the artists than I would on the graphic novel side. And there are fewer places where I can give notes. Like when I'm working with another illustrator on a graphic novel I usually have a chance to give notes at the thumbnail sketches phase, the pencil stage, and the ink stage. With a superhero comic the turnaround is so fast that sometimes the art is done and I didn't get a chance to give any notes.

RB: Were the scripts that you were turning in more like the Dark Horse scripts, or were they more the Marvel style?

GLY: Yeah, I didn't do Marvel style. It was pretty detailed. There were some artists that I worked with that asked me to take out the panel indicators. They just wanted all the action and dialogue on a page to just read as a single page. But most of the artists I've worked with so far have wanted me to break it up into panels. All but one.

RB: Did you indicate the shape of the panel?

GLY: No, I might say, these three panels are the same size if I wanted a certain rhythm, or I might say this is the largest panel on the page. I wouldn't give any more details than that.

RB: Why do you love comics?

GLY: My love of comics comes—it's like a pre-logical love. I loved comics even before I thought about why I loved them. I started collecting comics when I was in the fifth grade, and pretty soon after that I started writing and drawing my own. I really appreciate the combination of words and pictures. Comics is a single unified medium that is made up of two different media and the relationship between the words and pictures can be really complex and you can use that relationship to get all sorts of narrative and emotional effects. It just seems like the possibilities are endless. You can achieve a lot through prose or pictures by themselves, but there's something about that relationship that I really like.

RB: Are you in favor of more comics and graphic novels being used in English classes as serious literature?

GLY: Sure, yeah, absolutely. I think the comics medium is just another way humans communicate. And it's another form of telling stories. I'm not in favor of comics replacing prose books at all, but I am in favor of comics being taught alongside books in other formats. I just think by the time kids graduate from high school they should have done one deep reading of a fiction prose book, of a book in verse, of a graphic novel, and of a nonfiction book. They should do one deep reading of every different kind of literature.

RB: What are some of your favorite graphic novels and why should they be used in schools?

GLY: I really love *Maus*, by Art Spiegelman. So far it's the only graphic novel that's won a Pulitzer Prize. It's a graphic biography of the author's parents, who were both Holocaust survivors. He does so many complex things in that book. He basically uses cartoon animals as metaphors. All the Jews are mice, all the Germans are cats, all the Americans are dogs, all the Poles are pigs. And he really is able to use the visuals of that book to make you think about the issues and the situations that the people were in. I think that's a wonderful book. I think *Persepolis* is another staple in classrooms, written by Marjane Satrapi. She's a French Iranian who grew up in Iran during that country's transition into a fundamentalist government. And what she does with her pictures is she establishes an intimacy between her and her reader. So when you read that book it really feels like you're reading something out of her personal journal. I think that's a wonderful example.

RB: Are you encouraged by the increased number of ethnic characters in graphic novels, especially in superhero comics? And would you like to see more?

GLY: Yeah, I really like the current conversation that we're having in storytelling in general, and in comics in particular, about diversity. We live in an incredibly diverse world. It's pretty much impossible to get through life without caring about somebody who's from a different cultural background than you. And in a lot of ways our stories are supposed to prepare us for life, right? So it makes sense that we have stories about characters of every different kind of background. I don't think we're there yet. The representation in our stories is growing, but it's definitely not the same as it is in real life. But just the fact that we're having a conversation about it is very encouraging.

RB: What would teens need to remember if they want to do their own comic?

GLY: At the beginning it's more about the discipline of writing, and the discipline of making stories than it is about the final product. That means setting aside time to draw, setting aside time to write, definitely every week, better yet every day. And also, early on, you have to learn how to silence your critic. Later on your critic can help you improve. But in the beginning that critic can be paralyzing. So don't ever let the pursuit of the perfect get in the way of finishing a project.

RB: Where might teen writers find artists to help them put their dream onto the page?

GLY: I'd look around their school first. There are actually a number of stories of comic book creators coming into the industry together. One of the friends is a writer and the other one is an artist. The most prominent probably is Robert Turkman and Tony Moore, the creators of the *Walking Dead* comics. I believe they were friends in high school. So if you're a writer and you're creating stories, just look around your school, I'm sure there's some kid who's really into art. Another place to go is a comic book convention. At a lot of comic book conventions all around the country they have what they call Creator Connection where writers and artists meet, it's almost like speed dating. So the writers and artists go, and the format is you'll get five minutes to talk to each other. And at the end, if you're interested in working with someone else, you tell the host, and if the interest is mutual, the host will give contact information to the two of you.

RB: Say you're a teen who is majority race but you want to write characters of other ethnicities, but you're afraid of getting it wrong or stereotyping, should you just forget it and write all white characters?

GLY: As a writer, I know how hard it is to get over the fear of just writing, period. You have that blank page or that blank screen staring at you. And it is just hard to put your soul onto that page or screen. So I'm very reluctant to add any sort of fear onto anyone's plate. If you have a story that is in your heart and that story happens to feature a character that is different than you, I would never tell someone not to write that story. I would tell them, if it's in your heart you should write it. But at the same time there's a balance, right? If that character is different from you, you have to be very diligent in your homework. You've got to make sure you read a lot, you've got to make sure you talk to people who are insiders in that culture that you're writing. You've got to be diligent and do your homework. I don't think you should be afraid of making any sort of mistake in your first draft. That includes story-building mistakes, that includes grammar mistakes, but that also includes cultural mistakes. But make sure you get someone who knows what they're talking about to read over that draft for you. Make sure you fix it before you're done.

RB: Anything else you want to say to teen authors and artists?

GLY: You've got to get over the fear. I don't think that fear ever goes away. You wake up every morning and you've got to fight it all over again. When I talk to other writers, it seems like it's universal. All of us have to do it every day.[a]

Coming Up with a Story

This may seem obvious, but the first item you need to make a comic is a good story. It has to introduce a main character (or several characters) and launch into a series of obstacles that the main character(s) must work through. A story with high stakes will be more interesting to your readers than a story about someone's life in which she or he encounters very few problems to solve. A high stakes story

"Numbers and figures don't matter if none of the characters are likable and have relatable motives."—Ayinde R., Owing Mills, Maryland[b]

doesn't have to be life or death, it could be trying desperately to secure a date to the prom or dealing with a parent who moves out of the house. Real-life issues can generate a ton of anxiety, as you well know. So first you need a gripping story.

There is one sure-fire method of coming up with a story: create a memorable character. I heard one writer say that she imagines a setting first, and then characters present themselves. But most authors I've talked to dream up their character first, and then create a story for that person (or animal, or robot, or alien species, or whatever). Characters come in all shapes and sizes, limited only by our imagination. Many people who write comics are intrigued with superheroes, so let's start with that.

Superpeople

Maybe you have imagined a superhero you want to get out into the world. That's great; the last century has proven that people love superhero stories. You need to make sure yours is different from the ones already written about—you don't want to violate copyright laws. If you want to write about existing characters, there are fan fiction sites that let people write without violating copyright laws. But to distribute an original comic, your character needs to be unique.

So what is your superperson's backstory? How did your character get extraordinary powers or abilities? You don't necessarily have to answer that question right away in your story, but you need to know so that you will be consistent in the things your character can do. In the old days, a hero's backstory would occur in the first issue, but that is not necessarily true anymore. Now a person's history can come in the form of flashbacks a few episodes in if you choose—see *Silk* for a good example. Don't keep the audience waiting too long, though; their curiosity might cause them to read ahead, or worse, give up on the story, if you don't give them enough information.

An important part of a character's history is his or her relationships. What type of family is the character from? Is the original family still around, or have the person's relationships shifted? Who are the character's friends and associates? How closely does he or she depend on them? No story is interesting without an interaction with others. In fact, the interaction with others can be a source of great conflict and movement of a story's plot—see any *Green Lantern* book as a good example of this.

Of course, you will have to indicate to your artist how your character is dressed. If you have created a superhero, think about costume or uniform. Some of that will be dictated by the times in which the person lives. In one recent issue of *Superman*, written by Gene Yang and illustrated by Jack Herbert, they had the Man of Steel dressed in jeans and a tight-fitting T-shirt. This obviously had a much more contemporary feel than the billowy cape and red boots. That issue also featured Wonder Woman, having ditched the swimsuit look, in her new full-body armor. (Fans must have protested, because very soon both heroes went back to more traditional threads.) Will your superhero be part of a team that wears matching uniforms like the original X-Men, or will each wear his or her own fashion, as the mutants did later in their evolution?

You will need to specify a setting for your character. If the setting is a fictional city like Metropolis, you will need to have a clear picture of the landscape and describe it for the artist. An urban setting is going to lead to very different adventures and graphic elements than a suburban, rural, or jungle setting. Science fiction stories give even more freedom—you can decide what types of creatures and environment exist on the planet(s) your characters hang out on. Just like in prose science fiction, make sure the rules of your world are consistent: the role of technology, religious or philosophical beliefs, amount of government involvement in daily life, family structures and traditions, and other important world-building issues.

Stories about Everyday Life

Maybe your characters are not superheroes; maybe they are students at a school similar to yours, like in the graphic novels *Awkward* and *Nothing Can Possibly Go Wrong*. The considerations mentioned in the preceding paragraphs—backstory, relationships, clothes, and setting—are important to think about no matter who your characters are. So how do you come up with believable details for your characters? There are two ways to do this:

1. *Be a planner.* This is when you sit down and plan before you write. You can make a list of character attributes and details so that when you start writing, you'll have an idea of where characters live, what they wear, who they associate with, how they talk, what they eat, and many other details. After your list of attributes has been started, write a broad outline of the plot to guide you. For some people, knowing this information before they start writing helps them through the difficult process of beginning the story.

2. *Be a pantser.* This word comes from the old idiom about flying by the seat of your pants, or acting according to instinct without any planning. Writ-

ers who are pantsers don't start with lists or outlines; they just sit down and start writing, letting the characters materialize from their brain onto the page. I saw author-illustrator Kazu Kibuishi (*Amulet*) at a book festival in Atlanta once, and a student asked him if he outlined his stories before he began to draw. He answered that no, he drew first and created the story as he drew. Of course, he goes back and edits his rough drafts, but this process could properly be called pantsing. In this method, characters will not necessarily come out fully developed; they will change and morph over the first few pages (and drafts) until the writer gets a clear picture of who they are.

Neither of these methods is better or worse than the other. It just depends on your personality and writing style. Writers who work better knowing where they are going are going to be planners. Writers who love the discovery process and can't wait to see what is going to appear on the page will be pantsers. The world needs the stories of both styles of creators.

Whatever your process is, don't be afraid to let your characters experience pain. In fact, if your characters don't endure some pain, suffering, embarrassment, humiliation, heartbreak, betrayal, or personal failure, your story probably won't be very interesting! Writing coaches use the phrase, "Raise the stakes!" What they mean is that, as an author, you have to be willing to subject your characters to as much personal trauma as possible in order to give them the greatest distance to travel until they learn something or change for the better (or worse).

Writing the "Other"

Maybe you've seen discussions on social media or on television about majority race authors writing characters of color. Or criticisms of male authors writing female characters.

These are important discussions, so I want to say a word about this. Every author uses his or her imagination to create characters different than himself or herself. Even characters who are from your racial and cultural background will be different from you in many ways. That said, if you are creating a character who is substantially different from you in gender, culture, race, religion, body profile, or in any other way, you need to do your homework to make the character authentic. And then, for safety, you should give your work to someone from that background to check over to see if you got it right.

Brian Michael Bendis, the great comics writer whom I quote quite a bit in this chapter, faced criticism when he created Riri Williams, star of *The Invincible Ironman*. Bendis is a European American male, while Riri is an African American woman. Even though he created the character, some fans felt the stories should have been written by an African American female. On his Tumblr account, he answers this criticism. (Note: I have cleaned up some of the grammar and capitalization in Bendis's answer.)

> But I am not a person of color. I never will be. Nor am I a blind Catholic lawyer from Hell's Kitchen [Daredevil], nor have I been bitten by any spider, let alone a radioactive one, I am not a raccoon-like creature with bad grammar and a rocket pack, and I never was a homicide detective that used to be an immortal super hero. But I am a writer. Writers write stuff. All kinds of stuff. And if I was a person of color it would still be the same job. I would write all kinds of flavors and tones and perspectives. I write to discover things outside my perspective Every writer does.[1]

So if one or more of your characters is different from you, be brave and write about it. Just be sure to follow Gene Luen Yang's advice (found in my interview with him) and do your cultural homework and then have someone read it to see if you're on the right track.

Outlining

Most authors I have talked to like to wrestle out their story in an outline before they begin a script. An outline allows you to work out the kinks in your story line before you go through the process of breaking it down into panel-sized bites. Don't be nervous—I'm not talking about one of those Roman numeral outlines where you never know what the next level of numbers or letters should be. This outline is more like an extended summary in paragraph form where you explain the major incidents in your story. It's similar to a film "treatment."

Veteran writer and editor Brian Michael Bendis emphasizes the importance of an outline in his awesome script writing book *Words for Pictures*:

> A story outline is a somewhat more involved document [than a pitch document] that goes into more detail about story beats and character arcs. . . . You're basically writing a book report for a book that doesn't exist, a synopsis of something that is only in your head. . . . It can take you just as long to write a very good outline as it would to write three entire issues of a comic. But you have to remind yourself that you are not going to get to write that comic unless you first nail the outline. And when all is said and done, no matter what the circumstances, you are always, and I mean *always*, better off for having organized your thoughts in a succinct manner.[2]

"The common perception of comic book characters is that the heroes are good and the villains are evil. It's that easy and few think much further of them than that. Perhaps this phenomenon was born from the school of thinking that comics are for children. Children who are naïve and incapable of understanding the moral gray areas that are associated with the adult world. But as all artistic mediums produced by intelligent adults do, comic book writing and illustrating developed over time. As the audience grew to incorporate older readers, the writers realized the inadequate depth that their characters were boasting so publicly. The readers craved for something more from these sparkling heroes and dirty villains. They turned to the outside world and chose to introduce the more realistic idea that the line between good and evil is not so effortless to discern. Put some dirt on that hero, clean some off our villain, and let the reader interpret what they must."—Kori E., Seattle, Washington[c]

When Bendis uses the word "beats" he explains, "A story *beat* is a described beat of action. A series of beats creates a story's intended form." A beat might be, "the boy runs after the accelerating school bus" or "his sister throws his homework in the fireplace." He concludes by saying, "The outline process is writing, and you will discover things about the story as you create its outline."[3]

An outline/summary will help you discover if your plot is complex enough to fill an entire book, or if it is just an episode of a larger story. The outline will also introduce all the major characters and their roles in moving the plot forward. Relationships and conflicts will be explained so that when you begin the script, all the nuances of relationships and actions will be clear in your mind. As you write the script, new characters and twists will appear that were not included in the outline—and that's okay—but the overall direction and cast of characters will be firmly set as a goal.

A Second Pair of Eyes

After you write a draft of the outline/summary, let a few trusted friends or mentors read and critique your outline/summary. Ask them specific question, such as the following:

- Do these characters seem real to you?
- Do you know what the main character(s) want and what's motivating them?
- Is my story line interesting and believable?
- Is the climax exciting?
- Is the setting right for this story? Is the setting clear?

Those questions will give your readers something specific to talk about. If you're lucky, they will give you honest feedback about weak points in the story or questions they have. Let these friendly critiques help you as you revise the outline to make it tighter and stronger. Most stories require several revisions before they are strong enough to be put into script format. Like any job, the work you do in preparation will improve the final outcome.

Let me say something here about criticism and rejection. I have been a professional writer for three decades and let me tell you, writers face constant criticism. Some of it is friendly, others not so much. The *only* criticism that you need to listen to when it comes to your story is the wisdom that comes from friendly sources: smart friends, mentors, teachers, fellow writers, editors, agents—people who know the kind of books you want to write and who want to help you improve. Anyone can be critical, but there are only certain people who know what they're talking about when it comes to books and comics. Listen to those people.

"Wonder Woman reflects an independent woman who does not need a male character to vow revenge for her sake, due to that fact that she can fight her own battles. Her strength without a man is a highly relatable topic as more women find themselves living their lives single, raising families without fathers, or taking executive jobs that years ago was only considered to be man's work. The values that Wonder Woman promoted to the comic book community were very similar to the values reflected onto America's more modern society. She symbolized the empowerment of women, and labeled anything lesser as sexism. . . . Her mission has changed to bring the ideals of love, peace, and sexual equality to a world torn by the violence of men. Her role as a female icon has changed as rapidly and significantly as that of America's modern woman."—Caroline A., Syosset, New York[d]

Having said that, if you want to write or illustrate, *you need to develop a thick skin* and not get depressed or defensive when your work is criticized by those smart people. Just because your work receives criticism, that doesn't mean it isn't good. Every story can be improved. So take suggestions courteously and grate-fully, with an eye toward applying them as you can. Ask yourself, "What can I learn from this?" Throw out the criticism that seems wrong or contradictory to where you're going with the story and get back to work improving on your next revision. Comics author Neil Gaiman has a great quote on criticism: "Remember: when people tell you something's wrong or doesn't work for them, they are almost always right. When they tell you exactly what they think is wrong, and how to fix it, they are almost always wrong."[4] I believe he means that it's helpful to know where readers are having problems, but trust yourself to correct and revise your story to fix the problem.

Script Format

Once you have a solid outline or summary, get going on writing a script for your illustrator. If you are your own illustrator, you may want to skip this step and go straight to thumbnails, which is discussed later in this section on script format. But chances are you will want a script for your illustrator.

You have lots of options when it comes to formatting a script. There is no one standard format, but there are three general types of scripts: the full script (which has many formats); the brief synopsis (often called the Marvel style); or the thumbnail sketch (frequently called a storyboard). Some teams will even use a hybrid method of all of these formats to communicate with each other. Each method shifts the workload to a different member of the creation team.

Full Script Format

The full script is the most popular method of communicating in the comic book industry today.[5] There are many reasons for this, including speed of production—in the serial comic book industry, finished books ship out every month. Another reason is that many stories start with an author, then move to an illustrator to give it flesh. The full script gives the illustrator a clear vision of what the author intends. If there is anything like a standard script formatting, it comes from Dark Horse Comics, which offers this style guide on its website (images.darkhorse .com/darkhorse08/company/submissions/scriptguide.pdf). On pages 256–57 you can find the actual Dark Horse Comics script format.

Book Title, Issue # • Writer's Name (should appear at the top of each page) page number here, 1

SCRIPT FORMAT AND SPECIFICATIONS. Please create your scripts as follows.

WRITER'S NAME (name, address, and phone should appear only on the first page of your script)

Street Address City, State and Zip

Phone Number

PAGE ONE (five panels) (Begin each new story page on a new sheet of paper, label it, and indicate how many panels make up that page.)

Panel 1. Number your panels. Panel descriptions should be typed in standard upper and lower case. Please do not use tabs, alternate fonts, or any other formatting.

CHARACTER:

The "attribution" (the name of the character speaking) should appear in all caps on a separate line from their dialogue. It used to be that all comics were lettered by hand. These days, much of the lettering is done on computer.

OTHER CHARACTER:

Typing the dialogue in standard upper- and lowercase, flush-left, with no tabs or other formatting makes it easy for dialogue to be copied and pasted onto the comics page.

Panel 2. There is no set limit for how much or how little information should be included in each panel description; generally a sentence or two is enough. If there are specific character traits, objects, or placement of either that you need, make sure you tell the artist. The most important thing to remember: if it isn't in the script, don't expect to see it in the art. You'll get best results if you list characters in your panel descriptions in the order (left to right) that they need to speak in the panel.

SFX:

Sound effects are indicated just like dialogue.

CAP:

Captions are indicated the same way. All dialogue, sound effects, and captions should be listed in the order in which they should be read in the final art.

CHARACTER (thought):

Thought balloons are indicated in this fashion. Captions and dialogue should be limited to approximately 25 words per balloon, and about 50 words per panel, max.

Book Title, Issue # • Writer's Name (should appear at the top of each page) page number here, 2

Panel 3. Exact panel layout is usually left to the artist, but if you have something specific in mind, put it in your description. If absolutely necessary, you can draw a sketch of what you want.

CHARACTER (OP):

Characters speaking from off-panel are indicated this way.

OTHER CHARACTER (whisper):

If a character is whispering, the letterer needs to know. Other common indications for modified lettering or word balloons are (small), (burst), and (weak).

Panel 4. For action sequences, you'll get best results if you limit yourself to three or four panels per page. Remember: the more spectacular your action description, the less room you'll have for other panels on that page. In comics, space is your major limiting factor. If you have two characters speaking to one another in a panel on a page containing five or more panels, chances are there won't be room to show something happening simultaneously in the background. Also, except in rare cases, the most "back-and-forth" dialogue that will comfortably fit in a panel is a comment, a response, and a counter-response.

CHARACTER: [comment]

Dialogue that carries over from one balloon, or from one panel to another is indicated by double dashes at the end of the first dialogue section —

OTHER CHARACTER: [response]

— and another set at the beginning of the next. Interestingly, long dashes and semicolons are not used in comics punctuation. Colons are used only on rare occasions.

CHARACTER: [counter-response]

Double dashes can also be used to indicate a speech that is cut-off by events in the story —

Panel 5. For non-action scenes, you can have more panels per page, but keep in mind how many characters and props are necessary in a scene as you're writing. The more panels on a page, the smaller each of them will have to be. Trying to cram too much information into small panels will result in a comic that's difficult to read and visually uninteresting.

CAP/CHARACTER

"— a caption can be used to carry over dialogue from a previous scene to a new setting by placing the speech in quotation marks."

NEW CHARACTER: underline words that you want to emphasize. Ellipses (three periods) indicate a pause between . . . sections of a speech, or a speech that trails off . . .

Marvel Style

Many illustrators will appreciate this level of detail so that they can concentrate on bringing the story to life without worrying about plot, characters, story arc, and all that. Some illustrators, however, find this type of full scripting too restrictive. Stan Lee famously worked out a system at Marvel in the 1960s that left more room for creation by the artists. Stan Lee's scripts were generally one page long—that was the entire script! Some artists appreciate this kind of trust and freedom, while others want more of the author's vision so they can concentrate on the art.

Whatever style of script you choose to use, remember that it must be written so that the artist can bring the story to life. Editor Diana Schutz explains it this way: "Comics scripts are *not* written for the reader! That sounds strange, but it's true. A comics script is written for the artist, and the writer has to give the artist all the important story information, information that may be withheld from the reader until, say, the last page of the printed story or even a later issue."[6] So make sure the artist understands your vision.

The Marvel Method in Stan Lee's Own Words

On the blog titled *Dial B for Blog*, the authors include a speech that Stan Lee gave at Princeton University in March 1966. In the speech he explains his famous Marvel Method for writing scripts:

> We don't work the same as other outfits . . . up 'til five years ago, the writer writes a script just as a playwright writes a play, then the playwright gives it to a director, who gives it to the producer. And the director will be the equivalent of the artist.
>
> But we don't do it that way. We have what I think is a much better system—that we stumbled into because of necessity! I marvel that everybody doesn't do this. I had been writing all the stories myself, and I just didn't have time.
>
> If I was writing a story for Jack Kirby, Don Heck might be sitting on his hands, waiting to do something. And we're so—our schedule is so tight, we can't afford to have Don be sitting around. And yet, I had to

finish this story. So I said, "Look, Don, I can't give you a script, I've got another day's writing to do, because Jack needs it. But the next story would be Iron Man goes here, he does that, he meets that guy. You go ahead and draw it, draw it any way you can, I'll put the copy in later."

Don went ahead and did it. And ah, his drawings were like crossword puzzle, I didn't know what was going on. But anyway, I put the copy in. And I found, as I was doing it, it made it much more enjoyable. Because I wasn't looking at blank paper in a typewriter, but I was writing copy for people, for drawings that I was looking at, with expressions and actions, I felt carried away. . . . Now I give the artist a synopsis, and he draws the story himself. I have no idea what I'm going to get. Sometimes it comes out so far removed from what I'd expect.[e]

Some people dispute how much involvement Stan Lee actually had in creating these early Marvel comic books. The writers of *Dial B for Blog* state in a tongue-in-cheek way that the definition of the Marvel Method should actually be "An artist opens a vein and pours out their life's blood onto a blank page, creating the characters and their world, the plot, pacing, and setting—in short, creating ABSOLUTELY EVERYTHING. Then Stan Lee adds captions, sound effects and dialogue. That's the REAL definition of the Marvel Method."[f]

However much involvement the writer and the illustrator had, this method—a simple synopsis that allows the illustrator much more freedom—has become an alternative to the full script.

Thumbnails

A third method of scripting is a series of thumbnail sketches in the form of a storyboard (figure 8.1 shows a sample thumbnail sketch). Most comics get to the storyboard level *after* the script is written, but in some cases the storyboard *is* the script. This is very time-consuming for writers who do not draw, so it is rarely used. But for an illustrator who is drawing his own story, this might speed up the production time. The outline/summary will keep the story on track as the events and characters make their way onto the paper in the form of rough panels.

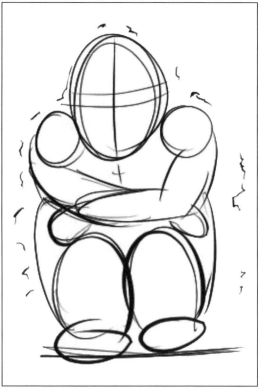

Figure 8.1. Thumbnail sketch by teen artist Christopher Burns. *Illustration courtesy of Chris Burns*

Books on Script Writing

Brian Michael Bendis is one of the most prolific and best-loved comics writers of our times. He has written for many DC and Marvel titles. Bendis was asked on his Tumblr account what books a prospective graphic script writer should read (besides his own book *Words for Pictures*), and this was his answer:

- *Story: Substance, Structure, Style and the Principles of Screenwriting* by Robert McKee
- *Comics and Sequential Art* by Will Eisner
- *On Writing* by Stephen King
- *Graphic Storytelling and Visual Narrative* by Will Eisner
- *Understanding Comics: The Invisible Art* by Scott McCloud[g]

Panel Principles

As you write your script, here are a few tips to keep in mind.

1. Include Only One Action or Emotion Per Panel

This is pretty clear when it comes to action: one dropped plate, one punch in the face, one hit into the outfield per panel. Any more actions and the time element would throw off the reader. If your batter cracks a ball into the outfield, you can't have the outfielder catching it in the same frame. Most of the time, the constraints of the panel will keep you in line here.

Emotions, however, present a challenge. Because of the cost of creating comics, some writers are tempted to put long conversations in one panel to save space. Truth be told, some authors do that once in a while to change the pacing, as I mentioned in chapter 2. That kind of panel cramming is the exception, not the rule. Try to stick with one emotional beat per panel. If one person admits she hates another character, don't include the other person's response of undying love in the same frame—that's too much in too little space. Take your time. Let the words and illustrations combine just right to create the proper emotional rhythm for your scene.

A corollary to this panel principle is that you should only include one word balloon per panel, or one exchange with one emotional beat. Any more than that will strain the panel.

2. Don't Repeat with Words
What You Are Already Saying in Pictures

Sometimes writers and illustrators show they don't really trust their readers by explaining in dialogue or via a caption what is happening in the art. Early superhero comics do this to a maddening degree. A character in an early Aquaman comic (*More Fun Comics* #73, 1941) says, "A hand—from out of the sea!" as the panel shows a gloved hand . . . coming out of the sea. Alternately, some comics and manga don't include enough dialogue or narration and the reader is constantly wondering what in the world is going on.

Scott McCloud, in his book *Making Comics*, says, "The relationship of word balloons to the drawings that surround them has always been an uneasy one."[7] He recommends asking a series of questions about this relationship:

- Are both pictures and words contributing something of value?
- Could the two together be more than the sum of their parts?

- Could the words and pictures carry a vastly different message to deliver a special effect or emotion?

Including the right balance of dialogue and art takes time and practice. Listen to the people you ask to critique your work; they may help you see an imbalance that you cannot see.

3. Use Fewer Panels for Faster Action Sequences

Most graphic novel pages contain four to six panels. Although this varies widely, readers are accustomed to that number. If you want to increase the speed of a scene, include fewer panels on the page. Jamming a page with a whole bunch of little panels will slow the reader down, which will slow the pace of your scene.

The action scenes in superhero comics will demonstrate this. When the action gets really intense, the panels tend to get bigger and there are fewer on the page. After the climax, as the scene winds down emotionally, the panels get smaller and more numerous. Also, the focus tends to shift from a wider view during intense action to more close-ups as the tension resolves. Of course, there are exceptions to this rule like any other, but generally the faster you want the reader to move, the fewer panels you will include on the page.

4. Include as Many Senses in Every Panel as Possible

Yes, comics is a visual form of storytelling. But the more senses you can include in your panels, the more involved your readers will be. Comics writing legend Chris Ware was quoted in an interview that appeared in the *Paris Review* as saying, "Comics, in some ways, are already structurally more synesthetic than 'text-only' writing, with their combination of pictures and words inducing a flowing sense of movement and sound and sometimes even smell."[8]

The popular manga *Kitchen Princess*, by Natsumi Ando and Miyuki Kobayashi, works with multiple senses in a spectacular way. When the main character, Najika Kazami, makes a delicious flan or a fruit parfait, the art actually makes your mouth water as you look at the page! All stories have texture but sometimes writers can get so caught up in the action that they forget to include the visceral details that draw the reader in.

5. Use the Language of Film to Tell the Illustrator What to Draw

As noted in chapter 2, film and comics are similar in some respects. Both are primarily visual mediums, as opposed to music and speech, which are primarily aural. Both also use a sequence of images in frames, or panels, to tell their story. Because of these two similarities, the scripts used to direct the visuals use some common language. Your script needs to let the artist know what to include in the frame and how far away the "camera" is, so use a modified version of film language to explain your vision. Here are some terms that will be useful:

- *Close-up.* This normally means that only one person is included in the panel. The focus is drawn in to one character, usually the speaker. An extreme close-up would be an even tighter shot; for instance, only the face of the speaker or some other aspect of an object. A perfect example of this occurs on page 5 of Brian Michael Bendis's *Powers: Who Killed Retro Girl?* In the graphic novel, the publisher includes a portion of the script in the back of the book. Notice what is happening as the page progresses:

PAGE 5—
1-PAUSE.
2-SAME SHOT, BUT IT IS GETTING SLIGHTLY TIGHTER ON WALKER [dialogue excluded]
3-SAME BUT EVEN TIGHTER. [dialogue excluded]
4-PAUSE. SAME EVEN TIGHTER
5-SAME EVEN TIGHTER. THIS IS NOW A CLOSE UP ON WALKERS DETERMINED FACE. JUST ONE BEAD OF SWEAT. [dialogue excluded][9]

Panel five is the last one on the page. As the shot gets tighter and tighter, the tension on the page rises dramatically. Finally, the last panel is amplified by the suspenseful page turn. This is masterful use of both an incremental close-up and a cliff-hanger page turn.

- *Wide shot.* This is just what the name implies: a frame that includes more characters or more of the space in which the characters are interacting. This is often used to establish location or when action occurs. An establishing shot is a wide shot used on the first page of a comic or a chapter to establish the location of the action—also called a splash page because it is often "so spectacular that it draws the reader into the story."[10] The splash page for Kazu Kibuishi's *Amulet*, book 2: *The Stonekeeper's Curse* shows three people (very tiny) from behind as they walk toward a hulking, dark city stacked on the side of a steep mountain. The person in the middle is being held by the two others, and every window in the ominous city has two lighted windows, making it look like the houses are alive and watching the approaching individuals. With an establishing shot like that, you can't help but launch into the book!

- *Medium shot.* Several characters appear in the shot, with minimal background to establish place and ambience. Many American comics use this type of shot more often than any other. Gene Luen Yang told one rookie author, "You can eliminate all instances of 'medium shot of' in your script. Medium shot is the most common type of shot. It's the default."[11]
- *Overhead or helicopter shot.* This is a panel seen from directly above the characters. It provides a change in perspective to keep the reader interested during a long scene of dialogue or action.

In figure 8.2, you can see the value of different shot distances. As the camera moves closer to the main character, the mood changes. When the reader sees the title of the book in a close-up shot, she experiences empathy for the main character, who is not just casually reading at a coffee shop—she is experiencing a huge emotional change in her life.

Neil Cohn, in *The Visual Language of Comics*, describes panel framing differently. He describes them in terms of the active entities within the frame:

- *Macro*—depicts multiple active entities
- *Mono*—depicts single active entities
- *Micro*—depicts less than one active entity (as in a close-up)
- *Amorphic*—depicts no active entities (i.e., only inactive entities)

According to Cohn, your choice of framing can determine whether your comic seems more Western or more manga-like, because "American comics seem to use more Macros, while Japanese manga seem to use more Monos."[12]

6. Be Specific in the Details You Think Are Important for the Illustrator

If one of your characters is wearing a yellow sundress, you've got to let your illustrator know. There are many decisions illustrators will make on their own, but if a detail is important to the story, let them know in the script. Remember to include the details about the reactions of the other characters when they are not speaking. The illustrator will not necessarily know that what is being said makes one of the characters jealous, while another will laugh. It's your job to explain each important detail.

7. Choose an Alternating Perspective in Longer Scenes

Many films will cut back and forth between close-ups of characters talking. That can get monotonous in a comic book. An overhead shot or a long shot or even a

Figure 8.2. The power of camera distance. *Illustration courtesy of Chris Burns*

cutaway to the exterior of the building will help break up the monotony of the scene. In manga, illustrators often provide a close-up of an inanimate object in the scene such as a cup or a scenic element. Scott McCloud, in *Understanding Comics*, calls that an aspect-to-aspect panel change. It provides intrigue and interest in a longer scene.

The Five Questions of Scott McCloud

If you are going to create comics, you will need to read Scott McCloud's books. *Understanding Comics* is his best and most widely read book, in which he explains—in a comic format—the brilliance and challenges of sequential art storytelling. For comics creators, he wrote *Making Comics* a few years later. In that book, he outlines five questions writers and illustrators need to ask as they are putting their vision down on paper (or tablet).[h]

1. Choice of moment—which moments best tell your story and which moments can you leave out without hurting the story?
2. Choice of frame—each moment needs to be displayed as if from a camera, so where will you put the camera, at what angle, and how far away?
3. Choice of image—once you've chosen the angle and framing, which objects or character(s) in the frame will be highlighted?
4. Choice of word—what words propel the story and work with the art, and which are unnecessary?
5. Choice of flow—this concerns the pacing of the story; in which order the reader will actually follow along?

Building Suspense Using Visual Tools

The most basic rule in creating graphic novels and comics is *keep the reader reading*. There are many tools at your disposal for keeping the reader reading, including great dialogue and art, loveable characters, humor, and a gripping story. Gripping stories use the element of suspense to draw readers in and keep them guessing what comes next. Suspense isn't just for crime tales and superhero action stories. The question of whether the main character is going to find out that her boyfriend is cheating on her can hold incredible suspense. A boy breaking in to his father's computer to find out why he stays out late every night can build tangible suspense.

Comics from the past have used a variety of tools to build suspense. Four of the most popular are a

"They symbolize the two paths that a person can take, sometimes stumbling helplessly down the wrong path whatever that may be for them. The Batman and the Joker symbolize the struggle in all of us to overcome the potential for evil that we all have blooming deep inside of ourselves."—Kori E., Seattle, Washington[i]

1. Virtual or actual ticking clock
2. Gradual moving in toward the subject until the frame is a close-up
3. Point-of-view switch that shows two or more scenes simultaneously
4. Climactic page turn

There are many other ways to build suspense, and more are created all the time. But let's look at these classic suspense techniques so that you'll be able to incorporate them into your layouts.

A Ticking Clock

In *Brotherman: Revelation*, creators Dawud Anyabwile and Guy Sims build suspense at the end by including an actual ticking clock on a time bomb. As the characters find out their meetings are canceled and drive toward the house, the words "TIK . . . TIK . . . TIK . . ." appear at the bottom of every page (see figure 4.4). We "hear" it with every panel we read, and the dread builds as we turn pages toward the inevitable. This is what a ticking clock refers to. But it can be more subtle: a deadline when an assignment is due online, the panic that occurs leading up to a dance, or the number of tickets available for a concert dwindling down on a telephone app. Every interesting character has something they want—a ticking clock simply adds more urgency and suspense.

Scott McCloud also produces a powerful ticking clock element in his graphic novel *The Sculptor*. In the story, an artist makes a deal with Death to achieve the power to sculpt anything he can imagine for a period of three hundred days. Time moves slowly at first as he makes new friends, forms a romantic relationship, and creates the illusion of normality. But as the three-hundred-day deadline gets closer and closer, the last few scenes in the book are almost frantic with desperation.

There are many types of ticking clocks. A prom can set the clock moving—will he get up the courage to ask his crush before someone else does? A test, a championship baseball game, a performance of a play at school—almost anything can set a time sequence in the mind of a reader. If you do want to add suspense in this way, do your readers a favor by referring to the time sequence regularly (either visually or in dialogue) and don't distort the time sequence by making it unbelievable. Setting up a ticking clock is like signing a contract with your readers. They agree to willingly get emotionally involved in your story if you stick to the rules of the time sequence you've created.

A Gradual Close-Up

Films often use this technique to build tension. Using a series of panels to draw closer and closer to a subject can achieve a similar effect in comics. This technique is used in the hybrid graphic/prose novel *The Invention of Hugo Cabret* by Brian Selznick. In one amazing graphic sequence, the scene starts with a wide shot of the main character falling in the path of a train. At first, the train is far away. As you move through the panels, the train gets closer and closer, giving the reader an almost palpable feeling of panic. Although comics cannot show true motion, a gradual close-up can create great suspense.

Switching between Scenes

You may want to create suspense by showing two different scenes happening simultaneously. Of course, readers want to follow one story line in a linear fashion. When you interrupt that by switching to another location or character, you are making the reader wait to find out what happens, which can build suspense. Especially if the two scenes are linked in some way. Cohn calls this a "convergence construction." He notes that "an important feature of this construction is that we only view the common environment of these characters at the final panel. Before that, we must inferentially build the conception of these characters belonging to

> "For the first time I noticed the foreshadowing in the earlier issues. A lot of the drama and a frank humor I write in dialogue today were inspired by the way the Runaways speak to each other. The characters are dynamic. They start out naïve and innocent and eventually come to be independent and brave. They realized that there is good and evil in all people, including their parents."—Emma S., Plymouth, Minnesota[j]

a common environment."[13] In other words, you can build suspense by making the readers try and figure out the connection between the two sequences.

For instance, say you're writing about a student who breaks in to his school to change a grade on a teacher's computer. Think about the effect of switching to the principal's house, with the principal saying to her husband, "Oh crap, I forgot my briefcase. Let me run down to the school and get it." You have her get into her car and start driving. Back to the student at the school. Back to the principal pulling into her parking spot. What effect would that have on your story?

Finding an Illustrator

Needless to say, a good illustrator is critical to a comic or graphic novel. If you don't draw yourself, you're going to have to find an artist. Ideally, you need to find someone who not only enjoys working in comic form, but can work in the style you have envisioned. In other words, if you have a realistic vision in your head, you don't want the illustrations to look like a minimalist comic strip or so abstract that it's hard to follow the story. If your story is very action oriented, you want someone who is adept at kinetic art. So the choice of an illustrator is perhaps the most important choice you will make.

There are many artists out there who would like to make a name for themselves. Maybe an art student in your school would like to collaborate with you. Many sites on the Internet also feature illustrators for hire. Gene Luen Yang says in the interview in this chapter, "If you're a writer and you're creating stories, just look around your school, I'm sure there's some kid who's really into art."[14]

If you have money to pay, finding a good illustrator will not be much of a problem. If money is tight (and when isn't it?) you may have to strike a deal with an illustrator to pay half of whatever comes in. Also keep in mind that the art in graphic novels happens in stages, so you'll probably need several kinds of artists to turn your vision into reality.

Different Jobs in Creating Artwork

Graphic novel art happens in stages. The first stage is to translate the written script into a character gallery and thumbnail sketches, which some people call a storyboard. Right away, the artist needs to create a character model sheet. This is a gallery that includes all the major characters, with facial details, wardrobe choices, typical gestures, and so on. Authors have been visualizing these characters for a long time, so they need to work with the illustrators to bring them into the world with the proper look and style.

Next comes the series of thumbnail sketches that roughly lays out the story. If the author of the script is good at storyboarding, this stage might be done by the author. Author storyboards have benefits and drawbacks, just like illustrator storyboards. Needless to say, if the illustrator receives a written script and a set of thumbnails, the art will come quite a bit faster. But the panel and page layout may be weak, since authors usually don't have graphic design experience. If, on the other hand, the artist creates thumbnails after reading the script, this creates an extra step with the requisite added time. But the quality of the layout will probably be improved.

Panel design and page design are integral parts of the thumbnail process. Each panel, each series of panels, each page, each two-page spread, each series of spreads, needs to work together to create an immersive and seamless reading experience. So if you are the author doing your own thumbnails, be prepared to have the illustrator make changes to your design. You can speed the process by coming up with ideas, but be flexible enough to let your illustrator help with the visual aspects. A good resource for panel design is *Panel Discussions: Design in Sequential Art Storytelling* by Durwin Talon, Will Eisner, Walter Simonson, Mark Schultz, and Mike Mignola.

After the thumbnails and character sketches have been agreed to by the author and illustrator, the artist proceeds with pencil sketches. That's why the illustrators of comic books are often called pencillers. Pencillers do not have to slavishly follow the thumbnails, but they give them a feel for the pacing and flow of the story.

"One time my brother bought some comic books and I read some of it and it was amazing. After that, I thought to myself and what if I can make my own comic. It will be incredible. I started to draw a character and make a story about it as my first mini comic. After a while, it finished and I showed it to my sisters. They interested with it and I was glad. Then I make more comic stories and my sisters will help me to give some ideas for the story.

"One day, my sisters started to make their own comic stories. I read some of it and I was really impressed with it. On that day, my sisters and I make our own comics and gave it to one another. It was very fun to read each other's comics. We usually make comics about comedy, romance, school-life, friendship and others more. From now on I will make more stories for my comics."—Nur Afrina A., Kuala Lumpur, Malaysia[k]

Because the art is done in pencil, small changes can be incorporated if the author feels strongly about any concerns.

After pencil sketches are done, the inker follows the penciller's lines in ink, making the art bolder and easier to follow with the eye. When the budget is tight or the author and illustrator are a team, the penciller can also be the inker. Then the colorist adds color to the art in the palette of colors agreed to by the author and illustrator. Each person in the process needs to have the story's world and details firmly in mind so that the author's original vision is honored.

A Word to the Artists

Most of my advice in this book has been directed toward authors or author-illustrators. But some of you reading this book think of yourselves primarily as illustrators, or as an illustrator first, then a writer. Obviously, art quality and art style are distinguishing features of any comic or graphic novel. The book *The Graphic Novel: An Introduction*, by Jan Baetens and Hugo Frey, has a lot to say to the artist, so I recommend reading that book. In chapter 6, the authors write about the artist's struggle to find his or her individual style while in training:

> Most authors want to draw "personally," rather than to draw "well," and perhaps the frequent fictionalizations of their nightmarish experiences in art school, where individual style is allegedly sacred but where cartooning is systematically and stubbornly rejected as silly and childish, may be a symptom of their struggle to achieve an individual style that does not have to comply with the constraints of what the art system considers good drawing.[15]

The point here is that every artist is different—and that's a good thing. Your art style is appropriate for a particular kind of story that only you can tell. So, yes, learn the basics of art and experiment with various techniques, but try to develop a style that is particular to you. Comics legend Chris Ware explains this artistic individuality: "All cartoonists have a signature 'style' that exists beyond the look of their art or the quality of their writing—a sense of experience, a feeling of how they see the world—as expressed in how their characters move, how time is sculpted."[16] So, artists, be individual! Be great! Let the world see your stories!

Distribution

In the old days, when comics were exclusively print publications, a creator would have to produce hard copies of a comic and distribute them to fans either by hand at a convention, at a local comics shop, or through a distribution deal. Copies were sometimes run off by hand at a local school or print shop. Now that many comics go straight to online distribution, print shops have to compete for the rare print projects. That's good news for you if you want hard copies—there are a number of professional printers who specialize in comics and their prices are reasonable (in a manner of speaking).

Getting Your Books Printed

The market changes rapidly, but comics blogger Tom Humberstone suggests finding a local printer. "Make sure you know what you want," he suggests, "how many pages your comic is, how many copies you want, and whether you want full bleed, etc. Start calling around printers for quotes. Browse the Internet for the number of printers nearby. . . . A couple of main things you'll want to find out is whether they deliver the comics to you . . . and what the unit cost will work out at."[17]

Because printers change their products and pricing so often, no definitive list of printers will be much good a year from now. But blogger Lora Innes gives a helpful comparison of several of the biggest print-on-demand (POD) printers who specialize in comics. POD printing allows you to print as many books as you want (even if it's just one), and most will ship directly to customers. For the same hypothetical project, the following printers provided the following prices. For more information, read the blog at chrisoatley.com/how-do-i-pick-the-print-on-demand-publisher-that-is-right-for-my-ccomic/. Please note that this comparison is from 2011—I only included it to give you an idea of how to pursue your own investigation. Here are the printers Lora lists, and their prices for the same project.

- *Ka-Blam* (www.ka-blam.com). Cost for hypothetical project: $1,351 plus shipping. Ka-Blam's biggest strength is that it caters directly to comic creators. One look at the site and you can see that printing comics is the company's specialty.
- *CreateSpace* (www.createspace.com). Cost for hypothetical project: $1,759 plus shipping or $1,009 with the Pro Plan. CreateSpace is the POD division of Amazon. Through it you can create DVDs, digital videos, books, and comic books.
- *LightningSource* (www.ingramcontent.com/publishers/lp/lightning -source). Cost of hypothetical project: $905 plus shipping and ISBN. Lighting Source is the POD division of Ingram, one of the biggest book distributors in America. The company does excellent work, has a turnaround time of under a month, and has excellent customer service.

- *360 Digital Books* (www.360digitalbooks.com). Cost of hypothetical project: $988 plus shipping. 360 Digital Books also does excellent work and has excellent customer service. The company offers fulfillment services that work directly with your own website.[18]

There are several more prominent printers who specialize in comics. A simple Internet search will reveal them. The important thing is to do your research.

Getting Your Books into Readers' Hands

The easiest way to distribute your comics is to rent a table at a comics convention such as Comic-Con and sell them there. All conventions have a special place for creators to sell directly to the public. Many creators print signs and banners to decorate their table and attract attention. Some even sell other paraphernalia such as T-shirts or mugs to keep their title in front of attendees. Making money at conventions is hard work, says comics creator Christian Sager on CNN's *Geek Out!* blog:

> DIY comics rarely turn a profit when you add in the cost of printing and table fees if you're settling up at conventions. . . . [That refers to] the cost of setting up a space at a comic book convention to sell wares. Most creators today barely break even and it's incredibly difficult to make a living from it.[19]

Fortunately, most teens don't have to make a living, you just have to pay for the printing costs!

National Distribution: Print or Online?

Some readers may want to get their hard-copy books listed with a national distributor. The largest distributor was, and is, Diamond Comic Distributors. They distribute comics, graphic novels, and related merchandise to direct buyers such as comics specialty shops. So if you get listed with Diamond, your potential customer base might be large. But unless you can generate a large number of sales as a preview in its catalog, Diamond is probably not going to be a viable option for most first-timers. When deciding upon independents that it would like to list, Diamond considers things like quality of art, content, and marketing plan. Keep in mind that even if you get listed in the catalog, Diamond still requires publishers (you, in this case) to do their own marketing to ensure higher sales. The company's website contains all the information: www.diamondcomics.com. There are other print distributors that carry independent books, but they are much smaller than Diamond.

Thank goodness, independent creators don't have to depend on print distributors anymore. The online marketplace is booming with independents who have dropped their old-fashioned insistence on printed books. One such creator, Grigoris Douros, producer of a series about a rock band trapped in a dystopian Texas, advises creators to reexamine the idea that their comic must come out in hard copy. "Think about your goals when creating comics and rate your priorities," he writes on his website. "Some people think success is having a physical copy in hand. I understand the appeal, but if your top goal is to get people reading your work, then going the digital only route makes a lot of sense and you avoid a lot of financial burden."[20]

If you decide to publish your comic online, you have quite a few options. The aforementioned writer, Grigoris Douros, lists these online publishers in the same post:

- Comixology
- Amazon
- iTunes/iBookstore
- Scribd; Tapastic
- iVerse/ComicsPlus
- PulpFree
- Gumroad
- Selz
- Sellfy
- IndyPlanet[21]

Each distribution site has its own submission process and offers a different percentage of profits to the creator, so do your homework before you submit.

Superstar comics creator Jeff Smith (*Bone*) interviewed superstar author-illustrator Faith Erin Hicks (*Nothing Can Possibly Go Wrong*) about online distribution in an article for Comic Book Resources online. Hicks explained why she started out with web comics and how it has launched her career:

> The nice thing about webcomics is anyone can do them, and the bar to entry is extremely low. . . . In order for me to make comics, and find a readership, if I had to self-publish and go to comic conventions, especially right at the beginning, I would not be doing comics, but the fact that the internet was there, it was free, it was really useful for someone if you are incredibly shy and socially awkward, as I still am, and definitely was back in 1999. This was a great way for me to start making comics without meeting scary people and talking to people.[22]

The article goes on to say that Hicks didn't make any money from her free web comics. But they did lead to paying jobs, and publisher First Second has serialized two of her graphic novels online: *Friends with Boys* and *Nothing Can Possibly Go Wrong*.

Can I Be Picked Up by a Publisher?

Most readers of this book who want to distribute their own comics will be happy with a local audience made up of family, friends, and any online readers they can generate. But some readers will want to take the next step and try and get their comics in front of an editor or talent scout at one of the major comics publishers. The biggest names in comics are DC and Marvel, of course, but there are a few other strong competitors. Table 8.1 provides a list of the top ten comic book publishers (in 2014) according to the *Wall Street Journal*:[23]

Table 8.1. Top 10 Comic Publishers (2014)

Publisher	Dollar Share of Marketplace
Marvel Comics	34.38%
DC Comics	28.86%
Image Comics	9.23%
IDW Publishing	5.69%
Dark Horse Comics	5.07%
Dynamite Entertainment	2.57%
Boom! Studios	2.23%
Eaglemoss Publications	1.30%
Avatar Press	0.97%
Random House	0.95%
All Other Publishers	8.75%

If you want to get your work into the hands of editors, there are a few ways to do it. One is to send it through the mail or email. In the prose book world, you need the help of a literary agent to get your manuscript in front of editors. But comics publishers are still (somewhat) open to unsolicited manuscripts. I say somewhat because comics has grown so quickly over the past twenty years that editors are busy and swamped, so they don't have a lot of time to read unsolicited work. All the more reason to make your work as tight and professional as possible. Find the editors who are overseeing work you love, in the same genre as you've written, and send it to them.

If you're sending a snail-mail copy, bind it nicely and include a well-written (and concise) cover letter with their name on it.

In his great book *Words for Pictures: The Art and Business of Writing Comics and Graphic Novels*, author and comic book legend Brian Michael Bendis asks several editors for their advice on submitting work. The following are some big don'ts and dos when sending work to a publishing house.

- Don't send work that looks sloppy or unprofessional; make good copies and bind them nicely.
- Don't send your original art work—you will *not get it back*. Make copies to send out.
- Don't scattershot your submissions—choose the editors working on books you like, in the genre you have created.
- Don't address the cover letter to "Dear Editor"; include the editor's name and do some research as to what he or she is working on right now.
- Don't send a children's comic to a horror editor—it shows you haven't done your homework and your submission will most likely be thrown into "File 13."
- Don't send a pile of books or manuscripts—send your one best work that shows you can tell a story and have studied the comics medium.
- Don't beg. Be professional and polite.
- Don't nag—follow up a submission every four to six weeks with a polite email. Yes, it will take that long to be looked at.

The alternative to sending an unsolicited work to the desk of an editor is to attend a convention and try to meet the celebrity editor while you're there. Don't hand him a bunch of books, just give the one best example of your work. Some conventions and workshops even offer an option to have an editor critique your work. Even if that doesn't lead to a sale, you will get some valuable feedback on your work from a trusted professional.

If you are interested in getting your work to a publisher, be sure to read *Words for Pictures*. Actually, if you're writing a script for any reason, the book is indispensable. For the book he gathers a number of these editors together in a roundtable to answer questions from prospective creators. As he says in the book, that section alone is worth the price of the book. Here is a further smattering of the advice the editors give.

- Don't pitch a story to Marvel or DC comics with Marvel or DC characters. Because of copyright laws, they are not allowed to read them. Submit a sample of your own work.

- Submit a comic with visuals, not a script with words alone. Editors don't have time to wade through long manuscripts—that's why they went into comics in the first place! A story laid out graphically will tell them everything they need to know within a page or two. If you're at a convention, hand over a hard copy of a finished comic they can read on the ride home. If you are submitting via email, provide a link to your online publication.

- If you're an artist, give an example of storytelling, not just gorgeous cover work. Splash pages are impressive but publishers want to see if you can tell a compelling story.

- This should go without saying, but if an editor gives you an assignment, don't miss the deadline. You are unlikely to get a second chance.

- Be professional, polite, and upbeat when you meet an editor. "Comics is a relatively small and interconnected community, so keep this in mind: you don't get a second chance to make a first impression," says Lauren Sankovitch, former editor for Marvel Comics.

- Don't plan any gimmicks or antics to get yourself "remembered" by editors at a convention. "Nothing succeeds like the work itself . . . it all comes down to how good you are on the page, right now—not how good you were years ago or how good you might one day be," says Tom Brevoort, Marvel Comics.

- Research the books an editor has worked on before you send or hand something over. Be selective.

- Be educated about the graphic format. Be aware of how much information you can fit in a panel or on a page. Rewrite a story until it flows seamlessly. "And, most of all, having something to say that stirs an emotional reaction of some kind. That's at the heart of why we read stories in the first place," according to Brevoort.

- Find out the publisher's submission guidelines by going to its website and doing your homework. If the company only accepts electronic submissions, it goes without saying that a package in the mail will never reach an editor's desk.

- Before you send something to an editor, says editor and educator Diana Schutz, "I recommend going to local conventions or establishing an online presence . . . getting your name out there is important: networking."

- A "minicomic" is a good marketing tool. Typically eight pages, it gives a flavor of the story and art. It should have a complete story arc, even if it is part of a longer story.
- If your comic is not picked up, take the rejection as a stepping-stone that all authors experience. Diana Schutz gives advice to authors: "[Y]ou have to be compelled to write, so that even if some editor slaps you down and says, 'No, you're not ready yet,' you have to keep going until you are ready."[24]

I will close this chapter, and the book, by quoting three of my favorite authors again: Faith Erin Hicks, Gene Luen Yang, and Brian Michael Bendis. First, Faith Erin Hicks: in this interview, which she did for *Comic Book Resources*, she explains her process when she creates a comic.

> I usually spend a lot of time nailing down the story outline and figuring out where the emotional beats go, then I do a rough pass at the graphic novel; drawing and writing all of it in thumbnail form on a few spiral notebooks. . . . Some cartoonists just start with a script, but I have to thumbnail my comics out while I'm writing the script, so I can figure out the pacing. It's a nice way to make sure the art and writing are developing in lockstep. Then I go and type up that rough handwritten script, editing it as I go. I guess it's about three drafts before I reach something to hand in to my editor, but each draft has a different shape: outline, thumbnails, then typed script. . . . I like drawing emotional scenes, moments where characters are struggling with internal conflict or emotions running under the surface. It's just something that really interests me.[25]

What interests you? What do you have to say to the world through a comic or graphic novel? As Gene Luen Yang says, you've just got to sit down and do it: "If you have a story that is in your heart, you should write it."[26]

And finally, let Brian Michael Bendis encourage you to work hard: "There are no shortcuts or magic tricks. The only way to make comics is to sit down and make comics. . . . If you're a real writer there is nothing ANYONE can say or do that will stop you. There is literally nothing to be afraid of. Nothing. It's an illusion. Go write."[27]

Appendix:
Final Purely Subjective Top Ten
Lists from Randall Bonser

I will leave you with my top ten lists. Okay, they're actually top twelve lists because there is so much richness to choose from. Remember these are purely subjective—you would probably choose different ones, for different reasons—but here they are!

Randall's Top Twelve Superhero Graphic Novels

1. *Superman: Kingdom Come* (Waid, Ross)
2. *Miles Morales: The Ultimate Spider-Man, Ultimate Collection* (Bendis, Pichelli)
3. *Runaways: The Complete Collection*, volume 1 (Vaughn, Alphone, Miyazawa)
4. *Guardians of the Galaxy*, volume 1 (Abnett, Lanning, Pelletier, Walker, Craig)
5. *The Saga of the Swamp Thing* (Moore, Bissette, Totleben)
6. *Aquaman*, volume 1: *The Trench* (Johns, Reis, Prado)
7. *Ms. Marvel*, volume 1: *No Normal* (Wilson, Alphona)
8. *Wonder Woman: Spirit of Truth* (Ross, Dini) tied with *Sensation Comics Featuring Wonder Woman*, volume 1 (Simone, Hernandez, Sciver, To, et al.)
9. *Green Lantern, Rebirth* (Johns, Van Sciver)
10. *JLA: The Deluxe Edition*, volume 1 (Morrison, Porter)
11. *X-Men: The Dark Phoenix Saga* (Claremont, Byrne, Autin)
12. *Civil War: A Marvel Comics Event* (Millar, McNiven, Vines, Hollowell)

Randall's Top Twelve Graphic Novels
Every Middle School Library Should Carry
(not including superheroes or manga)

1. *Roller Girl* (Jamieson)
2. *Awkward* (Chmakova)

3. *A Wrinkle in Time* (adapt. Larson)
4. *Amulet* (Kibuishi)
5. *Boxers and Saints* (Yang)
6. *March* (Lewis, Aydin, Powell)
7. *Smile* (Telgemeier)
8. *Nat Turner* (Baker)
9. *Maus* (Spiegelman)
10. *Nimona* (Stevenson)
11. *Bone* (Smith)
12. *Yummy* (Neri, DuBurke)

Randall's Top Twelve Graphic Novels Every High School Library Should Carry (not including superheroes or manga)

1. *Nothing Can Possibly Go Wrong* (Hicks, Shen)
2. *American Born Chinese* (Yang)
3. *Persepolis* (Satrapi)
4. *This One Summer* (Tamaki, Tamaki)
5. *Blankets* (Thompson)
6. *Anya's Ghost* (Brosgol)
7. *Maus* (Spiegelman)
8. *Through the Woods* (Emily Carroll)
9. *Tomboy* (Prince)
10. *Chasing Shadows* (Avasthi, Phillips)
11. *Nimona* (Stevenson)
12. *Skim* (Tamaki, Tamaki)

Randall's Top Twelve Manga Every Middle and High School Library Should Carry

1. *Black Butler* (Toboso)
2. *Bleach* (Kubo)
3. *Ranma 1/2* (Takahashi)
4. *Maximum Ride* (Lee)
5. *Fruits Basket* (Takaya)
6. *Kitchen Princess* (Ando Kobayashi)
7. *Dragonball* (Toriyama)

8. *Vampire Knight* (Hino)
9. *Tsubasa Reservoir Chronicle* (CLAMP)
10. *Naruto* (Kishimoto)
11. *Parasite* (Iwaaki)
12. *Boys over Flowers* (Dango)

Notes

Chapter 1

1. Neil Cohn, *The Visual Language of Comics: Introduction to the Structure and Cognition of Sequential Images* (London: Bloomsbury Academic, 2013), 153.
2. John Jackson Miller, "Comic Book Sales by Year," ComiChron, www.comichron.com/yearly comicssales.html, accessed September 27, 2016.
3. Heidi MacDonald, "How Graphic Novels Became the Hottest Section in the Library," *Publisher's Weekly*, May 13, 2013, www.publishersweekly.com/pw/by-topic/industry-news/ libraries/article/57093-how-graphic-novels-became-the-hottest-section-in-the-library.html, accessed March 15, 2016.
4. Will Eisner, *Comics and Sequential Art* (New York: W.W. Norton: 2008), 1.
5. Scott McCloud, *Understanding Comics* (New York: William Morrow, 1993), 9.
6. McCloud, *Understanding*, 12.
7. McCloud, *Understanding*, 17.
8. John Petty, *A Brief History of Comic Books* (Dallas, TX: Heritage Auction Galleries, 2006), 2.
9. Karen Glynn, "Early Comic Strips 1898–1916," Duke University Library, library.duke.edu/ exhibits/earlycomicstrips/, accessed July 12, 2016.
10. R. C. Harvey, "The Orphan's Epic," *Comics Journal*, May 20, 2013, www.tcj.com/the -orphans-epic/, accessed July 12, 2016.
11. Harvey, "Orphan's."
12. Randy Duncan, Matthew J. Smith, and Paul Levitz, *The Power of Comics: History, Form, and Culture* (London: Bloomsbury Academic, 2015), 14.
13. Duncan, Smith, and Levitz, *Power*, 16.
14. Miller, "Chronicles."
15. Duncan, Smith, and Levitz, *Power*, 22.
16. Duncan, Smith, and Levitz, *Power*, 23.
17. Duncan, Smith, and Levitz, *Power*, 23.
18. "Crime Comics and Books," Comic Book Plus, comicbookplus.com/?cbplus=crime, accessed August 2, 2016.
19. Duncan, Smith, and Levitz, *Power*, 25.
20. Ron Goulart, *Over Fifty Years of American Comic Books* (Lincolnwood, IL: Publications International, 1991), 216, quoted in Duncan, Smith, and Levitz, *Power*.
21. Duncan, Smith, and Levitz, *Power*, 26.
22. Stan Lee, quoted in Duncan, Smith, and Levitz, *Power*, 34.
23. Duncan, Smith, and Levitz, *Power*, 42.
24. Duncan, Smith, and Levitz, *Power*, 42.
25. Duncan, Smith, and Levitz, *Power*, 41.
26. Duncan, Smith, and Levitz, *Power*, 46.

27. Duncan, Smith, and Levitz, *Power*, 51.

28. Duncan, Smith, and Levitz, *Power*, 54.

29. Michael Dean, "Fine Young Cannibals: How Phil Seuling and a Generation of Teenage Entrepreneurs Created the Direct Market and Changed the Face of Comics," *Comics Journal*, July 2006, 49–59.

30. Duncan, Smith, and Levitz, *Power*, 65.

31. Lev Grossman, "All-Time 100 Novels," *Time*, January 11, 2010, entertainment.time.com/2005/10/16/all-time-100-novels/slide/watchmen-1986-by-alan-moore-dave-gibbons/, accessed February 9, 2017.

32. Duncan, Smith, and Levitz, *Power*, 70.

33. Rich Johnston, "Karen Berger Confirms DC Characters to Leave Vertigo," Bleeding Cool, July 23, 2010, www.bleedingcool.com/2010/07/23/karen-berger-confirms-dc-characters-to-leave-vertigo/, accessed July 15, 2016.

34. Dan Mazur and Alexander Danner, *Comics: A Global History, 1968 to the Present* (London: Thames & Hudson, 2014), 237.

35. Mazur and Danner, *Global History*, 230.

36. Arie Kaplan, *Masters of the Comic Universe Revealed!* (Chicago: Chicago Review Press, 2006), 203.

37. Kaplan, *Masters*, 208.

38. Bryn Bailer, "The First Comic Book with an All-Native American Superhero Team Returns," *High Country Ness*, February 17, 2014, www.hcn.org/issues/46.3/the-first-comic-book-with-an-all-native-american-superhero-team-returns, accessed March 15, 2016.

39. Duncan, Smith, and Levitz, *Power*, 83.

---

a. "There Has Been an Awakening," *Teen Ink*, www.teenink.com/nonfiction/academic/article/851271/There-Has-Been-an-Awakening/, accessed June 21, 2016.

b. "The Ultimate Hero Handbook," *Teen Ink*, www.teenink.com/nonfiction/heroes/article/71348/The-Ultimate-Hero-Handbook/, accessed July 2, 2016.

c. "What Is a Superhero?" *Teen Ink*, www.teenink.com/college_guide/college_essays/article/63590/What-is-a-Superhero/, accessed April 19, 2016.

d. Arie Kaplan, *Masters of the Comic Universe Revealed!* (Chicago: Chicago Review Press, 2006), 5.

e. Kaplan, *Masters*, 6.

f. Kaplan, *Masters*, 8.

g. Scott McCloud, *Understanding Comics* (New York: William Morrow, 1994), ii.

h. Kaplan, *Masters*, 5.

i. "Comic Book Superheroes and the End of the Idyllic Era," *Teen Ink*, www.teenink.com/nonfiction/academic/article/404259/Comic-Book-Superheroes-and-the-End-of-the-Idyllic-Era/, accessed June 25, 2016.

j. "Batman and Joker, A Literary Examination," *Teen Ink*, www.teenink.com/opinion/movies_music_tv/article/566553/Batman-and-Joker-A-Literary-Examination/, accessed June 25, 2016.

k. Noelle Stevenson, Grace Ellis, and Brooke Allen, *Lumberjanes: Beware the Kitten Holy* (Los Angeles: Boom! Box, 2015).

l. "There Has Been an Awakening."

m. "There Has Been an Awakening."

Chapter 2

1. Scott McCloud, *Understanding Comics* (New York: William Morrow, 1993), 29.
2. Neil Cohn, *The Visual Language of Comics: Introduction to the Structure and Cognition of Sequential Images* (London: Bloomsbury Academic, 2013), 1.
3. Chris Ware, quoted in Jan Baetens and Hugo Frey, *The Graphic Novel: An Introduction* (New York: Cambridge University Press, 2015), 134.
4. Arie Kaplan, *Masters of the Comic Universe Revealed!* (Chicago: Chicago Review Press, 2006), 5.
5. Will Eisner, *Comics and Sequential Art* (New York: W.W. Norton, 1985, 2008), 2.
6. Cohn, *Visual Language*, 56, 58.
7. Andre Carrington, "Drawn into Dialogue: Comic Book Culture and the Scene of Controversy in Milestone Media's *Icon*," in *The Blacker the Ink: Constructions of Black Identity in Comics & Sequential Art*, ed. Frances Gateward and John Jennings (New Brunswick, NJ: Rutgers University Press, 2015), 164.
8. Sean Tulien, "Out From the Gutter: How Psychic Distance and Closure Come Together to Elevate Comics," master's thesis for Hamline University, 2016, p. 6.
9. Tulien, "Out From the Gutter," 4.
10. McCloud, *Understanding*, 68–69.
11. McCloud, *Understanding*, 31.
12. Eisner, *Comics and Sequential*, 64.
13. Lisa Rojany Buccieri and Peter Economy, *Writing Children's Books for Dummies* (Hoboken, NJ: Wiley Publishing), 172.
14. McCloud, *Understanding*, 111.
15. Cohn, *Visual Language*, 158.
16. Cohn, *Visual Language*, 159.
17. Eisner, *Comics and Sequential*, 103.
18. McCloud, *Understanding*, 191–92.
19. Baetens and Frey, *Graphic Novel*, 135.
20. Baetens and Frey, *Graphic Novel*, 136.
21. Frances Gateward and John Jennings, "Introduction: The Sweeter the Christmas," in Gateward and Jennings, *Blacker the Ink*, 4.

---

a. Zachary B., "Why I Love Comics," school paper, November 10, 2016.
b. "There Has Been an Awakening," *Teen Ink*, www.teenink.com/nonfiction/academic/article/851271/There-Has-Been-an-Awakening/, accessed June 21, 2016.

Chapter 3

1. Randy Duncan, Matthew J. Smith, and Paul Levitz, *The Power of Comics* (New York: Bloomsbury Academic, 2015), 12.
2. Brian J. Robb, *A Brief History of Superheroes* (Philadelphia: Running Press, 2014), 32.
3. John Petty, *A Brief History of Comic Books* (Dallas, TX: Heritage Auction Galleries, 2006), 3.
4. Duncan, Smith, and Levitz, *Power*, 203.
5. Robb, *Brief History*, 73.

6. Daniel Wallace, *Superman: The Ultimate Guide to the Man of Steel* (New York: DK Publishing, 2013), 20.

7. Lauren P., "What Is a Superhero?" *Teen Ink*, www.teenink.com/college_guide/college_essays/article/63590/What-is-a-Superhero/, accessed April 19, 2016.

8. Robb, *Brief History*, 99.

9. Petty, *Comic Books*, 6.

10. Robb, *Brief History*, 111.

11. Robb, *Brief History*, 118.

12. John Wells, *American Comic Book Chronicles: The 1960s (1960–1964)* (Raleigh, NC: TwoMorrows Publishing, 2015), 46.

13. Petty, *Comic Books*, 8.

14. Pete Doree, "Green Lantern/Green Arrow," *The Bronze Age of Blogs* (blog), bronzeageofblogs.blogspot.com/2009/04/green-lantern-green-arrow.html, accessed June 9, 2015.

15. Robb, *Brief History*, 168.

16. Robb, *Brief History*, 201.

17. Keith Dallas, *American Comic Book Chronicles: The 1980s* (Raleigh, NC: TwoMorrows Publishing, 2013), 136.

18. Robb, *Brief History*, 204.

19. Robb, *Brief History*, 267.

20. Ryan Lambie, "How Marvel Went from Bankruptcy to Billions," Den of Geek!, February 13, 2015, www.denofgeek.us/books-comics/marvel/243710/how-marvel-went-from-bankruptcy-to-billions, accessed August 29, 2015.

21. Brett Schenker, "Market Research Says 46.67% of Comic Fans Are Female," *The Beat* (blog), February 5, 2014, www.comicsbeat.com/market-research-says-46-female-comic-fans/, accessed August 28, 2015.

22. Dorian Lynskey, "Kapow! Attack of the Feminist Superheroes," *Guardian*, March 25, 2015, www.theguardian.com/books/2015/mar/25/feminist-superheroes-she-hulk-ms-marvel-thor, accessed August 29, 2015.

23. Lynskey, "Kapow!"

24. Matthew Jent, "Captain Marvel: The Surprising History of How Female Superheroes Came to Be," KQED Pop, November 6, 2014, ww2.kqed.org/pop/2014/11/06/captain-marvel-the-surprising-history-of-how-female-superheroes-came-to-be/, accessed August 29, 2015.

25. Dave Gonzales, "Spider-Man Is Black in the Comics but Peter Parker Can Never Be Gay in the Movies," Geek, June 22, 2015, www.geek.com/news/spider-man-is-black-in-the-comics-but-can-never-be-gay-in-the-movies-1625934/, accessed June 22, 2015.

26. Michael Cavna, "Read This: Gene Luen Yang's Rousing Diversity Speech at the 2014 National Book Festival," *Washington Post*, September 1, 2014, www.washingtonpost.com/news/comic-riffs/wp/2014/09/01/read-this-gene-luen-yangs-rousing-comics-speech-at-the-national-book-festival-gala/, accessed August 29, 2015.

27. Carrie Jung, "Native American Superheroes Take Comic Books by Storm," *Aljazeera America*, June 28, 2015, america.aljazeera.com/articles/2015/6/28/native-american-superheroes-storm-comic-books.html, accessed September 1, 2015.

28. Robb, *Brief History*, 228.

29. Robb, *Brief History*, 228.

30. Mark Waid and Alex Ross, *Kingdom Come* (New York: DC Comics, 2008).

31. Nick Spencer, Daniel Acuña, and Paul Renaud, *Captain America: Sam Wilson*, vol. 1: *Not My Captain America* (New York: Marvel Entertainment, 2016).

32. Gene Luen Yang and Sonny Liew, *The Shadow Hero* (New York: First Second, 2014).

33. Ryan North and Erica Henderson, *The Unbeatable Squirrel Girl*, vol. 1: *Squirrel Power* (New York: Marvel Characters, 2015).

34. Neal Adams and Denny O'Neil, *Superman vs. Muhammad Ali* (New York: DC Comics, 1978).

35. G. Willow Wilson and Adrian Alphona, *Ms. Marvel*, vol. 1: *No Normal* (New York: Marvel Entertainment, 2014).

36. Robbie Thompson, Stacey Lee, Annapaola Martello, and Tana Ford, *Silk*, vol. 1: *The Life and Times of Cindy Moon* (New York: Marvel Entertainment, 2015).

37. Brian K. Vaughan and Adrian Alphona, *Runaways*, vol. 1: *Pride and Joy* (New York: Marvel Worldwide, 2016).

38. Neil Gaiman, Sam Kieth, Mike Dringenberg, and Malcolm Jones III, *The Sandman*, vol. 1: *Preludes & Nocturnes* (New York: DC Comics, 1991).

39. David Mack, *Daredevil/Echo: Vision Quest* (New York: Marvel Worldwide, 2010).

---

a. "What Impact Have Superheroes had on Popular Culture?" *Teen Ink*, www.teenink.com/nonfiction/academic/article/323794/What-Impact-have-Superheroes-had-on-American-Popular-Culture/, accessed September 16, 2016.

b. "Top 100 Comics July 2016," Diamond Comics, October 2, 2016, www.diamondcomics.com/Home/1/1/3/597?articleID=182669, accessed October 4, 2016.

c. "There Has Been an Awakening," *Teen Ink*, www.teenink.com/nonfiction/academic/article/851271/There-Has-Been-an-Awakening/, accessed June 21, 2016.

d. "What Impact?"

e. "Defender of Comics," *Teen Ink*, www.teenink.com/nonfiction/memoir/article/492862/Defender-of-Comics/, accessed June 24, 2016.

f. Brian J. Robb, *A Brief History of Superheroes* (Philadelphia: Running Press, 2014), 124.

g. John Wells, *American Comic Book Chronicles: The 1960s (1960–1964)* (Raleigh, NC: TwoMorrows Publishing, 2015), 46–47.

h. "Stan Lee Biography," Biography, www.biography.com/people/stan-lee-21101093, accessed August 29, 2015.

i. "Stan Lee Biography."

j. Randy Duncan, Matthew J. Smith, and Paul Levitz, *The Power of Comics* (New York: Bloomsbury Academic, 2015), 220.

k. Duncan, Smith, and Levitz, *Power*, 220.

l. Brian Michael Bendis, *Words for Pictures* (Berkeley, CA: Watson-Guptill Publications, 2014), 28.

m. "What Impact?"

n. Ralph Contreras, "Comic Book Terms—Crossover," Comic Book Graphic Design, October 20, 2011, comicbookgraphicdesign.com/comic-book-terms-crossover/, accessed September 15, 2016.

o. Trevor Van As, "Glossary of Comic Book Terms," How to Love Comics, January 21, 2013, www.howtolovecomics.com/comic-book-glossary-of-terms/, accessed September 15, 2016.

p. "The Ultimate Hero Handbook," *Teen Ink*, www.teenink.com/nonfiction/heroes/article/71348/The-Ultimate-Hero-Handbook/, accessed July 2, 2016.

q. "Wonder Woman: A Symbol of Sexism and the Modern Woman," *Teen Ink*, www.teenink.com/nonfiction/academic/article/244900/Wonder-Woman-A-Symbol-of-Sexism-and-the-Modern-Woman/, accessed April 30, 2016.

r. "Kelly Sue DeConnick," *Comic Vine*, www.comicvine.com/kelly-sue-deconnick/4040-52169/, accessed October 22, 2015.

s. Arie Kaplan, *Masters of the Comic Universe Revealed!* (Chicago: Chicago Review Press, 2006), 199.

t. Kaplan, *Masters*, 200.

u. Kaplan, *Masters*, 203.

v. Kaplan, *Masters*, 204.

w. Consuela Francis, "Blackness and the American Superhero," in *The Blacker the Ink: Constructions of Black Identity in Comics and Sequential Art*, ed. Frances Gateward and John Jennings (New Brunswick, NJ: Rutgers University Press, 2015), 141.

x. "Defender of Comics."

y. Kaitlin Miller, "Best-Selling Superhero Comics of All Time," *Sun Times National*, March 10, 2016, national.suntimes.com/national-entertainment/7/72/2729470/best-selling-superhero-comics-all-time-batman-superman/, accessed October 4, 2016.

Chapter 4

1. Randy Duncan, Matthew J. Smith, and Paul Levitz, *The Power of Comics: History, Form, and Culture* (London: Bloomsbury Academic, 2015), 77.

2. Jan Baetens and Hugo Frey, *The Graphic Novel: An Introduction* (New York: Cambridge University Press, 2015), Kindle Edition.

3. Baetens and Frey, *Graphic Novel*, Kindle Edition.

4. Baetens and Frey, *Graphic Novel*, Kindle Edition.

5. Art Spiegelman, *Maus: A Survivor's Tale* (New York: Pantheon Books, 1986).

6. Gene Luen Yang, *American Born Chinese* (New York: Square Fish, 2006).

7. Victoria Jamieson, *Roller Girl* (New York: Dial Books, 2015).

8. Raina Telgemeier, *Smile* (New York: Scholastic, 2010).

9. Prudence Shen and Faith Erin Hicks, *Nothing Can Possibly Go Wrong* (New York: First Second, 2013).

10. Svetlana Chmakova, *Awkward* (New York: Yen Press, 2015).

11. Alan Moore and David Lloyd, *V for Vendetta* (New York: DC Comics, 1990).

12. Jeff Smith, *Bone* (New York: Graphix, 2005).

13. Dawud Anyabwile, Guy A. Sims, and Brian McGee, *Brotherman: Revelation* (Atlanta, GA: Gig City Entertainment, 2015).

14. Shaun Tan, *The Arrival* (New York: Arthur A. Levine Books, 2007).

15. Neil Gaiman, Andy Kubert, and Richard Isanove, *Marvel 1602* (New York: Marvel Worldwide, 2010).

16. Jimmy Gownley, *The Dumbest Idea Ever* (New York: Graphix, 2014).

17. Mariko Tamaki and Jillian Tamaki, *Skim* (Toronto: Groundwood Books, 2008).

18. Vera Brosgol, *Anya's Ghost* (New York: Square Fish, 2014).

19. Jillian Tamaki and Mariko Tamaki, *This One Summer* (New York: First Second, 2014).

20. Noelle Stevenson, *Nimona* (New York: HarperTeen, 2015).

21. Doug TenNapel, *Cardboard* (New York: Graphix, 2012)

22. Ray Bradbury and Tim Hamilton, *Fahrenheit 451* (New York: Hill and Wang, 2009).

23. Madeleine L'Engle, *A Wrinkle in Time*, adapted and illustrated by Hope Larson (New York: Square Fish, 2012), 407.

24. Mary Shelley and Gris Grimly, *Gris Grimly's Frankenstein* (New York: Balzer & Bray, 2013).

25. Gareth Hinds, adapt., *Beowulf* (Cambridge, MA: Candlewick Press, 1999).

26. Neil Gaiman, *The Graveyard Book* (New York: Harper, 2014).

a. "Imagination," *Teen Ink*, www.teenink.com/nonfiction/personal_experience/article/521552/ Imagination/, accessed June 25, 2016.

b. "What Is a Superhero?" *Teen Ink*, www.teenink.com/college_guide/college_essays/article/ 63590/What-is-a-Superhero/, accessed April 19, 2016.

c. "2016 Great Graphic Novels for Teens Top Ten," Young Adult Library Services Association, www.ala.org/yalsa/2016-great-graphic-novels-teens-top-ten, accessed September 15, 2016.

d. "Why I Love Comics," school paper, November 10, 2016.

e. Hillary Brown, "10 Great Comics for Adolescent Girls," *Paste*, November 10, 2014, www .pastemagazine.com/articles/2014/11/10-great-comics-for-adolescent-girls-graphic-novel .html, accessed September 15, 2016.

f. Brown, "10 Great Comics"; Brigid Alverson, "SDCC: Jeff Smith Interviews Faith Erin Hicks," Comic Book Resources, July 30, 2013, www.cbr.com/sdcc-jeff-smith-interviews -faith-erin-hicks/, accessed July 22, 2016.

g. Cory Doctorow and Jen Wang, *In Real Life* (New York: First Second, 2014).

Chapter 5

1. John Lewis, Andrew Aydin, and Nate Powell, *March: Book One* (San Diego, CA: Top Shelf Productions, 2013).

2. Gene Luen Yang, *Boxers and Saints* (New York: First Second, 2013).

3. Roy Boney, *Mighty Code Talkers: We Speak in Secret* (Digital: Native Realities Press, 2015).

4. Arigon Starr, *Tales of the Mighty Code Talkers: Annumpa Luma Code Talker* (West Hollywood, CA: INC Comics, 2014).

5. G. Neri and Randy DuBurke, *Yummy* (New York: Lee and Low Books, 2010), 63.

6. Ethan Hawke and Greg Ruth, *Indeh* (New York: Grand Central Publishing, 2016).

7. Kyle Baker, *Nat Turner* (New York: Abrams, 2008).

8. Jeff Jensen and Jonathan Case, *Green River Killer: A True Detective Story* (Milwaukie, OR: Dark Horse Books, 2011), epilogue.

9. "What Is a Memoir? Memoir Writing Interview Part 1" an interview with Kendra Bonnett and Matilda Butler, *Creative Writing Ideas Blog*, www.creative-writing-now.com/what-is-a -memoir.html, accessed February 18, 2016.

10. Liz Prince, *Tomboy* (San Francisco, CA: Zest Books, 2014), 240–41.

11. Marjane Satrapi, *Persepolis* (New York: Pantheon, 2003).

12. Joe Sacco, *Palestine* (Seattle, WA: Fantagraphic Books, 1993), 285.

13. Josh Neufeld, *A.D.: New Orleans after the Deluge* (New York: Pantheon, 2010).

14. Derf Backderf, *Trashed* (New York: Abrams ComicArts, 2015), 167.

15. Alan Moore, Stephen Bissette, and John Totleben, *Saga of the Swamp Thing* (New York: DC Comics, 2012).

16. Doug TenNapel, *Bad Island* (New York: Graphix, 2011), 57.

17. Emily Carroll, *Through the Woods* (New York: Margaret K. Elderry Books, 2014).

18. Joe Hill and Gabriel Rodriguez, *Locke and Key*, vol. 1: *Welcome to Lovecraft* (San Diego, CA: IDW Publishing, 2009).

19. Van Jensen and Dusty Higgins, *Pinocchio, Vampire Slayer* (San Jose, CA: SLG Publishing, 2009).

20. Ben Hatke, *Zita the Space Girl* (New York: First Second, 2010).

21. Linda Medley, *Castle Waiting* (Seattle, WA: Fantagraphics Books, 2006).

22. Jane Yolen and Mike Cavallaro, *Foiled* (New York: First Second, 2010).

23. Kazu Kibuishi, *Amulet*, bk 1: *The Stonekeeper* (New York: Graphix, 2008).

24. Quoted in Kat Kan, "Returning Heroes and Others," Graphically Speaking column, *VOYA*, February 2013, 556.

25. Duane Swierczynski and Simon Gane, *Godzilla: History's Greatest Monster* (San Diego, CA: IDW Publishing, 2014).

26. Matt Hawkins and Rahsan Ekedal, *Think Tank* (Berkeley, CA: Image Comics, 2013), Chapter 2.

27. Brian Selznick, *The Invention of Hugo Cabret* (New York: Scholastic Press, 2007).

28. Swati Avasthi, *Chasing Shadows* (New York: Alfred A. Knopf, 2013).

29. Kate DiCamillo, *Flora and Ulysses* (Somerville, MA: Candlewick Press, 2013).

30. Neil Babra, *No Fear Shakespeare Graphic Novels: Hamlet* (New York: SparkNotes, 2008).

31. Conor McCreery, Anthony Del Col, Andy Belanger, and Ian Herring, *Kill Shakespeare: Backstage Edition* (San Diego, CA: IDW Publishing, 2015).

32. Tetsu Saiwai, *The 14th Dalai Lama: A Manga Biography* (New York: Penguin, 2010).

33. Ben Avery, Noval Hernawan, Lisa Moore, and Zach Matheny, "Beauty Queen: The Story of Esther," in *The Kingstone Bible* (Leesburg, FL: Kingstone Comics, 2011).

34. Sharon E. McKay and Daniel Lafrance, *War Brothers: The Graphic Novel* (Toronto: Annick Press, 2013).

35. Louis L'Amour, Charles Santino, Beau L'Amour, Katherine Nolan, and Thomas Yeates, *Law of the Desert Born* (New York: Bantam, 2013).

a. "Don't Judge a Book by Its Cover," *Teen Ink*, www.teenink.com/opinion/all/article/209520/Dont-Judge-a-Book-by-its-Cover/, accessed July 15, 2016.

b. "Defender of Comics," *Teen Ink*, www.teenink.com/nonfiction/memoir/article/492862/Defender-of-Comics/, accessed June 24, 2016.

c. Survey received by email, July 15, 2016.

d. "Comic Book Superheroes and the End of the Idyllic Era," *Teen Ink*, www.teenink.com/nonfiction/academic/article/404259/Comic-Book-Superheroes-and-the-End-of-the-Idyllic-Era/, accessed June 25, 2016.

e. "Don't Judge a Book by Its Cover."

f. Phone interview with author, July 15, 2016.

g. Email interview with author, December 4, 2016.

h. William Strunk Jr., E. B. White, and Maira Kalman, *The Elements of Style (illustrated)* (New York: Penguin, 2005).

i. Jim Ottaviani and Maris Wicks, *Primates* (New York: Square Fish, 2015).

Chapter 6

1. Brigitte Koyama-Richard, *One Thousand Years of Manga* (Paris: Flammarion, 2007), 6.

2. Neil Cohn, *The Visual Language of Comics: Introduction to the Structure and Cognition of Sequential Images* (London: Bloomsbury Academic, 2013), 6.

3. Helen McCarthy, *A Brief History of Manga* (Lewes, East Sussex, UK: Ilex Press, 2014), 6.

4. Kristin Fletcher-Spear and Merideth Jenson-Benjamin, *Library Collections for Teens: Manga and Graphic Novels* (Bowie, MD: E. L. Kurdyla), 24.

5. Fletcher-Spear and Jenson-Benjamin, *Library Collections*, 24.

6. McCarthy, *History of Manga*, 12.

7. McCarthy, *History of Manga*, 14.

8. Paul Gravett, *Manga: Sixty Years of Japanese Comics* (New York: Collins Design, 2004), 23.

9. McCarthy, *History of Manga*, 18.

10. McCarthy, *History of Manga*, 20.

11. "Program for Teaching East Asia," University of Colorado, 2008, www.colorado.edu/cas/tea/curriculum/imaging-japanese-history/late-twentieth-century/pdfs/handout2.pdf, accessed March 8, 2016.

12. Gravett, *Sixty Years*, 24.

13. Gravett, *Sixty Years*, 23.

14. Charles Solomon, "Astro Boy was role model who revolutionized manga," *Los Angeles Times*, October 23, 2009, articles.latimes.com/2009/oct/23/entertainment/et-astroanime23, accessed March 8, 2016.

15. McCarthy, *History of Manga*, 30.

16. Gravett, *Sixty Years*, 76.

17. McCarthy, *History of Manga*, 18.

18. McCarthy, *History of Manga*, 18.

19. McCarthy, *History of Manga*, 28.

20. McCarthy, *History of Manga*, 28.

21. Gravett, *Sixty Years*, 80.

22. "Manga/Sally the Witch," TV Tropes, tvtropes.org/pmwiki/pmwiki.php/Manga/SallyTheWitch, accessed May 10, 2016.

23. Gravett, *Sixty Years*, 78.

24. Ryan Holmberg, "Tatsumi Yoshihiro, 1935–2015," *Comics Journal*, March 12, 2015, www.tcj.com/tatsumi-yoshihiro-1935-2015/, accessed May 10, 2016.

25. McCarthy, *History of Manga*, 44.

26. McCarthy, *History of Manga*, 60.

27. Fletcher-Spear and Jenson-Benjamin, *Library Collections*, 37.

28. Gravett, *Sixty Years*, 54.

29. Fletcher-Spear and Jenson-Benjamin, *Library Collections*, 37.

30. McCarthy, *History of Manga*, 46.

31. Fletcher-Spear and Jenson-Benjamin, *Library Collections*, 40.

32. Gravett, *Sixty Years*, 80.

33. Fletcher-Spear and Jenson-Benjamin, *Library Collections*, 42.

34. Cohn, *Visual Language*, 154.

35. Cohn, *Visual Language*, 154.

36. Cohn, *Visual Language*, 156.

37. Yana Toboso, *Black Butler*, vol. 1 (New York: Yen Press, 2010), 176–78.

38. Matsuri Hino, *Vampire Knight*, vol. 1 (San Francisco, CA: VIZ Media, 2007).

39. Natsuki Takaya, *Fruits Basket*, vol. 1 (Los Angeles: TokyoPop, 2004).

40. Tite Kubo, *Bleach*, vols. 1–3 (San Francisco, CA: VIZ Media, 2011).

41. Rumiko Takahashi, *Ranma 1/2*, vols. 1–2 (San Francisco, CA: VIZ Media, 2014).

42. Natsumi Ando and Miyuki Kobayashi, *Kitchen Princess 1* (New York: Del Rey, 2007).

43. CLAMP, *Tsubasa Reservoir Chronicle* (New York: Del Rey, 2004).

44. NaRae Lee, *Maximum Ride: The Manga*, vol. 1 (New York: Yen Press, 2009).

45. Nobuhiro Watsuki, *Rurouni Kenshin: Restoration* (San Francisco, CA: VIZ Media, 2013).

46. Hitoshi Iwaaki, *Parasite* (New York: Kodansha Comics, 2013), 88–89.

a. "Manga vs. Comics," *Teen Ink*, www.teenink.com/opinion/sports_hobbies/article/603559/Manga-vs-Comics, accessed June 24, 2016.

b. "Creator/CLAMP," TV Tropes, tvtropes.org/pmwiki/pmwiki.php/Creator/CLAMP, accessed May 10, 2016.

c. Lisa "Skuld" Wu, "The Legend of CLAMP," *Miteiru! Japanese Animation Journal of the Massachusetts Institute of Technology*, February 2003, p. 4, web.archive.org/web/20090902100424/web.mit.edu/anime/miteiru!/2003–02–15.pdf, accessed June 25, 2016.

d. "Review of xxxHolic by CLAMP," *Teen Ink*, www.teenink.com/reviews/book_reviews/article/447814/XxxHolic-by-CLAMP/, accessed June 25, 2016.

e. "Dr. Slump," *Wikipedia*, en.wikipedia.org/wiki/Dr._Slump, accessed September 27, 2016.

f. "Shueisha Establishes New Department Focused on Dragon Ball," October 13, 2016, *Anime News Network*, www.animenewsnetwork.com/news/2016–10–13/shueisha-establishes-new-department-focused-on-dragon-ball/.107591, accessed September 27, 2016.

g. Helen McCarthy, *A Brief History of Manga* (Lewes, East Sussex, UK: Ilex Press, 2014), 46.

h. "Akira Toriyama," *Wikipedia*, en.wikipedia.org/wiki/Akira_Toriyama, accessed September 27, 2016.

i. "Manga vs. Comics."

Chapter 7

1. Rick Gekoski, "What's the Definition of a Great Book?" *Guardian*, December 23, 2011, www.theguardian.com/books/2011/dec/23/definition-great-book-rick-gekoski, accessed August 10, 2016.

2. Kristi Romo, interview with the author, August 27, 2016.

3. Brigid Alverson, "Teaching with Graphic Novels," *School Library Journal*, September 8, 2014, www.slj.com/2014/09/books-media/the-graphic-advantage-teaching-with-graphic-novels/, accessed August 10, 2016.

4. Heidi MacDonald, "New Study Shows That Graphic Novels Really Do Help People Learn," *The Beat* (blog), January 28, 2013, www.comicsbeat.com/new-study-shows-that-graphic-novels-really-do-help-people-learn/, accessed August 10, 2016.

5. Gene Luen Yang, "History of Comics in Education," Comics in Education, 2003, www.humblecomics.com/comicsedu/history.html, accessed April 19, 2016.

6. K. Haugaard, quoted in Yang, "History of Comics in Education."

7. Katherine Polak MacDonald, "Batman Returns (to Class)," in *Teaching Comics and Graphic Narratives: Essays on Theory, Strategy and Practice*, ed. Lan Dong (Jefferson, NC: McFarland, 2012), Kindle Edition.

8. Neil Cohn, Martin Paczynski, Phil Holcomb, Ray Jackendoff, and Gina Kuperberg, "The Impact of Structure and Meaning on Sequential Image Comprehension," Visual Language Lab, 2012, www.visuallanguagelab.com/P/NC_pn&b_abstract.pdf, accessed April 19, 2016.

9. Carl Zimmer, "The Brain: The Charlie Brown Effect," *Discover Magazine* online, October 25, 2012, discovermagazine.com/2012/dec/29-the-charlie-brown-effect#.ULkMd4UX4cp, accessed April 19, 2016.

10. Randy Duncan, Matthew J. Smith, and Paul Levitz, *The Power of Comics: History, Form, and Culture* (London: Bloomsbury Academic, 2015), 333.
11. Kristin Fletcher-Spear and Merideth Jenson-Benjamin, *Library Collections for Teens: Manga and Graphic Novels* (Bowie, MD: E. L. Kurdyla), 52–54.
12. MacDonald, "Batman Returns," Kindle Edition.
13. "Using Comics and Graphic Novels in the Classroom," *Council Chronicle*, September 5, 2007, www.ncte.org/magazine/archives/122031, accessed August 10, 2016.
14. "Using Comics."
15. Adrielle Anna Mitchell, "Exposition and Disquisition: Nonfiction Graphic Narratives and Comics Theory in the Literature Classroom," in *Teaching Comics and Graphic Narratives: Essays on Theory, Strategy and Practice*, ed. Lan Dong (Jefferson, NC: McFarland, 2012), Kindle Edition.
16. Mitchell, "Exposition," Kindle Edition.
17. Mitchell, "Exposition," Kindle Edition.
18. Craig Thompson, *Blankets* (Marietta, GA: Top Shelf Productions, 2003).
19. Lynda Barry, *One Hundred Demons* (Seattle, WA: Sasquatch Books, 2002), 70.

a. "Don't Judge a Book by Its Cover," *Teen Ink*, www.teenink.com/opinion/all/article/209520/Dont-Judge-a-Book-by-its-Cover/, accessed July 15, 2016.
b. "The Defender of Comics," *Teen Ink*, www.teenink.com/nonfiction/memoir/article/492862/Defender-of-Comics/, accessed June 24, 2016.
c. Survey received by email, July 15, 2016.
d. Various, *Mankind: The Story of All of Us*, vol. 1 (Horsham, PA: Zenescope, 2012).
e. Gene Luen Yang and Mike Holmes, *Secret Coders* (New York: First Second, 2015).
f. "Imagination," *Teen Ink*, www.teenink.com/nonfiction/personal_experience/article/521552/Imagination/, accessed June 25, 2016.
g. "Don't Judge a Book by Its Cover."

Chapter 8

1. From a post on www.brianmichaelbendis.tumblr.com, accessed September 15, 2016.
2. Brian Michael Bendis, *Words for Pictures: The Art and Business of Writing Comics and Graphic Novels* (New York: Watson-Guptill Publications, 2014), 24.
3. Bendis, *Words*, 24.
4. T. Henrik Edberg, "34 Inspiring Quotes on Criticism (and How to Handle It)," *The Positivity Blog*, www.positivityblog.com/index.php/2016/02/10/quotes-on-criticism/, accessed September 23, 2016.
5. Bendis, *Words*, 28.
6. Bendis, *Words*, 153.
7. Scott McCloud, *Making Comics: Storytelling Secrets of Comics, Manga, and Graphic Novels* (New York: HarperCollins, 2006), 142.
8. Chris Ware, "The Art of Comics No. 2," interviewed by Jeet Heer, *Paris Review*, no. 210, Fall 2014, bit.ly/1yJtKQo, accessed August 27, 2016.
9. Brian Michael Bendis and Mike Avon Oeming, *Powers: Who Killed Retro Girl?* (New York: Marvel Entertainment, 2014).
10. Mark Ellis and Melissa Martin Ellis, *The Everything Guide to Writing Graphic Novels* (Avon, MA: Adams Media, 2008), 194.

11. Email note to the author, October 2014.

12. Neil Cohn, *The Visual Language of Comics: Introduction to the Structure and Cognition of Sequential Images* (London: Bloomsbury Academic, 2013), 56, 59.

13. Cohn, *Visual Language*, 60.

14. Phone interview with author, July 16, 2016.

15. Jan Baetens and Hugo Frey, *The Graphic Novel: An Introduction* (New York: Cambridge University Press, 2015), 134.

16. Chris Ware, quoted in Baetens and Frey, *Graphic Novel*, 134.

17. Tom Humberstone, "Printing Your Small Press Comic," *Tom Humberstone: Blog*, July 10, 2009, ventedspleen.com/blog/2009/07/10/printing-your-small-press-comic/, accessed August 27, 2016.

18. Lora Innes, "How Do I Pick the Print-on-Demand Publisher That Is Right for My Comic?" ChrisOatley.com, chrisoatley.com/how-do-i-pick-the-print-on-demand-publisher-that-is-right-for-my-ccomic/, accessed September 15, 2016.

19. Christian Sager, "Thinking of Making Your Own Comic Book? Read This First," *Geek Out!* (blog), geekout.blogs.cnn.com/2011/08/31/thinking-of-making-your-own-comic-book-read-this-first/, accessed August 27, 2016.

20. Grigoris Douros, "Where to Sell Your Digital Comics: The List of Digital Platforms," Zeno Telos Press, July 24, 2015, www.zenotelos.com/digital-comics-distribution-platform-list/, accessed August 27, 2016.

21. Douros, "Where to Sell."

22. Brigid Alverson, "SDCC: Jeff Smith Interviews Faith Erin Hicks," Comic Book Resources, July 30, 2013, www.cbr.com/sdcc-jeff-smith-interviews-faith-erin-hicks/, accessed July 22, 2016.

23. Michael Rapoport, "Marvel Dominated Comic Sales in 2014," *Speakeasy* (*Wall Street Journal* blog), January 9, 2015, blogs.wsj.com/speakeasy/2015/01/09/best-selling-comics-2014/, accessed July 22, 2016.

24. Bendis, *Words*, 154.

25. Alverson, "SDCC."

26. Phone interview with author, July 16, 2016.

27. Bendis, *Words*, 205, 201.

a. Phone interview with author, July 16, 2016.

b. "There Has Been an Awakening," *Teen Ink*, www.teenink.com/nonfiction/academic/article/851271/There-Has-Been-an-Awakening/, accessed June 21, 2016.

c. "Batman and Joker: A Literary Examination," *Teen Ink*, www.teenink.com/opinion/movies_music_tv/article/566553/Batman-and-Joker-A-Literary-Examination/, accessed June 25, 2016.

d. I included this quote from Caroline A. because it celebrates Wonder Woman's complex character; creating an outline can help you develop the interior and exterior obstacles that produce such complex characters. "Wonder Woman: A Symbol of Sexism and the Modern Woman," *Teen Ink*, www.teenink.com/nonfiction/academic/article/244900/Wonder-Woman-A-Symbol-of-Sexism-and-the-Modern-Woman/, accessed April 30, 2016.

e. Dave Wood and Jim Mooney, "Secret Origins of the Amazing Spider-Man," *Dial B for Blog*, www.dialbforblog.com/archives/691/, accessed June 7, 2016.

f. Wood and Mooney, "Secret Origins."

g. From a post on www.brianmichaelbendis.tumblr.com, accessed September 15, 2016.

h. Scott McCloud, *Making Comics: Storytelling Secrets of Comics, Manga, and Graphic Novels* (New York: HarperCollins, 2006), 37.

i. This quote shows that superhero comics convey ideas as well as action. That's an important aspect to consider when writing your own stories. Considering McCloud's five questions can make your storytelling more precise, so your message can come through more clearly. "Batman and Joker."

j. Emma S., "The Defender of Comics," *Teen Ink*, www.teenink.com/nonfiction/memoir article/492862/Defender-of-Comics/, accessed June 24, 2016.

k. Nur Afrina A., "My Hobby," *Teen Ink*, www.teenink.com/fiction/all/article/885941/My-Hobby/, accessed June 25, 2016.

Index

Note: Page references for figures are italicized.

About the Author

Randall Bonser has been a professional writer for three decades, having worked on a wide variety of subjects, from lacrosse to weight loss. He only discovered the joy of comics as an adult, while working toward his master's degree in writing for children and young adults at Hamline University. One of the highlights of his life was working with Gene Luen Yang when the latter was an adviser on his creative thesis—a graphic novel script for middle school readers (on which he is still working). Metro Atlanta is home for Bonser, his wife, and two teenaged children. In addition to working on several in-progress books, he teaches creative writing workshops for kids, as well as college writing classes.